HOLY GROUND

HOLY THINGS FOR THE HOLY PEOPLE.
ONE IS HOLY, ONE IS LORD, JESUS CHRIST.
O TASTE AND SEE THAT THE LORD IS GOOD.

Liturgy of Jerusalem in
Cyril of Jerusalem
Mystagogical Catecheses 5:19-20

REMOVE THE SANDALS FROM YOUR FEET, FOR THE PLACE
ON WHICH YOU ARE STANDING IS HOLY GROUND.

Exodus 3:5

AFTER THIS I SAW FOUR ANGELS STANDING AT THE
FOUR CORNERS OF THE EARTH, HOLDING BACK THE
FOUR WINDS OF THE EARTH SO THAT NO WIND
COULD BLOW ON EARTH OR SEA OR AGAINST ANY
TREE. I SAW ANOTHER ANGEL ASCENDING FROM THE
RISING OF THE SUN, HAVING THE SEAL OF THE LIVING
GOD, AND THE ANGEL CALLED WITH A LOUD VOICE
TO THE FOUR ANGELS WHO HAD BEEN GIVEN POWER
TO DAMAGE EARTH AND SEA, SAYING, "DO NOT
DAMAGE THE EARTH OR THE SEA OR THE TREES,
UNTIL WE HAVE MARKED THE SERVANTS OF OUR GOD
WITH A SEAL ON THEIR FOREHEADS."

Revelation 7:1-3

HOLY GROUND

A LITURGICAL COSMOLOGY

Gordon W. Lathrop

Fortress Press

Minneapolis

HOLY GROUND
A Liturgical Cosmology

Fortress Press paperback edition 2009

Scripture quotations are from the New Revised Standard Version Bible, copyright © 1989 by the Division of Christian Education of the National Council of the Churches of Christ in the USA and used by permission.

Cover image: *The Angel Ascends from the Rising of the Sun* (Japanese stencil, 1967) by Sadao Watanabe (1913–1996) from *Biblical Prints of Sadao Watanabe*. Reprinted with permission of Masao Takenaka.

Cover and interior design: Ann Elliott Artz Hadland

Author photo: © 2002 Pamela Davidson. Used with permission.

"In Sacred Manner" © 1990 Susan Palo Cherwien, as found in *O Blessed Spring* (Minneapolis: Augsburg Fortress, 1997). Used with permission.

"There in God's Garden" by Király Imre von Pécselyi, trans. Eric Routley, © 1976 by Hinshaw Music Inc., Chapel Hill, N.C. Text used with permission.

SC ISBN 978–0–8006–9655–9
HC ISBN 978–0–8006–3590–9

The paper used in this publication meets the minimum requirements of American National Standard for Information Sciences — Permanence of Paper for Printed Library Materials, ANSI Z329.48-1984.

Manufactured in the U.S.A.

13   12   11   10   09   1   2   3   4   5   6   7   8   9   10

With love
for
Nathaniel *and* Vyshnavi
Anthony Tobias *and* Julianne
Miriam
Monica Rosemary
Kierthan Nicholas
and any who will join them as
keepers of the ground

CONTENTS

Preface

This book consists of reflections on the ways in which Christian worship may help us to imagine, understand, care for, and live in the world. It forms the third volume of a trilogy. That trilogy is comprised of three works of liturgical theology, all of which intend to consider how Christian worship means something in the present time and, most specifically, how such worship says something true about God and so also says something true about both the gathering called "church" and our context called "world." Thus, the first volume of that trilogy, *Holy Things: A Liturgical Theology* (Minneapolis: Fortress Press, 1993), concluded with a consideration of the implications of the *ordo* or pattern of Christian worship for both church order and world order. The second volume, *Holy People: A Liturgical Ecclesiology* (Minneapolis: Fortress Press, 1999), extended the consideration of *ordo* and church order, focusing on the meaning of "assembly" and on both liturgical ecumenism and liturgical contextualization.

The present volume extends the earlier interest in liturgy and world order. However, while this book continues the agenda of *Holy Things,* while its notes sometimes signal the earlier work, and while it is united in method with the other volumes, it may be read quite on its own. The questions about world order, about earth-care, about shared communal symbolization, about cosmology—about what world we think we are living in—are urgent ones for us now. Anyone interested in Christian worship and the relationship it may bear to these questions is welcome to these pages.

At first glance, one might think that the book should have been called *Only One Is Holy.* The dialogue of invitation to and warning about Holy Communion, from which both earlier volumes took their titles, has those words as the fascinating, contradictory, gracious response. But such a title could be misunderstood. In the first place, the phrase "only one is holy" was woven through both of the earlier books, as it is through the present one, meaning to invite us into a continuing critique of the holiness of things, people, liturgy, churches, symbols, worldviews of any sort. This book joins the others in that method. *Only One Is Holy* might be considered the hidden title of the whole trilogy. In the second place, however, that "only one" could lead us to imagine that therefore nothing else is holy, our earth included. But the character of the biblical God's holiness is found exactly in being given away, in continually gathering needy cosmos and needy humanity into wholeness, healing, holiness. Therefore: *Holy Ground*. The story of the burning bush (Exodus 3), from which these words are drawn, should be read as a story of the encounter with the unique holiness of God. Let that encounter stand for all worship or liturgy. But then that God speaks: "The place on which you are standing is holy ground."

The pre-Socratic philosopher, Heraclitus, whose fragmentarily preserved paradoxical thought has been one important source for some of the methods of these books, was said to have written a single book, *On Nature*, divided into three sections: on cosmology, on politics and on theology (Diogenes Laertius, *Lives of the Philosophers* 9:5). This present trilogy seeks to share with Heraclitus these subject divisions, though in reverse order. But it does not seek to share the overall title. Neither this book nor the others is about "nature." I hope, rather, that this book, like the others, may honestly be about God, as God is known in Christian worship. Liturgy and liturgical theology are the subjects. I hope that these subjects may then lead helpfully to renewed consideration of ecology, worldview, and "sarcophilic" ethics (see chapter 5) in Christian perspective.

The writing of this book was enabled by a one-year sabbatical from my direct responsibilities as professor and chaplain at the Lutheran Theological Seminary at Philadelphia. I wish to express my thanks to the board of that seminary, to its president, Philip Krey, to its dean, Paul Rajashekar, and to my colleagues on its faculty for so fully supporting this undertaking. This absence would simply not have been possible, however, without the gracious and remarkable work of the acting chaplain, Elizabeth Huwiler, the seminary cantor, Mark Mummert, and the seminary sacristan, Anna Mercedes. I thank them with all my heart.

Parts of the book were worked out in public lectures: the Godfrey Diekmann lecture at St. John's University in Collegeville, Minnesota, together with lectures at the Institute for Sacred Music in Yale University and at a seminar in the University of Uppsala, Sweden (chapter 1); the Feinstein Lecture at Providence College, Providence, Rhode Island (chapter 3); the Pastoral Liturgical Institute at Notre Dame University (chapter 4); and the Hein-Fry Lectures of the Evangelical Lutheran Church in America together with the Lutheran Heritage Lecture at Pacific Lutheran University (chapter 5). Much of the conception of the work was also discussed with the Liturgical Theology Seminar of the North American Academy of Liturgy. I want to thank the several people who enabled these invitations and who helped me by their consideration and discussion of the work-in-progress: Martin Connell, Kevin Seasoltz, Martin Jean, Bryan Spinks, Horace Allen, Per Hansson, Peter Bexell, Michael Tkasik, Anne Koester, Nathan Mitchell, Phyllis Anderson, Mary Collins, Samuel Torvend, Dwight Vogel, Ann Riggs, Don Saliers, and all the members of the Liturgical Theology Seminar.

Part of chapter 1 was earlier published in the essay, "How Awesome Is This Place!" in R. R. van Loon, ed., *Encountering God: The Legacy of the Lutheran Book of Worship for the 21st Century* (Minneapolis: Kirk House, 1998), 40-51. Chapter 3 was earlier published, in substantially different form, in the *festschrift* for Don Saliers: E. Byron Anderson and Bruce T. Morrill, eds., *Liturgy and the Moral Self* (Collegeville, Minn.: Liturgical Press, 1998), 41–53.

Several conversation partners were immensely important to me in the development of the book. Besides those already mentioned, I wish to thank Dirk G. Lange, Melinda Quivik, John Hoffmeyer, Jennifer Lord, Jerry Folk, Margaret Spring, Timothy Wengert, Glaucia Vasconcelos-Wilkey, Michael Burk, Kamala Suntharalingam, Kevin Schulz, Jann Boyd, Thomas Best, Gunnar Weman, and these: Raymond Lathrop and David Lathrop, with whom I first knew a liturgy in the wild; Jeffrey Truscott, who introduced me to Masao Takenaka and helped me find the print by Sadao Watanabe; Harold Rast and Michael West of Fortress Press, who have shown such kind hospitality to this book and its predecessors; Monica Rosemary Schmidt, who helped me read Job anew; Miriam Schmidt, who walks all this talk; Nathaniel Lathrop and Anthony Lathrop, with whom I shared both bread and homilies in the wilderness; Julianne Dwyer and Vyshi Suntharalingam, for their support of our walking; Thomas McGonigle, who listened to several chapters read aloud, deepening them in prayer; and Gail Ramshaw, who not only found all the trees with me but also encouraged me to look through that telescope at what could be seen of the cosmos.

Introduction
Liturgical Cosmology and Its Importance

What does Christian liturgy have to do with cosmology? How do the songs and spoken dialogues, the Scripture readings and the holy actions that Christian communities make the agenda of their assemblies propose or respond to a sense of ordered cosmos?

"Holy things for the holy people," cries out the eucharistic presider in the ancient communion rite preserved in the liturgies of the Eastern churches. Standing at the holy doors, the holy bread and cup in hand, this presider both invites and warns the assembly: "Come. Eat and drink freely. But take care. Come only if you are holy. Here is danger. Are you able to drink this cup?" Who could dare approach? But then the assembly itself takes up the word in faith, answering the presider. "One is holy, one is Lord, Jesus Christ," they sing out, in a kind of faithful contradiction, calling "holy" the one who was made utterly unholy in his death and so taking courage to find themselves included. And, according to the oldest report we have that tells us of this dialogue,[1] the cantor then begins to sing another text that bears the very grace that the people have claimed. The song floats over them as they do, indeed, approach to eat and drink: "O taste and see that the Lord is good."

This old Eastern Christian dialogue has thus accompanied since at least the fourth century one of the most central actions of all Christian liturgy: communal eating and drinking before God in active memorial of Jesus Christ. But such eating and drinking are not only Eastern. They are found

---

1. Cyril of Jerusalem, *Mystagogical Catecheses* 5:19–20; see Frank Leslie Cross, ed., *St. Cyril of Jerusalem's Lectures on the Christian Sacraments* (London: SPCK, 1966), 37–38, 78–79.

as a nearly universal Christian heritage, and various forms of warning and invitation, protection and open access, judgment expressed and mercy claimed are also nearly universal attendants of this heritage. For Christians also of other traditions, this pungent dialogue can stand as a symbol and evocation of the strong center and the gracious open door that need to mark all liturgy, not only this crucial eating and drinking. Indeed, it is possible for us to let the dialogue be a tension-laden symbol for many of the meanings of Christian assembly, East and West, Protestant and Catholic—for the "yes" and the "no" that Christian liturgy speaks to cultic values, for the importance of the assembly and yet for its neediness.[2]

But what does this exchange—what does the liturgy for which it may stand—have to do with the earth, let alone the cosmos?

Here is a burning question posed to Christian ritual practice by our current experience and knowledge. The question arises inevitably and forcefully when one puts together a desire to be faithful to the ritual tradition—or even simply a fascination with the liturgy or an imagination drawn by liturgical symbols—with the new awareness of the fragility and rarity of the earth's patterns of life, the almost daily encounter with new evidence of the immensity of the universe, and the current need for socially coherent ways to understand and walk together in the world. All these concerns—ecology, a physical account of the universe, and public symbolism—have been called *cosmology*. And, as we shall see, in many ways all three are urgently interrelated. So what does Christian liturgy have to do with cosmology?

Say the question this way: The communion meal and this dialogue text that interprets that meal seem to accentuate human eating and drinking and then, around this meal, the theological issues of worthiness, judgment, mercy, forgiveness, and therewith the history and meaning of Jesus. It seems as if human history, human sustenance, human redemption all have center stage. Is this ritual simply another form of the anthropocentric religion—even of the accent upon a "chosen" or "saved" and privileged remnant of humanity—that many commentators have recently described as the very ideology that has underwritten our current ecological crisis?[3]

---

2. So this dialogue has provided the central organizing theme of the two earlier volumes that this present third volume accompanies: my *Holy Things: A Liturgical Theology* (Minneapolis: Fortress, 1993) and *Holy People: A Liturgical Ecclesiology* (Minneapolis: Fortress, 1999).

3. Originally, Lynn White Jr., "The Historical Roots of Our Ecological Crisis," *Science* 155 (1967): 1203–7. See also Timothy C. Weiskel, "While Angels Weep . . . Doing Theology on a Small Planet," *Harvard Divinity Bulletin* 19, no. 3 (fall 1989). Compare Roy A. Rappaport, *Ritual and Religion in the Making of Humanity* (Cambridge: Cambridge University Press, 1999), 453.

It may be so, has been so. Even this exchange, with its fascinating dialectic, can be heard as if only human beings—their forgiveness, sustenance, inclusion—matter. More, liturgy generally can be read as if only certain human beings, only the present celebrants huddling together, matter. Christian liturgy, the liturgy for which this exchange may stand as a symbol, has been understood to serve an ideology in which humanity "crowns" the creation, a humanity being now continually restored to this preeminence by the sacramental grace celebrated in the liturgy. By such a reading, the world in which this liturgy occurs might just as well still be a world in which the earth is at the center of the universe, the sun and moon, planets and stars encircling it, and humanity engaged in the struggle to impose human order and utility upon the wilds that still surround us. The "cosmology" involved in such a reading would be a remnant of a pre-Copernican worldview, symbolically implied and literally imaged only in church, but with widespread and deleterious effects in public practice, in commerce, and in ethics.

But such a reading would be shortsighted. The open doors that the dialogue envisions may be open to more than we had thought. In the first place, holiness is not where we had thought it should be. The unholy—especially the unholy outsiders, the unholy poor, the *non*celebrants—are welcome, according to the contradiction of the dialogue. More: bread and wine, as many other texts of the liturgy celebrate, are themselves products of a remarkable collaboration between a fruitful earth and human cultures. The meal held here tends toward being a model of sustainable consumption in which everyone is welcome to eat with thankfulness, no one hoarding, no one hungry, no one excluded, just enough made available. More: tasting enables seeing. Participants come to see that "the Lord is good." If this is so, perhaps they see more. Perhaps they see a new order in the cosmos itself.

The warning cry, "Holy things for the holy people," closely resembles the warning given to Moses in the biblical story of his initial encounter with God: "Remove the sandals from your feet!" (Exod. 3:5). So the story goes on, "Moses hid his face, for he was afraid to look at God" (3:6). Then the old response of the people, "One is holy, one is Lord," stands next to the revelatory center of that older Exodus story: "I am God," come the words out of the heart of the bush that burns without being consumed. "I am the God of your ancestors. . . . I have observed the misery of my people. . . . I AM WHO I AM. . . . This is my name forever" (Exod. 3:6, 7, 14, 15). At the heart of the encounter of Moses—at the heart of the communion rite—at the heart of this biblical religion—there is one, majestic, holy God. But then comes the surprise: The very "holiness" of this God is the hearing of the cries of those who suffer, the acting on their behalf. And, then, in further surprise and in revelation of biblical holiness: "The place on which you are standing is holy ground." Not "I am holy and all else is not." Not "I am holy and you, mortal, can be too, if you imitate me." Not "I am holy and that is the human destiny, too—in the sky, away from here, with me." But "the place on which you are standing is holy ground."

One could argue that the story simply makes the land around the burning bush, the place of the theophany, into a sort of cult locale, a *fanum*, a temple surrogate. Such a holy, set-aside precinct only heightens the unholiness of all the rest of the land, all the *pro-fane*. But perhaps not. Rather, wherever the God of Israel, the God who saves the poor, is encountered, there even a bush is unharmed, being rather heightened, made magnificent and central as it becomes an instrument of revelation. And the ground itself is holy. In this central biblical story, the unique holiness of God does not exclude but rather entails the holiness of the ground, the bush, the surrounding ecology of things.

Similarly, in the symbolically important communion dialogue, the surprise springs forth in this: that the one holy, the one Lord is one who is no king, no lord, no Holy One at all, but rather a crucified man, tortured, degraded, utterly unclean. And so, holiness is redefined and the meal made open. Not "I am holy and nothing else is." Not "I am holy and you can take part in me if you are too." Not "you can come but make sure that the others do not." But "taste and see that the Lord is good."

What if that "taste and see" and that "holy ground" really do go together? What if authentic biblical religion and the liturgy that enacts and celebrates that religion really do mean to heal our eyes so that we may see the world itself held into holiness in God? What if the one whom the communicants encounter, the one who welcomes them, though unworthy, into redefined holiness, also shows them at the same time the holy ground, all things being held together in this mercy?

These questions will occupy this book. The book thus concerns that classic answer of the people in the Eastern communion dialogue: "Only one is holy." In the Western church, that same assertion has been sung through the ages in the entrance song called the *Gloria in excelsis:* "for you alone are the holy one, you alone are the Lord, you alone are the most high, Jesus Christ, with the Holy Spirit" *(quoniam tu solus sanctus, tu solus dominus, tu solus altissimus, Jesu Christe, cum Sancto Spiritu).* Hymnic stanzas have sung out numerous variations of this same theme, many a Protestant church using the early nineteenth-century words of Reginald Heber to open its service:

"Only thou art holy, there is none beside thee."[4] This unique holiness of God can be taken as a way to understand God as a great monad, a self-subsisting singularity beyond the world, unrelated to the world, denigrating the world. But the question to this hymn—indeed, to all of the public songs of the churches—must be whether the surprise of the holiness of God will genuinely come to expression in the liturgies that these songs fill. Do these hymns carry the surprise that arises from understanding the crucified and risen Jesus as the measure of "holiness," the surprise that includes a remembrance of what the biblical God's holiness inevitably entails: "remove the sandals from your feet, for the place on which you are standing is holy ground"?

So what does the Holy Communion—and with it all of Christian liturgy—have to do with the earth, we may begin to ask, emboldened by the holiness of the ground entailed by the holiness of the biblical God. But the questions are yet deeper, invested with all the senses of "cosmology." What kind of world does the liturgy propose that we live in? Is the only account of the universe actually present in Christian celebration really a pre-Copernican one, with sun and moon circling the earth and the layered heavens piled up beyond the stars? Are there any resources in Christian worship for connecting us to our immense new context, in which the earth appears as far from the center—for connecting us to galaxies and the redshift and the continuing "inflation" of space/time and the cosmic background radiation and the possibility of more than one universe? And would those connections matter? Indeed, this inquiry after meaning may be the deepest question: How do the words, symbols, and exchanges of Christian liturgy engage us in worldmaking? If we know that human ritual almost always carries cosmological implications, ways that societies find themselves oriented to the universe,[5] then what sort of "cosmos," what sort of "ordered world," does Christian liturgy imply? And, if that cosmos is intentionally archaic, how can it have effect in Christian ethics? In short, is there a "liturgical cosmology" that matters today?

---

4. For example, "Holy, Holy, Holy" is hymn 165 in *Lutheran Book of Worship* (Minneapolis: Augsburg, 1978).

5. This assertion is, of course, an essential inheritance from the work of Émile Durkheim, elaborated incisively, for example, in Mary Douglas, *Natural Symbols: Explorations in Cosmology* (New York: Random House, 1973), and elaborated cogently and most recently by Roy Rappaport, *Ritual and Religion*. Compare Catherine Bell, *Ritual: Perspectives and Dimensions* (New York: Oxford University Press, 1997), 50: For Mary Douglas, "ritual is always a matter of symbolic actions that express sociological truths in cosmological terms."

Cosmos in Postmodern Times

"Cosmos" transliterates κόσμος, the Greek word for "order." Or rather, from that same Greek word understood also as meaning "ordered world" or "universe," "cosmos" becomes the English word for "harmoniously patterned universe," "world" as a system. The word is, oddly enough, a cognate of such words as "cosmetics," since the order in question could sometimes be adornment, embellishment, even disguise. But made into "cosmology," it becomes the word for discourse about the ordered world, words that invite us into the ordered world, an account of the ordered world. Still, the "cosmetics" connection might help us to remember that these may well be only one's own accounts of the ordered world, one's own created embellishments for the sake of ordered life. This "cosmetics" connection recalls us to our postmodern context.

In current speech "cosmology" is used in three ways, and all three will be important to the considerations of this book. Perhaps most commonly these days, in newspapers and ordinary discourse, the word "cosmology" refers to that discipline of astrophysics that, in dialogue with many other disciplines, attempts to give an account of the universe in all its parts: its beginnings, its permutations, its projected futures, its microstructures and its macrostructures, its atoms and particles, its galactic webs and walls, even its tiny but included observing minds (us, as far as we currently know). This cosmology attempts to formulate and test a theory of everything, of "the whole shebang," as Timothy Ferris calls it.[6] Cosmology, then, is a kind of astronomy. But it is astronomy also aware of the smallest structure of matter or energy or light, wherever those things occur. It is astronomy attentive also to the earth itself and to us ourselves as parts of the system. Cosmology gives an account of the "big bang," the all-encompassing single event that more and more evidence supports as having begun everything, some 13 to 14 billion years ago. It also gives an account of how matter began to be formed and how light began to shine. It is currently trying out accounts of the endlessly continued expansion of space itself—the cosmic inflation—toward which expansion the evidence is also leaning. Truth to tell, a single "theory of everything" remains an elusive goal, an as yet unattained "holy grail." Einstein's relativity and Bohr's particle physics, for example, persist as unintegrated in any single theory. But that does not keep the cosmologists

6. Timothy Ferris, *The Whole Shebang: A State-of-the-Universe(s) Report* (New York: Simon & Schuster, 1997).

from trying. And the genuine excitement of current discovery, at least as it is reported in the hands of some masterful interpreters,[7] is profoundly interesting, even if its social significance and the reasons for our interest remain underdiscussed.

But the older, metaphysical meaning of "cosmology"—the inquiry about the social and personal sense of an ordered world, its establishment, its significance, its consequences—also survives. This older sense shows up not simply as quotations from Plato's *Timaeus,* the Greek philosopher's most extensive cosmological speculation, in modern astronomy texts,[8] but as an important theme in some recent philosophical work[9] and, especially, in ritual studies.[10] "Cosmology" here is an account of or an orientation to the universe as that account or orientation has public meaning and lived personal importance. Or "cosmology" is a statement of the principle or principles around which the universe is seen to be ordered, such principles also being understood as ways in which the wise will organize their lives. Of course, such an account may well be the current one on the pages of the "Science" section of the *New York Times* but turned now toward what seems to be the consequent social significance of the most influential scientific discoveries. The *Timaeus* also represented a report on the state of science in the mid-fourth century B.C.E., as well as an account of why the world should privilege philosophy and philosophers. In that sense, the *Timaeus* was intentionally both "science" and "worldview." But people actually live by many other cosmologies. They represent them and reinforce them in their rituals. They imply them by their languages and their stories. They use them in the ways they read the landscape or organize space. They pass them on to their children as they pass on their cultures. We may rightly ask about the "cosmology" of any given culture. If "culture" can be considered "the orientation necessary to survive and thrive in a place, the linguistic and symbolic but also the practical tools necessary for a human community to interact with the land and create a local order of meaning,"[11] then culture necessarily implies "worldview." "Culture," "ritual," "social space," and "worldview," by this

7. In addition to Ferris, one thinks of John Noble Wilford, George Johnson, James Glanz, or such first-rank participants in the research who are also interpreters as Stephen Hawking or Murray Gell-Mann.

8. Compare Ferris, *Whole Shebang,* 11, 40, 170.

9. For example, that of C. S. Peirce. See Roberta Kevelson, *Peirce and the Mark of the Gryphon* (New York: St. Martin's Press, 1999).

10. See, for example, Douglas, *Natural Symbols.*

11. Lathrop, *Holy People,* 66.

understanding, are indissolubly connected. And these cultural "worldviews," too, are cosmology.

A third use of the term has arisen in our own time. Arguing that the stars and their courses are too far away, too utterly beyond our influence to matter to the real organization of our days, some people have begun to speak of a new "cosmology."[12] For them, astronomy finally failed to give modern humanity a sense of ordered whole in which human life on the earth has its context. Such a sense of wholeness needs to be provided now by the more proximate but full system in which we live as a part. Here the "cosmos" is the earth itself—rocks and seas and weather and a huge but fragile variety of species of life—a habitable system that is indeed affected by human social action. Here is a "world" in which we may perceive ourselves as embedded, to which our thought and our action, our science and our poetry—our significant meanings—may be appropriately ordered in discovery, in self-understanding, and in urgent work for preservation and care. Here the appropriate "whole" that gives context to thought and direction for action—the "cosmos"—is the blue planet of which we are a self-reflective, speaking, ritualizing part. This cosmology has clear, reforming goals: Acknowledge that we are, indeed, part of the earth. Use our speech and our ritual to speak on behalf of our planet. Organize our economy to support ecological goals, not to be its own, independent and uncriticized, "worldview." Use our reason—we are the planet come to thought—to work for the well-being of the terran ecological net.

But all three uses of "cosmology"—in astrophysics, in philosophical and cultural studies, and in ecology—have disorienting new challenges from postmodernism. Granted that this latter term is notoriously vague, the truth remains that we are in a new era, one marked by distrust of authority, history, and any patterns too easily applied. Postmodernism evidences great uneasiness about any coherent systems at all, fearing that they may foreclose and exclude more than they assist. And postmodernism doubts the doctrine of progress. Rather, ours is a time of the great importance of actual, vivid experience, of multiplicity and multiculturalism in the valuing of that experience, and the assertion that every assertion (including the present one) has a self-interested author. We live in a hall of mirrors—or a brave new time, depending on your perspective—in which, nonetheless, the self can remain the relatively unassailed arbiter of meaning.

---

12. For example, Stephen Toulmin, *The Return to Cosmology* (Berkeley: University of California Press, 1982). Compare Roy Rappaport, *Ritual and Religion*, 456–59.

Such a time spells both difficulty and opportunity for cosmology. Astronomy and physics face the charge that the results of their discoveries are themselves the products and expressions of their Western cultural contexts, a current Western version of "myth," not the "truth."[13] Anthropology and ritual studies may similarly be accused, by both postmodernism and the allied postcolonialism, of imposing Western meanings, conceived in a Western-imposed hierarchy of cultures, on very diverse ritual data. Perhaps the word "ritual," even, is an imposition: does everything gathered under that name really fit?[14] And even ecology depends on your point of view: one culture's slash-and-burn agriculture for the sake of survival is another culture's destruction of the rain forest and contribution to global warming. Postmodernism asks: who is to say who is right? Furthermore, the environmental movement—a notable achievement of modern, not postmodern thought[15]—may itself be dependent upon deep but suspect faith in the progress of humankind. So a consequent postmodernism asks: who is to say that a huge die-off of the human species, like the die-off of the dinosaurs and other species throughout bio-history, ought not be considered "natural"? Cosmic collisions or a really nearby supernova could similarly wipe out or radically redo life on the earth. The order of our earth-cosmos is not isolatable from chaotic events in the networks of stars.

Indeed, for some forms of postmodernism, the category *cosmos* may itself be the problem, "order" being the creation of the human, even the Western human, mind. These postmodern thinkers might ask: are not chaos and chance at least equally our experience? Ought they not be welcomed into the dialogue of our thought?

But such counsel—when it becomes the charge that all we see when we look into the well is our own face—is finally a counsel of despair.[16] And it is ethically suspect to refuse to enter into the complex undertaking of evaluating cultures for their effect upon the whole of human life and the

13. Such has been one popular reading of the argument found in the important study by Thomas S. Kuhn, *The Structure of Scientific Revolutions* (Chicago: University of Chicago Press, 1982). See also Anthony Aveni, *Conversing with the Planets: How Science and Myth Invented the Cosmos* (New York: Kodansha, 1994).

14. Jack R. Goody, "Against 'Ritual': Loosely Structured Thoughts on a Loosely Defined Topic," in Sally F. Moore and Barbara G. Myerhoff, eds., *Secular Ritual* (Amsterdam: van Gorcum, 1977), 25–35.

15. Rappaport, *Ritual and Religion*, 460.

16. See the fine reflection on this very issue from the point of view of New Testament studies by John Dominic Crossan, *The Birth of Christianity* (San Francisco: HarperCollins, 1998), 40–46.

whole well-being of the planet. While rightly learning humility, wider thinking, openness to the other, and the honest yet critical inclusion of the perspective of the self from these postmodern, postcolonialist concerns, we may nonetheless dare more. Such commitment is also postmodern.

A reasonable proposal might be this: modern science is indeed an interactive combination of "discovery" and "construction," of observed and discovered "law,"[17] and constructed and communicated "meaning."[18] Scientists make up theories. Then they test them. Or the observation leads to the creative imagining of a modified theory or an entirely new proposal. Science is not only constructed in the human mind and in human discourse. There really are things to observe, and scientific theories, if they mean anything at all, must remain disprovable, vulnerable to counterevidence, open to the future. Still, observers do affect the observed, and humanity cannot live without the meanings. "Meaning" is not a marginal poetic extra, something quite beside the essential point of "fact." Meanings make up the characteristic markings of human life, and it will not do simply to dismiss them as "constructed." Fine human thought generally will involve a lively interaction between discovery and construction. And—here is an insight not frequently seen by scientists—ritual construction is one of the primary ways in which meanings occur among human beings. "Cosmologies"—astronomical theories of everything, social orientations to the world, ecological proposals—are indeed constructed. We will need to inquire, for example, what constructed meaning, what "cosmology," enables us to imagine that the care of the earth and all of its species is a primary value. We will need to dare to say that there are indeed primary values. And to keep living today and into tomorrow, we will need cosmologies, even though chastened postmodern ones, while newly inquiring how these cosmologies may listen to many other worldviews as they do their work. And if the cosmologies are reinforced in our rituals, then we will need to keep these rituals in interactive dialogue with the observations we can make of things as they are, including also the observations of those acute and practiced observers we call scientists, including the observations about, say, time and space that may sometimes challenge the easy cosmologies of our "common sense."

Such postmodern difficulties for the various meanings of "cosmology" in our time may pale next to yet another challenge. For many people, the

---

17. Even when the supposed "law" is discovered to change, as indeed it may! See George Johnson, "Suddenly, the Cosmos Looks More Fickle," *New York Times* (August 18, 2001), sec. 4: 1, 18.

18. Rappaport, *Ritual and Religion*, 453.

ruling worldview of the present time comes to expression in our economy. When that economy presents itself as a global system—and when monetary values are seen as primary values, the "bottom line" as the most basic knowledge about anything—then we have arrived at something like a cosmology.[19] We may feel that such an economic account of all things is a pervasive, comprehensive delusion, misrepresenting many of the things it seeks to describe and to order. We may ask if a person's education, the land in West Virginia, a single threatened species of frog, the archaeological discovery of an ancient Anasazi road, the discovery of another planetary system can be represented by their monetary value. But for many of us, while we may dabble in astrophysics or ecology or other public symbols, it is the relationship of our self to the economy that continues to be our practical, essential worldview.

Christian liturgical theologians have sometimes heard and reflected upon the challenge articulated by Susanne Langer in the mid-twentieth century: that we need a new public symbolism that would be able to hold and orient our lives in material and social realities, giving new grounds for hope and a social context for the functioning of the individual mind.[20]

Even more widely, liturgists have reflected upon the work of Mary Douglas. Perhaps with greater wisdom, this mid-twentieth-century sociologist had no illusions about "new symbolism" but did argue that the complex symbol systems held by modern, Western societies (the "elaborated code," she calls this system) had the ability to question themselves, opening toward values held by alternate, less "modern" cultures (for example, what she calls the "positional" pattern of "primitive" or "classical" peoples whose social organization is marked by very strong, essentially inescapable roles). Douglas writes that the argument of one of her books had been

> that the elaborated code challenges its users to turn round on themselves and inspect their values, to reject some of them, and to resolve to cherish positional forms of control and communication wherever these are available. This would seem to be the only way to use our knowledge to free ourselves from the power of our own cosmology.[21]

---

19. Ibid., 454–56.

20. Susanne K. Langer, *Philosophy in a New Key* (Cambridge, Mass.: Harvard University Press, 1978), 288–89. Compare David Power, *Unsearchable Riches: The Symbolic Nature of Liturgy* (New York: Pueblo, 1984), 5–34; and Lathrop, *Holy Things,* 3–4.

21. Douglas, *Natural Symbols,* 190; compare 50.

To find public symbols capable of holding and orienting us in the actual circumstances of the world and, at the same time, to free ourselves from the unbroken power of our own actual worldviews—such are the deepest post-modern challenges to the undertaking "cosmology."

But the problem is greater yet. The actual circumstances of the world in our times have included such tales of horror that it is difficult to imagine any account that is able to propose "order" to the wounded modern mind. The Nazi Holocaust of the Jews, the American incineration of Hiroshima and Nagasaki, the endless death marches and genocides and rapes from the Armenians to the Rwandans, from Nanking to Sarajevo, the destruction of the World Trade Center and people in captive airplanes: all these events have been told and shown to the public consciousness, destroying order. And there are the awful "natural" catastrophes—typhoons, floods, volcanic erup-tions, earthquakes, and famine-producing droughts—all of which make it difficult to hold any sense of a world that is concerned about the fate of humankind. Of course, there have always been such stories. But the sheer magnitude of these disorienting narratives and their wide, popular availabil-ity in the late twentieth century may be the very reasons that we have needed an agonizing appeal for "symbols to hold and orient" us anew in the universe. Such an appeal, of course, bears witness to the sense of the absence of the sought-for symbols. Our public symbols, Langer asserted just after the Second World War, have failed us. Or they work only by narrowed refer-ence, by forgetfulness in the face of the horrors, by being used exclusively for our intimate group, by setting aside the "actual circumstances of the world."

Is cosmology possible at all?

Say the matter in much smaller scope. The great tenth-century Anglo-Saxon epic *Beowulf* used, as an extended image for mourning and grief, the narrative of an old man "who has lived to see his son's body swing upon the gallows." For such a one, all wisdom, all song, all celebration seem worth-less:

> Alone with his longing, he lies down on his bed
> > and sings a lament; everything seems too large,
> > the steadings and the fields.[22]

---

22. Seamus Heaney, trans., *Beowulf* (New York: Farrar, Straus & Giroux, 2000), 167, lines 2460–62. In Anglo-Saxon: Gewīteð ꝥonne on sealman, sorh-lēoð gæleð ān æfter ānum; ꝥūhte him eall tō rūm, wongas ond wīc-stede.

"Everything seems too large." Ƿūhte him eall tō rūm. Such lament is the end of any easy cosmology. When the human community has seen many sons and daughters—and much else, besides—upon the gallows, everything seems far too large, uncontainable, beyond order.

We do urgently need all three forms of cosmology together, interacting honestly about the massive, observed universe, social meaning, and care for the earth. We do urgently need to be able to hold a legitimate care about the human self together with a legitimate concern about the economy of "household earth" together with these other systems of meaning. Such combinations are rare. How will we achieve them? In the process, how will we remember and respond to Beowulf's lament?

Liturgical Worldmaking amid the Cosmologies

Christian liturgy does not provide an automatic answer. Gatherings for worship will certainly imply some cosmology. That is, Christian rituals are also among the human rituals that construct a sense of world. Who and what we pray for, how we image earth and sky and all their creatures, what roles human beings are seen to have, how our social organization is seen to matter, how we share food, where God "is"—all these will leave us with a sense of "world," even if no mention is made of "cosmos." References to social order and enactments of social position—who gets to do what—will also for us have cosmic resonance.[23]

But the danger remains quite alive that the cosmology of the Christian liturgical assembly today will be archaic, shrunken, ultimately self-serving. Some people may think that biblical fidelity requires that the earth-centered, three-storie universe that seems to be reflected in biblical accounts needs to be reinforced in liturgical song and poetry. God is "up," the direction toward which the "ascension" has gone. So is "heaven." So are angels. "Hell," if it is mentioned, is "down." The sun rises and sets. Stars and even galaxies are lights beautifully hung in a sphere that travels around us, for our delight or our admonition. Such seems to some to be a language to speak in church. As a result, nothing said in church will have any connection with contemporary astronomy—and few connections to the actually

23. See above, n. 5. See also Lawrence A. Hoffman, *Beyond the Text: A Holistic Approach to Liturgy* (Bloomington: Indiana University Press, 1987), 173: liturgy involves the diverse media of the act of prayer, in which "the people, as living reality, act out the world as it sees it, and from which its members return to their several homes to shape their lives about the contours of the world as presented in prayer."

surrounding earth and its conditions. But then the absence of such connection may not much matter. The real "world" constructed in such liturgy may well be uncritically accepted, drawn from current individualism, one in which "you" (singular) and "I" are center of the universe. Prayers, sermons, and sacramental interactions that principally concern the hopes and dreams of the individuals present will be vulnerable to such a view. There will thus be little help for finding care for the earth rooted in Christian symbols. And it may be, after all, that the response to Beowulf's young man on the gallows—or to any other grief—will be rather like Matthew Arnold's prophetic, pathetic despair of any cosmology at all in his "Dover Beach":

> Ah, love, let us be true
> To one another! for the world, which seems
> To lie before us like a land of dreams,
> So various, so beautiful, so new,
> Hath really neither joy, nor love, nor light,
> Nor certitude, nor peace, nor help for pain;
> And we are here as on a darkling plain
> Swept with confused alarms of struggle and flight,
> Where ignorant armies clash by night.[24]

The single "order"—cosmos—that may remain to such an assembly will be the order of the small, intimate circle of "you and me" and the order of the poetry or liturgy itself. Such an individualist assembly may then be further subject to the uncriticized presence of the regnant, consumerist worldview. Shopping for the self in the diverse but troubled world is experienced as some comfort, a comfort reinforced if one's religion and religious ritual are also primarily about the self. So, in the "intercessions," we may plead only for our own happiness, and after the liturgy head for the mall.

What is more, the cosmological disorders and failings available to Christian liturgy are not limited to individualist or consumerist ones. Many other ways exist—as we shall explore[25]—in which unhelpful or even evil worldviews may be proposed by liturgical celebration.

---

24. Matthew Arnold, "Dover Beach," in Alexander Allison et al., eds., *The Norton Anthology of Poetry,* rev. ed. (New York: Norton, 1975), 851. The poem was first published in 1867.
25. See below, chapter 7.

But it need not be so.

The argument of this book is that the strong central symbols of Christian liturgy can stand in lively and helpful dialogue with the needs for a current cosmology. Indeed, when those symbols are celebrated in a strong assembly with a clear open door, when their use is refreshed in the ways that have been called "the ecumenical liturgical renewal," they can have a surprising cosmological resonance. Assembly gathered, the great bath enacted or remembered, Scripture read and preached and sung, many things prayed for, the holy meal held, assembly and its resources sent—these things can propose, reinforce, and, most importantly, radically and continually reorient our worldview. Liturgical renewal matters profoundly not only for historical, aesthetic, and theological reasons but also for that renewal's cosmological proposals. Christian liturgy can, indeed, orient us anew in relationship to the universe, can provide us with at least some public symbols that can enable public thought, can stand in helpful dialogue with yet other public symbols, can celebrate and call us to care for the planet. Christian liturgy, at its best, can do all this while also not foreclosing on the necessity for honest grief, for mourning unreservedly when "everything seems too large," for the experienced inadequacy of any cosmology at all.

These assertions, of course, have to be demonstrated. This book will try to do so.

These assertions also need to be made and nuanced with a good deal of modesty. Roy A. Rappaport was right when he argued that liturgy's capacity to claim and hold human beings and our ways of knowing the world has been considerably diminished since the Enlightenment.[26] Other commentators have argued that immodest claims have been made for "the liturgy" and its ability to heal our ills and order our world, inevitably fueling a massive disappointment in liturgical renewal.[27]

Of course, those claims may sometimes be attributable to the rhetoric of faith. A preacher calls an assembly to see the cosmological importance of the small actions in which the assembly is engaged, as if this particular liturgy were indeed *axis mundi,* all the trees of the wood and powers and

---

26. Rappaport, *Ritual and Religion,* 460. But note that Rappaport also devoted this final, massive work to creating a kind of handbook for a ritual that will matter to human interaction with the world.

27. Compare Rodney Clapp, "At the Intersection of Eucharist and Capital: On the Future of Liturgical Worship," *Proceedings of the North American Academy of Liturgy* (2000): 29–45, esp. 35. Clapp also quotes Catherine Bell and Michael Aune.

principalities of the cosmos clapping their hands around this little, local action that seems so marginal to society. When Alexander Schmemann says of the eucharist, "here we see the world in Christ, as it really is,"[28] or when Aidan Kavanagh describes the liturgy as "the Church doing the world as God means it to be done in Christ,"[29] these cosmological claims are not, at first glance, modest. Still, we might best take them to be invitations to faith and assertions about the connections between liturgy and life. Nonetheless, when an immodesty in our claims is connected with an actual privatization of our ritual practice, the result may well be an unintended—or, at least, uncriticized—reinforcement of the prevailing worldview of the market.

But the great tradition of the liturgy itself, of actual liturgical celebration, is marked by a deep-going modesty, a critique of our own claims to coherent meaning, and a constant conversion to hope in God's meaning. In the Christian assembly, modesty comes to expression in a whole variety of symbolic gestures. The central liturgical moments frequently involve an *epiclesis,* an invocation of God's free Spirit, over which our liturgy has no control. Advent is as important a description of the world as is the feast for which it prepares, and, when the Light does come, it is always hidden in surprising places, under the form of its contrary, in identification with the marginalized and the godless. The texts of prayer frequently express, in their biblical or Cranmerian parallels and repetitions, a kind of stammering before God, "the overall casting of liturgy as the *hope* that there might be a liturgy."[30] The liturgy accords with its central prayer, the Lord's Prayer, crying out for the coming of the day of righteousness and, at the same time, experiencing the present little meal and the local mutual forgiveness, about which we speak in that prayer, as a down payment (as eschatology puts it) on God's promise, on God's conception of the world, not as full description of all that is.

But is such a modest undertaking destined to let the current world order—say, a global consumerist economy—go unchallenged? And will such a modest liturgy be silent about our cosmology? On the contrary. Precisely the symbol of modesty before God—and the modesty of our liturgical symbols—may function like contradictory parables to all of our

---

28. Alexander Schmemann, *For the Life of the World* (New York: St. Vladimir's Seminary Press, 1973), 44.

29. Aidan Kavanagh, *On Liturgical Theology* (New York: Pueblo, 1984), 176.

30. Catherine Pickstock, *After Writing: On the Liturgical Consummation of Philosophy* (Oxford: Blackwell, 1998), 214.

consequent narratives, including the current narratives of consumer happiness or whatever else we use as a picture of our world. The down payment of forgiveness and bread in the assembly[31] indeed casts a light over the world. Baptism is not a polity. It is an identification with the crucified Christ who identifies with all the peoples of the world, including especially the marginalized ones of forgotten and silenced sufferings. As such, baptism is a constant criticism of all politics, a constant hole in our political, religious, and cosmological systems, calling those systems away from absolutizing tendencies. The central narratives in the assembly, if we use the lectionary and if we will listen, are scriptural words of reversed expectations and of surprising grace, one passage against another, an antinarrative to our cultural narratives and a new openness to the "holy ground." Eucharist is not an economy, but it is an economic proposal: founded upon the astonishing presence of God within the limits of our flesh, it is a sharing of food within limits, enough for everyone and for sending into the streets to the absent and the hungry, blowing a hole in our usual patterns of supply and consumption, our buffets of "all you can eat." The eucharist is not public order itself, but it is public order publicly and openly criticized. The lines that run out from these "down payments" are cosmological lines, in critical dialogue with all of our coherent accounts of the world and in critical dialogue with our lives.

Liturgical cosmology, as it is conceived here, does its work in a manner analogous to the parables. Those New Testament tales of reversal and grace frequently assume a wider narrative and a set of religious assumptions (for example, holy bread is unleavened and baked by priests in the temple) in order to speak the surprise of grace by subversion (the dominion of God is like leavened bread made by a woman).[32] In that use of surprise and reversal, the parables carry the deepest biblical tradition, resembling the dialogues of both the holy ground and the holy things with which we began. So, we will see, the classic actions and words of the Christian assemblies can be seen to set out reversals and subversions to many of the coherent accounts we may use to hold our world together, to construct our cosmologies. In fact, it will be the argument of this book that the principal cosmological contribution of the Bible itself is not so much a full-blown cosmology—three-storied and earth-centered, or not—as it is a quiet contrary word, a surprise, a breaking of cosmologies, a reversal toward new possibilities, a subversion

---

31. See Lathrop, *Holy People,* 76–77.
32. Matt. 13:33; Luke 13:20 and following. Compare Lathrop, *Holy Things,* 24–27.

of expectations, a reconfiguring of the-self-in-the-world. The Christian liturgy, also in this, is biblical: word and sacrament can be seen as enacting this same subversion. Such subversion—and not a closed account of the order of things—must be seen as the locus of God's revelation. The crucified one is the only holy one. Sinners are welcome. All persons, all things are equal in need and in grace. The bush is not burned. The ground is holy. Such turns mark the presence of the biblical God, leaves from the tree of life in our very midst, intended for the healing of the nations.

Liturgical cosmology, by this account, will not be the consequent narration of the true structure of things as if that narrative and our control of that narrative were to be identified as the revelation of God. Nor will it be the subsequent polemical defense of this presumed "true narrative" in the marketplace of cosmologies that surrounds us. Rather, it will be the actual and surprising experience of standing before God and discovering that the bush is not burned and the ground is holy. And it will be the further reflection about what that experience means.

As people of such liturgical parables, with their theological and cosmological modesty, Christians ought to join with all people of goodwill in the constant reform of the social order and in continuing research about the nature of the world. Liturgical cosmology ought not be in competition with astrophysics—let the research go on!—or with differing accounts of the importance of earth-care. Nor will it present itself as the only public symbolism that matters.

But precisely because of its parabolic character, liturgical cosmology will have much in common with several different cosmologies, listening to them as it is possible to do so, learning questions from them, using them to relativize the power of any regnant worldview. Take, for example, astrophysics. When astronomy does not present itself as theology, when physics does not try to prove "God" or "the soul," when the "big bang" is not seen as the latest revelation, the material for a new "natural religion," Christian theologians should rejoice. It is remarkable and very useful that Ferris has appended to his consideration of "the whole shebang" a "contrarian theological afterword," in which "God, questioned about cosmological matters, responds with his customary silence."[33] Liturgists know about this silence. It lives at the heart of the most important liturgical interactions, and its acknowledgment in a work of astrophysics can inspire confidence and enable deeper dialogue. In fact, several characteristics of some of the best astronomical

---

33. Ferris, *Whole Shebang,* 10, 303–12.

cosmology demonstrate affinity, though *not* identity, with the method of liturgical cosmology as understood here: paradoxes as a source for thought,[34] broken symmetries as primary structures,[35] the refusal of "progress" as a universal principle,[36] and the postmodern struggle to ask how human beings—these creatures on the third rock from the sun, a relatively small star in a marginal arm of a marginal galaxy in a second-class cluster of galaxies—are involved as observers and participants in the universe.[37]

Or, take the cosmological accounts of the indigenous peoples of the world, of Douglas's "positional" cultures. The Bible itself is full of fragments of a variety of diverse creation stories. It is useful to listen to all of them, coming as they do from ancient and very different cultures than our own. We think most quickly of the seven days of Genesis 1. But there are also the garden story of Genesis 2, the echoing of the Babylonian account of a cos-mogonic conflict with the sea-monster in Psalms 74 and 89, the positing of the Canaanite storm-god as creator in Psalms 29 and 104. We could add yet other material from Job, Proverbs, and Isaiah. The argument in this book is that the major cosmological point in the Bible is made when these stories are both received and turned to radically new purpose. The storm-god of Psalm 29 now becomes the God of Israel, praised for giving the people peace. The one who ordered the world through the sea-conquest in Psalm 74 is now begged for new order in the face of the chaos of Jerusalem.

Such a reading should prepare Christians to encounter yet other cre-ation stories in the world, looking also for reversals and reorientations. Christian liturgists who know that "order" is not just an ancient achieve-ment or an unchangeable imposition but a current proclamation and gift should be prepared to encounter affinities—not identities—to their work in a variety of indigenous sources: in Australian Aboriginal attachment to the land being vastly different from a Western sense of ownership;[38] in Navajo creation stories embracing both Balance—"Beauty," *hózhó*—and Coyote,

---

34. See ibid., *passim*.

35. Ibid., 214–16.

36. Ibid., 170–203.

37. Involved here among other things are the "Weak" and the "Strong Anthropic Prin-ciples," as well as the "Copenhagen" interpretation. See ibid., 255–58, 290–302.

38. See Ronald M. Berndt and Catherine H. Berndt, *The Speaking Land: Myth and Story in Aboriginal Australia* (Ringwood: Penguin Books Australia, 1989).

39. See Paul G. Zolbrod, *Diné bahane': The Navajo Creation Story* (Albuquerque: Univer-sity of New Mexico Press, 1984).

the great unbalancer;[39] in the *kachina* cult being enacted by the whole pop-
ulace of a village, not just the elite or the priests;[40] in all of these stories
having radically different resources for respect for other species and for the
earth. We will want to explore some of these dialogues with indigenous
senses of cosmos as we ask how Christian liturgy relates to the land, the
peoples of the land, the earth, the directions, the sky, and ethics under the
sky—to cosmology generally. In fact, such indigenous accounts, threatened
as they are in most instances by the worldviews of the surrounding dominant cultures, may stand as primary examples of three of our interests: public symbols that hold a culture in a significant world; shared accounts that
assist in the care of the earth; and laments in the face of a space that is now
too large, beyond our ordering.

This Book: Liturgical Theology as Liturgical Cosmology

But liturgical cosmology is not ethnography. It is also not astronomy or
ecological ethics. It is not ritual studies or philosophy or theories of social
meaning. It is also not systematic theology as that discipline turns to the
doctrine of creation and its implications. Nonetheless, to the extent possible,
liturgical cosmology needs to be in dialogue with all of these things.

What is it then? In this book, liturgical cosmology is, first of all, the
experience of the assembly itself being gifted with a sense of "world" as that
assembly engages in the interactions of the liturgy. The assembly's liturgy
thus provides the "account"—the "logos"—that holds us into "cosmos," in
all its meanings. This book will offer an invitation to its readers to come
again into that account, into participation in the interactions of communal
liturgy. Then, liturgical cosmology, in a secondary sense, is somebody's further reflection upon that liturgical event, upon the ways in which liturgy
makes—or does not make—cosmological proposals and upon the implications of those proposals. But since "cosmology" signifies a collection of
urgent matters for us in the present time, this "secondary liturgical cosmology" cannot be content to remain description or critique. It needs to propose again how liturgical assemblies can so make the symbols strong and the
doors wide open that the interactions of liturgy do indeed provide public

40. On the inclusivity of *kachina* ceremonialism, see Stephen H. Lekson, *The Chaco
Meridian: Centers of Political Power in the Ancient Southwest* (Walnut Creek: Alta Mira, 1999),
147–48. For an example of the cosmological stories related to this ceremonialism, see Dennis
Tedlock, trans., "When Newness Was Made," *Finding the Center: The Art of the Zuni Storyteller*,
2nd ed. (Lincoln: University of Nebraska Press, 1999), 245–318.

symbols, orient us in the actual universe, engage us in the care of the earth. Such reflection upon and counsel toward symbolic practice, such secondary and pastoral liturgical cosmology, will make up the balance of this book.

Of course, one might ask at this point, "*What* liturgy exactly? And *whose* liturgy?"[41] While there are dangers in generalizations, this book will continue to reflect upon Christian assemblies in which bath and word, prayer and table take central place amid a participating people. That simple outline is what is meant here by "the liturgy." Nothing more but also nothing less. These ideas need not be seen as esoteric or rare and certainly not as elitist. Almost all Christian assemblies, throughout the ecumenical Christian world, have some contact with an *ordo* in which word, bath, and table—supported and surrounded by prayer—play at least some role. And, once again, this book will argue that very role needs to be recovered as central, not only on biblical and theological grounds but also out of cosmological need. Nor are the reflections here in any sense the normative or official meanings, endorsed by ecclesiastical hierarchies or liturgy committees but questionable as reports of what participants really think. Here is the report of one participant. If that report is helpful for you, a spur to your own reflections and counsel for your community's next liturgy, the author is content and grateful.

In what follows, attention will first be given to some of the ways in which cosmology occurs in the Bible. Since Christian liturgy can be regarded as the enactment of central material from the Bible in a present assembly, these considerations will also point to the principal ways in which cosmological proposals are made by the liturgy (chapter 1). The book will then proceed to considering these ways concretely: first, liturgical "world-making" (chapters 2–3); then, the implications of liturgical cosmology for ethics and for dialogue with other forms of cosmology (chapters 4–6); finally, the dangers and the opportunities that are alive in a liturgical poetics attuned to the cosmos (chapters 7–9). In the second section of the book,

---

41. These are the questions asked in part to earlier work in this trilogy of books—and asked carefully and well—by Michael Aune, "Ritual Practice: Into the World, into Each Human Heart," in Thomas H. Schattauer, ed., *Inside Out: Worship in an Age of Mission* (Minneapolis: Fortress, 1999), 153, and by James White, "How Do We Know It Is Us?" in E. Byron Anderson and Bruce T. Morrill, eds., *Liturgy and the Moral Self* (Collegeville, Minn.: Liturgical Press, 1998), 56–57. In response to those questions, one ought also to look at Don Saliers, "Afterword," in *Liturgy and the Moral Self,* 209–24; Maxwell Johnson, "Can We Avoid Relativism in Worship? Liturgical Norms in the Light of Contemporary Liturgical Scholarship," *Worship* 74, no. 2 (March 2000): 135–55; and E. Byron Anderson, "The Claims We Make about Worship," in *Proceedings of the North American Academy of Liturgy* (2001): 77–93.

reflections on baptismal practice will be set in dialogue with cosmology as public symbolism, reflections on eucharistic practice will be set in dialogue with cosmology as ecology, and reflections on the liturgical use of time and space will be set next to the worldview of current astronomy. In the third section, the false worlds and cosmological failures of some Christian liturgy will be acknowledged (chapter 7), and consideration will be given to the liturgy's ability to hold us in meaning even when there is no map, no cosmos, and everything is too large (chapter 8). Concrete suggestions for practice will be made throughout, though especially in chapters 4–6 and 8. The whole of the book will stretch between two great biblical trees, both of which can be seen as metaphors for the triune God's presence in the liturgy: the unburned burning bush with its holy ground (Exod. 3:1-5) and the tree of life with its leaves and fruits, its roots and branches, healing the nations and holding all things under the Mercy (Rev. 22:1-2). In the process of thinking about these trees—about the presence of God in the Christian liturgical assembly—the book will be seeking to consider what that assembly has to do with the actual trees of the earth that surround us, the ones the angel of Revelation seeks to protect (Rev. 7:1-3).

One other central biblical image will recur in this writing as well: the hole in the heavens at the baptism of Jesus. Also here we may find a metaphor for the assembly's encounter with the living God and for the understanding of cosmos that follows. The hole in the heavens, the burning bush with holy ground all around, the very leaves of the tree of life, the angel calling out God's protection for earth and sea and trees—all of these images, and the powerful presence of the triune God that they proclaim, may be known in the assembly.

For the presence of God in the assembly is the whole source of authentic liturgical cosmology. That is why liturgical cosmology is a kind of liturgical theology, an attempt to see again how the liturgy speaks and signs God, an effort to see the public and social and cosmological significance of that speech and those signs, a search "to make the liturgical experience of the church again into one of the life-giving sources of the knowledge of God."[42] Come into the church. Sing out, "Only one is holy!" If the liturgy is biblically faithful, you will hear the cosmological surprise. You will hear, "taste and see that the Lord is good." You will hear, "the place on which you are standing is holy ground."

---

42. Alexander Schmemann, *Introduction to Liturgical Theology,* second edition (New York: St. Vladimir's Seminary Press, 1975), 19. See also Lathrop, *Holy Things,* 4–8.

PART ONE

Cosmos
Liturgical Worldmaking

FIRE IS BOTH WANT AND FULLNESS.
COMING UPON ALL THINGS,
IT WILL JUDGE AND SENTENCE THEM.

—Heraclitus

1

A Hole in the Heavens:
Biblical Reorientation in the Universe

A handful of written works might be considered as the world classics of cosmology. Among them, in the Western world, no written philosophical cosmology has had more influence than Plato's *Timaeus*. Its "discourse of the nature of the universe"[1] has hovered, acknowledged or unacknowledged, on the edge of continuing philosophical and scientific reflection concerning the nature and order of all things from its fourth-century B.C.E. origin, through the Renaissance work of Johannes Kepler, right up to current astrophysics.[2] In dialogue with interpretations of Genesis, the *Timaeus* has also played a central role in some Christian theological thought—in the work of Alexandrians and Cappadocians in the East and of Boethius in the West, even in the formulations of the Nicene Creed.[3] Its teaching that all things form a perfect sphere even shows up as paintings on the walls of medieval churches, God sometimes being depicted as the "demiurge," as Plato calls the maker of all things, measuring out that very sphere. Indeed, among ancient educated people in the Hellenistic world, the *Timaeus* would have been the most likely work, after Homer, to have been read in Greek.[4] It is thus no surprise to find references to the *Timaeus* in the

---

1. *Timaeus* 27c: τοὺς περὶ τοῦ παντὸς λόγους ποιεῖσθαι. Jowett translation in Edith Hamilton and Huntington Cairns, eds., *The Collected Dialogues of Plato* (New York: Pantheon, 1961), 1161. Greek from *Platonis Timaeus et Critias* (Leipzig: Teubner, 1888).

2. Ferris, *Whole Shebang* (see above, intro. n. 6), 11, 24, 40, 170, 171, 206.

3. Jaroslav Pelikan, *What Has Athens to Do with Jerusalem? Timaeus and Genesis in Counterpoint* (Ann Arbor: University of Michigan Press, 1997).

4. D. T. Runia, *Philo of Alexandria and the Timaeus of Plato* (Leiden: Brill, 1986), 57: "the *Timaeus* was the only Greek prose work that up to the third century A.D. every educated

New Testament itself, notably in the Letter to the Hebrews (for example, 11:3, 10), where the ideas of "creation out of nothing" and of that "demiurge," significant Timaean themes, recur. Furthermore, the *Timaeus* "was the only dialogue of Plato known in anything near its entirety to the Latin Middle Ages, and, therefore, it has had the longest continuous influence of any of the dialogues in the West."[5]

We, too, should take this work seriously. We should do so obviously not for the speculative fruits of its deductive reasoning, many of which will seem ludicrous to us—for example, souls come from the stars and return to the stars; birds are recycled human beings who had "airy" minds in their first life—but as a symbol of massive, engaged human thought about the origin and structure of things. Still, now and then, a line from the *Timaeus* will stun us with its nearly contemporary insight and remind us why astronomers still read the book. There is, for example, this: "Time, then, and the heaven came into being at the same instant, in order that, having been created together, if ever there was to be a dissolution of them, they might be dissolved together."[6] Such a line may sound to us like Einstein or like accounts of the "big bang."

Unlike what is found in other Platonic dialogues, Socrates appears in this work not as the major voice, the stand-in for Plato's thought or for Plato's synthesis of his own work with that of his great teacher, but primarily as interlocutor and as audience. That fact may indicate a certain distancing of Plato himself from the content of the work, a certain relaxation or playing of the mind. In any case, the work represents the later Plato (after 361 B.C.E. and before Plato's death in 347 B.C.E.) and seems to have been intended as part of a trilogy of works of which we possess only the *Timaeus* and a fragment of the *Critias*.

The *Timaeus* begins with Socrates briefly summarizing the *Republic* as a way to invite his companions to keep their promise to entertain him with further reflections on the history of all things (17a–20b). Critias, presented as a widely recognized Athenian leader, then proceeds to tell a story about the earliest history of Athens, about its connections with Egypt and its conflict with Atlantis (20c–27b). This story is given as a down payment on the

---

man could be presumed to have read." Bas van Iersel and Jan Nuchelmans, in "De zoon van Timeus en de zoon van David," *Tijdschrift voor Theologie* 35 (1995): 107–24, also assert that "between 100 before Christ and 100 after Christ no single dialogue of Plato drew as much interest as did the Timaeus" (118).

5. Pelikan, *Athens*, 23.

6. *Timaeus* 38b; Jowett translation in Hamilton and Cairns, *Plato*, 1167.

human history—specifically the history of the city and its worthy wars—
that he engages to tell after Timaeus first recounts the origin of the world
itself. The bulk of the book is then given over to that account of the gen-
eration and order of the cosmos. If Critias is an important Greek leader,
Timaeus is another. Timaeus appears as a Pythagorean philosopher, a states-
man from the Greek city of Locri in Italy, and an astronomer who "has
made the nature of the universe his special study."[7] The agreement among
the speakers is that Timaeus should first recount the genesis of the cosmos,
down to and including the creation of humanity, and that Critias will then
again take up human history.

Timaeus's account is divided into two parts.[8] Each of these parts is
begun clearly (27c–d and 47e–48e), with a strong verbal indication of
beginning—"so, now, let us begin"—and with a strong invocation for divine
assistance. The first part (27c–47d) considers the great, perfect pattern of all
things (Plato's "ideas," differently expressed) and the imitation of that pattern by the demiurge in making the things that are generated and visible.
The classic four elements—earth, air, fire and water—are discussed, and
from their subsequent combinations all else is posited. Timaeus then proposes the great sphere that is all things, discussing the motions of the sun
and moon and planets within the sphere of heaven and demonstrating the
extent of the observations of such movements in ancient Greek astronomy.
He then moves on to speculations on the making of the stars and the birth
of time, the birth of the gods, and the making of souls. Lesser gods, "younger
gods," now made the bodies for these souls, not always doing so with perfection. Nonetheless, in imitation of the great sphere of all things, the human
head was made—"being the most divine part of us and lord of all that is in
us"[9]—the rest of the body being appended as servant to the head. Then, into
this head are inserted the organs of the senses, to create the face and front
of the head and to minister to the needs and well-being of the soul. The first
and chief of these senses is sight, and the first part of Timaeus's account
closes with an encomium on the immense importance of sight.

If the first part proceeds in a way that edges into narrative and myth—a
"likely story" (τὸν εἰκότα μῦθον), as Timaeus asserts (29d)—the second

---

7. *Timaeus* 27a; ibid., 1161. Compare 20a.

8. Some scholars see three sections: 29d–47d, 47e–68e, 69a–92c; compare Pelikan, *Athens*, 25 n. 14. But the text itself calls attention to only the two divisions we note here, doing
so especially with the twice-repeated invocation of divine help (27c; 48d).

9. *Timaeus* 44d; Jowett translation in Hamilton and Cairns, *Plato*, 1173.

part of his account (47e–92c) waxes more philosophical. Timaeus begins again. Now he discusses necessity, the dialectic between "the one" and nothing, the passive material receptacle for all generations, and whether there are of necessity many worlds or one world. But here, as well, Timaeus moves from the macrocosmos toward the creation of the human body, just as he is supposed to have agreed to do, just as he did also in the first part of his account. So he goes on to the affections (παθήματα) and, again, to the faculties of sense (αἰσθητικός), including finally, and importantly, sight. The treatise then becomes a reflection on medicine and, at the end, a brief account of the creation of women (regarded as very much lesser human beings, as recycled cowardly males), sexuality, and the other animals. And so it closes.

Exactly at the juncture of the two parts of Timaeus the astronomer's account of the cosmos, summing up his first part and anticipating the similar movement of the second part also toward the human senses, there is found the little speech in praise of sight (47a–c). The Jowett translation of this speech of Timaeus reads as follows:[10]

> The sight in my opinion is the source of the greatest benefit to us, for had we never seen the stars and the sun and the heaven, none of the words which we have spoken about the universe would ever have been uttered. But now the sight of day and night, and the months and the revolutions of the years have created number and have given us a conception of time, and the power of inquiring about the nature of the universe. And from this source we have derived philosophy, than which no greater good ever was or will be given by the gods to mortal man. This is the greatest boon of sight, and of the lesser benefits why should I speak? Even the ordinary man if he were deprived of them would bewail his loss, but in vain. This much let me say however. God invented and gave us sight to the end that we might behold the courses of intelligence in the heaven, and apply them to the courses of our own intelligence, which are akin to them, the unperturbed to the perturbed, and that we, learning them and partaking of the natural truth of reason, might imitate the absolutely unerring courses of God and regulate our own vagaries.

So, says Timaeus, philosophy ultimately derives from sight. The very words of his cosmology depend upon sight—wise sight, sight made the basis

10. Ibid., 1174–75.

of reflection, but sight nonetheless. According to him, the wise will take what they see in the orderly progression of the stars in their courses and apply that to their own minds, seeking to follow and imitate such movements in peaceful reason. Similarly, near the end of the second part of his discourse, Timaeus returns to the same theme: let the wise man follow the thoughts and revolutions of the universe, learning the harmonies of the sphere, "so that having assimilated them he may attain to that best life which the gods have set before mankind, both for the present and the future" (90d).[11] Summarizing the goal of each part of the discourse, then, the Timaean praise of sight points both to the scientific basis of his cosmology—observation, followed by deductive reason and mathematics—and to the ethical implications of this cosmological reflection: Let the philosopher's mind learn and follow what he sees; let the philosopher's mind imitate "the absolutely unerring courses of God,"[12] thereby attaining the good life. The praise of sight gives a center to both the structure and the content of this cosmology.

It is, of course, painful to think about that "ordinary man." Timaeus himself does not spend much breath upon him, briefly running past the one whose blindness might cause him to bewail the loss of even the simple gifts of sight, let alone its philosophical and cosmological heights. For him, this nonphilosopher does not matter to the argument. Still, the careful modern reader, especially the reader who rejoices in the general tenor of this praise of sight, might be more troubled. In fact, the seemingly thrown-away comment of Timaeus is even sharper than the Jowett translation allows to appear. A more literal translation would read:

> But those [gifts of sight] which are lesser, why should we hymn them here? Those very gifts, even if they are lamented with wailing by the blind person who is not a philosopher are certainly lamented in vain![13]

The "ordinary man" of Jowett is in fact, in the Greek, a blind man, thus one incapable of being the kind of philosopher Timaeus envisions, incapable of attaining the good life, not able to follow those divine courses in the sky. If such a one bewails the loss of the "lesser gifts" of ordinary vision, certainly

11. Ibid., 1209.
12. 12. *Timaeus* 47c: μιμούμενοι τὰς τοῦ θεοῦ πάντως ἀπλανεῖς οὔσας (See above, n. 1).
13. *Timaeus* 47b: τἆλλα δέ, ὅσα ἐλάττω, τί ἂν ὑμνοῖμεν; ὧν ὁ μὴ 'λόσοφος τυφωθεὶς ὀδυρόμενος ἂν θρηνοῖ μάτην (see above, n. 1).

that lament is foolish, μάτην, void of result, in vain. This problem with the cosmology of Timaeus was no problem at all to a worldview marked by the privilege and domination of certain upper-class, physically intact males. To us, however, this one sentence may seem like something of the lament of Beowulf, when "everything seems too large," edging into Plato's attempt at a comprehensive account of the cosmos and Plato's cosmological ethics.

What shall we do with this lament? And, if the *Timaeus* is really so important to Western cosmology, what shall we do, then, with our coherent accounts of all things, accounts for which the massive achievement of this ancient dialogue may stand as a symbol? Should we really let our uneasiness about the blind and lamenting "ordinary man" trouble us? Even more, is the role given to women in this dialogue—not to mention its idea that all the other animals are lesser and unworthy human beings recycled—a fatal flaw in its thought for us? And what does all this have to do with liturgy?

Mark:
Broken Myths, Broken Cosmologies

In the Gospel according to Mark, the name "Timaeus" appears again. At the junction of the two major parts of the Second Gospel, between this Gospel's "Galilee" and its "Jerusalem," exactly between the ministry narratives and the passion story, there stands the account of a blind man (Mark 10:46-52). He is called "the son of Timaeus." The name itself strikes us in at least three ways. First, this is the only recipient of the healing ministry of Jesus in the entire Gospel who is given a name at all. The name matters. Second, the name is intensified, this patronymic being repeated both in Greek and in Aramaic.[14] We are strongly invited to note doubly that this person is the son or descendant or heir of Timaeus, just as he himself doubly calls Jesus the son or descendant or heir of David (10:47, 48).[15] And third, as many com-

---

14. "Bartimaeus," presented here as if it were a given name, uses the Aramaic prefix "bar," meaning "son of," with the Greek name "Timaeus." Van Iersel and Nuchelmans, *Timeus,* also discuss the striking name and its likely connotations to those who knew something of Greek philosophy, but they do not consider the actual contents of the *Timaeus* or the structurally interesting location of the lamenting blind man in *Timaeus* 47b. See also Mary Ann Tolbert, *Sowing the Gospel* (Minneapolis: Fortress, 1995), 189 n. 21.

15. The first of the times that the blind beggar calls out to Jesus, the name is in the exact and strikingly unusual order that is used in first naming him. The reader is thus invited to see that the "son of Timaeus, Bartimaeus" is meeting the "son of David, Jesus," and so to understand, at the least, that one who carries the central identity of Greek philosophy and cosmology is calling out in need to the one who carries Jewish and biblical messiahship. See van Iersel and Nuchelmans, *Timeus,* 113.

mentators have noted, the name is very hard to place in a Jewish context.[16]
It is not a recognized, current Hebrew or Aramaic name. We ought to yield
the point. It is a Greek name and, in fact, one with a very specific and recognizable history. Here is the "son" of Timaeus, Plato's Timaeus, and, ironi-
cally, he is himself blind, crying out in lament, seeing nothing, going nowhere.
This cry for help occurs at the very place, structurally, that the lament of the
blind man occurs in the *Timaeus:* at the juncture of the two major parts of
the book.

The story, of course, is not some literal historical report. In fact, reading
it may help us to see more generally the creative, symbolic intention of
much of the Second Gospel. The evangelist could well have received the
account of a healing at Jericho or along the road as part of the oral tradition.
But it is Mark[17] who supplied the location of the account in the pattern and
flow of the book. And most probably, Mark provided the name of the beggar, not as a report of what happened to Timaeus's own descendants but as
a symbol and a breaking of symbols, an example of the Second Gospel's
address to our present time. The evangelist thereby made of the account an
explicit *mimesis* and reversal of Plato[18] and made the Gospel of Mark a profound contribution to cosmology.

That *mimesis* and reversal of Plato become clearer when one notes what
the story follows and where it leads. In Mark, the account comes just after
the last of the passion predictions, Jesus' words about sharing his cup and his
baptism, and his exhortation to his followers not to be like the leaders of the

16. See Earle Hilgert, "The Son of Timaeus: Blindness, Sight, Ascent, Vision in Mark,"
in Elizabeth Castelli and Hal Taussig, eds., *Reimagining Christian Origins* (Valley Forge: Trinity
Press International, 1996), 191.

17. We do not know the name of the author of this Gospel, called the "Second Gospel"
but most likely the first example of this genre, nor do we know that author's gender or number. This book will nonetheless call that author by the conventional name, hoping that the
readers remember that this "Mark" could well be a community or a particular woman or
man.

18. Dennis R. MacDonald, in the suggestive work *The Homeric Epics and the Gospel of
Mark* (New Haven: Yale University Press, 2000), 2, calls such *mimesis* used in reversal a "transvaluative hypertext" that "not only articulates values different from those in its targeted
hypotext but also substitutes its values for those in its antecedent." While MacDonald very
helpfully suggests several—perhaps too many?—such transvaluations of Homeric texts in
Mark, he misses this passage from Plato. He nonetheless articulates well (pp. 7–8) the criteria
needed to establish that we are actually dealing with "intertextual referencing": accessibility,
analogy, density, order, distinctiveness, interpretability. At least five of his six criteria are
strongly met by our proposal of linking the Bartimaeus story with *Timaeus* 47b. MacDonald
is also helpful in directing our attention to the Hellenistic—as well as the Hellenistic Jewish—cultural context of Mark. So, "accessibility": Plato's *Timaeus* would have been part of
the evangelist's world.

Gentiles (10:32–45). Timaeus and Critias, of course, were such leaders, and their attitudes toward women and "lesser" sorts of people were examples of the worldview of such tyranny. Now, the very descendant of Timaeus is presented as such a lesser sort. But unlike the figure in the *Timaeus,* this blind beggar does not lament in vain. Throwing off his cloak (the "philosopher's cloak"? is it philosophy itself that is blind?), he comes to Jesus (10:50). Calling Jesus "my teacher," he asks to see. And upon receiving his sight, he follows Jesus "in the way" (10:52). What follows immediately in the book is the beginning of the Markan passion account, the enacting of Jesus' cup and the baptism of his death. The "way" that Bartimaeus follows is the way into this death, not the unperturbed and reasonable courses of the heavenly bodies. Participation in this way seems to invite us to a different sort of cosmology, a different view of the constitution of the universe and a correspondingly different estimate of the good life.

One might assume that the figure of Bartimaeus then disappears from the Gospel. His name does not occur again. But given the crucial location of this figure in the structure of the Gospel, the open-ended report of his following on the way, and the narrative interest in both his clothing and his sight, it is not impossible to suggest that the evangelist sees this same figure recurring, first as the young man who is following Jesus (14:51; compare 10:52) and who runs off naked, then as the young man in the empty tomb, now dressed in a white robe, announcing where Jesus is to be seen (16:5, 7).[19] These latter two figures have been linked in recent exegesis of Mark, and the single "young man" has been seen as a type of the newly baptized, of those who are immersed in the death of Jesus in order to be clothed in his life and made witnesses of the resurrection.[20] Indeed, the youngest and the newest members of the Christian assembly, by this view, may be wiser and more insightful than Peter or the other leaders. But it may be important to extend this reflection by understanding the "young man" to be none other than Mark's "son of Timaeus." Then that beggar has been

---

19. At the least, Bartimaeus is the very first of a series of important marginal figures who now appear in the Markan passion account as counterparts to the misunderstanding disciples, figures who are beginning to understand the way of Jesus: Bartimaeus himself, going into the passion story and opening up the way for these figures, then the providers of the colt (11:6), the scribe who asks the good question (12:34), the widow in the temple (12:41-44), the anointing woman (14:9), the young man in the garden (14:51-52), Simon of Cyrene (15:21), the centurion (15:39), the women who come to the tomb (16:1), and the young man in the tomb (16:5). See van Iersel and Nuchelmans, *Timeus,* 113.

20. See Lathrop, *Holy People* (see above, intro. n. 2), 176.

fully stripped and clothed in the manner of ancient baptisms. Throwing off the cloak of philosophy or of begging, he has come to the teacher (10:50-51) and entered into the way of the catechumen. That way involves more than ideas and reason. It leads to naked need and immersion in Jesus' death (14:51-52). Finally, this very same figure, now clothed in resurrection life, bears witness to a new use of sight: beholding Jesus "in Galilee" as he promised (16:5-7). This new Timaeus also follows "the absolutely unerring courses of God" toward the "best life" as the philosopher advises, but those courses are not found in the sky but, hidden under the form of disorder and loss, they are found among us, on the earth, in the way of Jesus Christ, "seen" in faith. It may very well be that the author of the Fourth Gospel understood Mark clearly here: just after that Gospel reports that the Pharisees have said that "the κόσμος has gone after him" (John 12:19), the narrative continues, " . . . some Greeks . . . came to Philip . . . and said to him, 'Sir, we wish to see Jesus'" (12:20-21).[21] Cosmology itself, that old Greek undertaking, is restructured in beholding Jesus, the Crucified, who draws all to himself.

If this reading of the Bartimaeus story is correct, then Mark has intentionally created or borne witness to a hole, a tearing in the fabric, of the cosmology of the *Timaeus*. This hole occurs just at the place where the blind cry out for sight and are ignored, where, for the Christian, the lament is too strong for the cosmological business-as-usual to continue. And it occurs at a place that corresponds, in the *Timaeus*, to the ethical culmination of the argument, to the turning of the consideration of all things toward the ordering of the life of the wise. Only now the wise—together with everyone else—are invited to the wise folly of the cross. And the hole gets even larger.

It would not be true to assert that Mark entirely rejects either the *Timaeus* or the enterprise of cosmology. After all, the evangelist takes seriously the Platonic book by engaging in this reversal. One can assume that, for Mark, the great sphere, the courses of the heavenly bodies, and the rudiments of medicine—cosmological assumptions of Hellenistic culture—were all taken to be more or less as the *Timaeus* describes them. Even more, one can find a number of parallels between interests of the *Timaeus* and concerns of Mark. Timaeus asserts, "The father and maker of all this universe is past finding out, and even if we found him, to tell of him to all men

21. K. Hanhart, *The Open Tomb, A New Approach: Mark's Passover Haggadah* (Collegeville, Minn.: Liturgical Press, 1995), 125–26.

would be impossible" (28c).[22] Mark celebrates the "messianic secret." Only for Mark, that secret focuses around the Crucified One, and the utterly impossible thing nonetheless happens (10:27): people come to know him in faith and the readers of the Gospel book are invited to know the truth of who he is. The *Timaeus* praises the philosophical importance of sight. For Mark, sight is also centrally important (8:18; 9:4; 13:26; 14:62; 16:7). Only for Mark, the seeing can be blind and the blind may be able to see. At last, the sight of faith is invited to behold the Crucified as the Risen One. In the *Timaeus*, God brings order out of disorder (30a). In Mark, this assertion is made the theme of many narratives—for example, the great chapter of miracles: the stilling of the sea (4:35-41), the healing of the demoniac (5:1-20), the quenching of the woman's flow of blood (5:25-34), the quieting of the wailing for Jairus's daughter (5:38-40)—all down payments on the young man in the empty tomb at last announcing the greatest overcoming of disorder. Most importantly, the *Timaeus* is repeatedly interested in "the heaven" (οὐρανός, 28b and *passim*) as the location of the great courses of the heavenly bodies and the principal name for that perfect sphere of all things: "the sensible God who is the image of the intellectual, the greatest, best, fairest, most perfect—the one only-begotten heaven," as the last words of the dialogue have it (92c).[23] Mark, too, is interested in "heaven" (e.g., 1:11; 6:41; 8:11; 13:25; 14:62). Only in Mark, the hearers of the Gospel book, along with Jesus, "see" the heavens torn (1:10), and the "son of God" is not the sphere of the sky but is among us, sharing our death (1:1; 15:39), becoming our life.

A hole in the heavens, a tear in the perfect fabric of the perfect sphere, then the Spirit descending like a dove at the end of the flood and a voice coming from the heaven: there, at the outset of the book (1:9-11), is an image of the Markan cosmology.

The Gospel of Mark is not a full cosmology. Rather, the book involves, as at least part of its concern, a significant reorientation of Plato's work. This reorientation takes the "likely story" of Timaeus and deals with it as a "broken myth."[24] Such breaking receives the terms of the myth and its power to

22. Jowett translation in Hamilton and Cairns, *Plato,* 1161–62.
23. Ibid., 1211. See also 31b.
24. "Myths are stories that investigate the nature of the world. . . ." Robert Bringhurst, *A Story as Sharp as a Knife: The Classical Haida Mythtellers and Their World* (Vancouver: Douglas & McIntyre, 1999), 288. "Once the story is known, a single image or even a single word can evoke it." Ibid., 47. For the "broken myth," see Paul Tillich, *Dynamics of Faith* (New York: Harper, 1957), 52–54. For this idea applied to myths and symbols in Christian liturgy, see Lathrop, *Holy Things* (see above, intro. n. 2), 27–31, and *Holy People,* 69, 177 n. 50.

evoke and describe our experience of the world. But the coherent language of the myth, its consequent and contained system, is seen as insufficient, and its power is seen as dangerous. The myth, then, is both true and not true, capable of truth only by reference to a new thing, beyond its own terms. In Mark, that new thing is the word of God and the presence of the Spirit known in the Crucified and Risen One. In Mark, that new thing is the encounter with the God whom the church has called "the Holy Trinity." And in this broken myth, Bartimaeus and the hole in the heavens function as broken symbols: the philosopher is blind and then a candidate for baptism; the perfect sphere is torn as the triune mercy of God is made known on the earth. These symbols evoke the whole myth, and that account is seen as broken, in need, now referring beyond itself.

In just the same way, at least two other examples of broken cosmological symbols also function in Mark. These symbols arise not from Greek but from Jewish and Middle Eastern provenance. The mustard seed parable (Mark 4:30-32) receives the old cosmic image of the "tree of life"—the great tree that holds all things in order—and yet breaks that image to new meaning: the tree of life is an annual bush; the tree of life, making room for all things in its branches, is the cross.[25] More extensively, the Jerusalem Temple, that ancient symbol of the heart of the cosmos, the navel of all things, is also reinterpreted. The Temple is cleansed (11:15-19) and then held under the threat of destruction (13:2). But the cornerstone of a new temple (12:10-11) or its architect and builder (14:58; 15:29; compare 6:3) is the Crucified One. Such use of cosmological symbols exactly corresponds to the Markan use of soteriological terms as well: the Christ, the expected "anointed king," in Mark comes to serve, not be served, is anointed only for his burial by an unnamed woman, rules only from the cross, is hailed only in mocking or by his executioner.

Plato, too, remembers human fallibility and mortality. Timaeus reminds his hearers, "I who am speaker and you who are the judges are only mortal men" (29d).[26] His conclusion follows: "We ought to accept the tale which is probable—the likely story, the fairly reasonable myth—and inquire no further." Mark inquires further.[27] He uses precisely the failures and holes in the

---

25. See below, chapter 9.

26. Jowett translation in Hamilton and Cairns, *Plato,* 1162.

27. Actually, to be fair, Plato inquires further as well. Plato's interest, especially expressed in other dialogues like the *Phaedrus* or the *Symposium,* does really lie in continually finding the truth in dialogue, while for him the myth can only repeat its monologue over and over.

myths to praise the God who comes into our mortality with life-giving, world-holding mercy.

These broken myths invite the reader to explore and use such patterns and themes of world coherence as may be available to us, but also to find the deepest, all-including coherence not in any of our schemes or symbols but in the mercy of God. This broken cosmology makes room for the women, for the lament of the blind or anyone else to whom the world has become too large, for the need of the marginalized and forgotten, for the experience of the utterly disordered world. The Gospel of Mark itself contains several connecting lines out to the cosmos. There is a way in the wilderness (1:2-3). Crowds are drawn from many regions and from the four directions (3:8; 8:9). A new sense exists that all the houses, fields, and families of the earth can be seen as home to those who follow Jesus (10:30). But the heavens are torn, and the courses of the stars—while belonging to God—are not necessarily the reliable sign of peaceful reason: the sun can be darkened (13:24; compare 15:33), the stars can fall (13:25). Order—deep order for all things—is only to be found in the word and promise of God and in the encounter with the Risen One.

Such assertions ought not be used by Christians to shut down the undertaking of cosmology, in any of its senses. A Christian in the present time can rightly engage vigorously in the massive scientific inquiries needed to move toward an astrophysical account of the structure of things or a biological account of the structure of life, the massive social and political work needed to develop shared worldviews, the massive intellectual work needed to elaborate an accurate and responsible ecology. A Christian in the present time can rightly rejoice in the fruits of these labors. These are our versions of the *Timaeus*. But all of them have holes, silences, inabilities. None of them should be turned into comprehensive worldviews with an utterly consequent ethics implied. That way lies tyranny. Indeed, the Christian experience of the broken symbol makes a proposal to all worldviews—scientific, religious, philosophical: let them be held critically, with room for lament, room for the other, and room for mercy. Our worldviews—perhaps especially our religious worldviews—are not themselves God. Only one is holy.

My colleague, John Hoffmeyer, in a personal communication, has written, "Plato's caution against further inquiry is a warning against trying to find a μύθος that could somehow shake off its vulnerability. It is not an admonition to rest content with the μύθος. On the contrary, the Platonic task is to expose (and re-expose and re-expose) the μύθος (to the 'never-ending story' of διαλέγεσθαι)." The problem is that the widely known *Timaeus*, largely narrated not by Socrates but by a Pythagorian, was dealt with as final, all-encompassing myth by the Neoplatonists and others who used it.

This critique of worldviews is urgently needed in the present time. Cosmologies have been constructed that consign whole groups of people, whole parts of the world, whole ranges of species to evil or even to nonbeing. God or the gods have been made into guarantors of these constructions. Mass murder has ensued. Cosmologies are not all innocent, all of equal value, all beautiful. We need the scientific testing of hypotheses, the experimental vulnerability to actual evidence. But we also need the breaking of symbols, the breaking of myths.

Where are we to find the Christian experience of the broken symbol—or, more, the broken myth, the broken cosmology? Even the Gospel of Mark seems to conclude (16:8) with nobody understanding, except perhaps the young man in the tomb, and with the women running away, silent and afraid. By the end of the Gospel, there is no experience to counter the final word of death, except for the very ambiguous empty tomb. But the ending of the Gospel sends the reader or hearer of the book—sends us—back to Galilee where the Risen One is to be seen (16:7), that is, back to the beginning of the Gospel book itself (1:16).[28] There, shockingly if we know the *Timaeus,* we see again that this is a text about a "son of God" other than the perfect cosmic sphere. Indeed, we see the heaven itself torn open. And there, after once again coming across baptism and the call to follow, the reader or hearer encounters Jesus in the text, in a synagogue (1:21) and then in a house (1:29), receiving the crowd, teaching, healing. Hearing this text in the house of the church, house of the word, is then the very "seeing" of the Risen One that the young man in the tomb promises. Jesus lives in the text as it is present in the assembly. The Gospel book itself, read in the assembly, is the resurrection appearance. The whole assembly comes into the hidden meaning of the story, the now manifest, risen identity of the Crucified One. The whole assembly becomes the locus for seeing the torn heavens, receiving the Spirit, hearing the voice of God, being reoriented in the world. Even more, as the text continues, the reader or hearer comes to understand that the fragments of bread from Jesus' great meals (6:30-44; 8:1-10) are still being passed out. Eyes are healed in that shared bread to see the Crucified One as risen. Finally, we see that the way of Bartimaeus, the way of baptism, is open also to us. The house, the word, bread, baptism, the "way": the Gospel of Mark unfolds toward the exercise of the very symbols that give a center to the Christian assembly. The Markan reorientation of

---

28. For the significance of this assertion for eucharistic meaning and practice, see below, chapter 4.

cosmology comes to liturgical expression. Indeed, Markan cosmology is a liturgical reorientation, not an ideology, not an idea.

The importance of the Bartimaeus story in the Gospel comes to even greater clarity when one considers that the son of Timaeus is the second blind person to be healed in the story. The first is an unnamed man who is healed in a gradual process (8:22-26) just before the first passion prediction (8:27—9:1). Thus, the three passion predictions of Mark, those immensely important bearers of the meaning of the book and the meaning of Jesus, are exactly framed by accounts of the healing of the blind. Coming to "see" means coming to understand and encounter God's mystery in Jesus. Coming to see means coming to understand and encounter the hole in the philosopher's consequent account of the world. Coming to see means coming to trust that all things are held in the mercy of God. Furthermore, in the first case sight is given as a gift of Jesus just after the disciples have been accused of being "blind" in spite of their knowing about the basketfuls of bread left over, still available to be given away (8:18-21). In the second case, Bartimaeus is healed just after the word about sharing in Jesus' cup and Jesus' baptism. And Bartimaeus—or someone like him, another narrative figure meant to make room for us in the text—goes on to be stripped, immersed in Jesus' death and made a witness of the resurrection. The blind coming to see—and with them, we ourselves—are associated with the word about the death of Jesus and with the bread, cup, and baptism that hold out that death as a gift of life. That word, that bread and cup, that baptism have their central place in the Christian assembly. To exercise them is to be in the thing to which the Gospel bears witness, to be under the torn heavens, at the place where the mercy of the triune God begins to reconstitute our cosmology. The Christian liturgy, when it is faithful to these central things, holds us in a living cosmological proposal.

Biblical Words, Contrary Words

Mark's Gospel is not the only biblical text that has a contrary, transvaluative approach to cosmology. And Mark's Gospel is not the only biblical text where that reversal comes to liturgical expression. Although it is popularly assumed that Genesis gives us a single cosmogonic account with a single cosmological understanding and that the rest of the Bible simply supports and follows this Genesis account, the truth is much more complex. Many biblical texts are best read as reversals and transvaluations of a great diversity of worldviews. Mark uses and breaks the "likely story" of the *Timaeus*. But in doing so, Mark stands in the deepest biblical tradition. In other places in the Bible, yet other accounts of the origin of the world are presumed. Yet other ways of holding all things in coherence are in play. The biblical business, time and again, seems to be to propose a hole in these systems or to reverse their values while still using their strengths, to turn or reaim their words toward another purpose. The biblical concern seems to be to break these systems before the encounter with God and to fill biblical liturgy with just that encounter. Affirming such a contrary, subversive word seems the primary cosmological undertaking of the Bible.

Reversal may even have been the purpose of the first creation story in Genesis (1:1—2:3). In that great poem of creation, many things that other cosmogonies called "gods"—the sun and moon created on the fourth day, for example—are created quite secondarily and are peacefully called "good" by the one Creator. Furthermore, while other accounts of the origin of all things laid accent upon the deity conquering chaos like an enemy, here the cosmos arises peacefully, at the word of God, with no secondary evil power to overcome. Those reversals of common cosmologies are then given a liturgical base: every week through which we live is made into an image and witness of creation, the seventh day responding to God's work and rest with rest and praise.

Indeed, by this account, a liturgical transvaluation has been brought to the old Babylonian planetary week. That Babylonian way of marking time, a way known by the "priestly" writer of Genesis 1, was most likely created to reflect the power of the seven astral "wanderers" known to ancient observers of the sky—the sun, the moon, and the five visible planets—as well as the ancient fourfold division of the lunar period. If one understood the moon to have four phases, then each of those phases was more or less seven days long, confirming the use of the planetary week. For the Babylonians, the seventh day of this week was, however, an "unlucky day" on which nothing should be done since it would inevitably go wrong. The first creation account of Genesis utterly reworks the Babylonian week. The days witness to God's creation, not the power of the planets. The unlucky day has become a "sabbath," a witness to God's goodness as greater than any human work. The pattern of doing no work has been maintained but reaimed. Humankind is invited to refrain from work not out of anxiety but, rather, in rest, witness, and praise. Then, if the structure of the universe itself is recalled in course of the days of the week, the movement of the days toward the sabbath enacts the opening of all things toward God. Sabbath is a kind of hole in the old Babylonian sphere of the week.

A certain reversal may also have been the intention of the second creation story (Gen. 2:4 and following). In this story, many of the usual materials of ancient urban and agricultural myth—the garden, the tree of life, the four rivers—have been reworked to become the materials needed to tell of sex and work, sin and sorrow and death, all as background to the ongoing biblical story of God's promise and God's mercy. Indeed, the second story also stands in a certain tension with the first story. The cosmos itself is good, made so by the very word of God. But that cosmos is also the theater of sin and death. The way to the tree of life—the very axis or linchpin of the cosmos—is now shut off to humanity, guarded, beyond reach (3:24). The liturgical enacting of this story has always involved the various Jewish and Christian ways of making confession and praying for or announcing the forgiveness of sin. And, while Jews have sometimes seen the embracing of Torah—even the liturgical dancing with Torah (compare Prov. 3:18)—as a new access to the tree of life, Christians see coming to Christ and eating his meal as "nesting" in that tree (Mark 4:32; compare John 15:1-5) and eating from its fruit (compare Rev. 22:2). The liturgy begins to make accessible what the story forbids.

In any case, if one reads these two stories to imply the absolute preeminence of human beings in the scheme of things, as has sometimes been common for Christian interpreters, then other biblical voices exercise the reversal.[29] A chain of reinterpretation ensues. The climax of the book of Job (Job 38–42), for example, celebrates God's delight in all creation, even in Behemoth and Leviathan, those mythological beasts that stand for uncontrollable enmity to order as humans see it. God delights in the creatures quite apart from any relationship these creatures have with human beings.[30] The series of questions put to Job, leading him to humility, give great detail to the conditions of wind, sea, sun, stars, clouds, and seven species of wild animals, all rightly and utterly apart from any human domination or use. In Job, as surely as in the work of a modern evolutionary biologist, humankind is part of the natural fabric, not its swaggering, controlling lord: "Look at Behemoth, which I made just as I made you" (40:15). Job is a healthy anti-

---

29. The biblical cosmology should thus be seen as involving a dialogue of voices, not a monologue, and can be interestingly compared with other accounts of the origin of the universe that involve such dialogue. Compare Dennis Tedlock, ed. and trans., *Popul Vuh* (New York: Simon & Schuster, 1996), 211.

30. Monica Rosemary Schmidt, "Remembering the Humility of Job" (unpublished senior thesis, Davidson College, 1999).

dote not only to the orthodoxies of Deuteronomy[31]—the Bible against the Bible—but also to an overly anthropocentric reading of Genesis. Job may be a kind of hole in the creation stories of Genesis, a hole filled with the encounter with God (Job 38:1-3; 40:6-7; 42:5). Job has the greatest room for lament and disorder, for the time when everything seems too large. In addition, its description of the cosmos and the rich variety of life on earth makes room for human beings, but only as respectful and humble participants along with other species. And the center of the book, the only "answer to Job," is the encounter with God. That encounter is the central concern of any liturgy.

But the two stories of creation from Genesis, even with the important correction from Job, are not the sum of the matter, not the total biblical word on cosmology, as they are assumed to be. Far from it. We have seen that already with Mark and the *Timaeus*.

But we might also find it in Psalm 74. There, in a psalm that probably originates in the time of conflict with Greek or Seleucid invading armies but may be earlier, the creation account utilized is itself an account of conflict. Like many of the ancient Near Eastern cosmogonies and unlike Genesis 1, this psalm assumes that the world came into being through a battle between the deity and the chaotic sea, personified as the sea dragon Leviathan (Ps. 74:12-17). From this victory came tamed water—springs and rivers—but also the body of the earth, the stars and the sun and the seasons. But this mythological language is now turned to radically new purpose. The chaos here is not a primordial sea or sea creature, but the present chaotic need of invaded and subjugated people who have a sense of the absence of God. The ancient creative deed of God is itself collapsed into another deed, another conquest at sea: the story of the exodus of the people from slavery. A literal translation of the Hebrew of Psalm 74:14 would read, "You crushed the heads of Leviathan; you gave it as food to the people in the wilderness." Leviathan conquered becomes the manna. The exodus of the people to freedom before God becomes an act of new creation. Psalm 74, then, stands in the reinterpretive chain of biblical texts, beginning with the "Song of the Sea" in Exodus 15, that use the mythological language of creation through conflict to praise God's acts for salvation.[32] But here that language is also

---

31. The comforters of Job, Eliphaz, Bildad, and Zophar, speak lines that are directly dependent on Deuteronomic ideas. But God says to these comforters, "My wrath is kindled against you ... for you have not spoken of me what is right, as my servant Job has" (Job 42:7).

32. See Lathrop, *Holy Things*, 27–28.

used for beseeching. The hole in the mythic cosmology is the present bleed-ing need: "the dark places of the land are full of the haunts of violence. Do not let the downtrodden be put to shame; let the poor and needy praise your name" (Ps. 74:20-21). God is asked to create ordered cosmos again. Lament and intercessory prayer are the liturgical forms taken by this reori-entation of a mythic cosmology.[33]

But if one is tempted to turn a liturgical understanding of "world" into lament alone, the contrary word can be found in another psalm. Psalm 136 similarly places the creation of the cosmos, of earth, sea, and great lights (136:5-9), next to God's acts for salvation (136:10-24), but it does so as a prayer of thanksgiving. Here the liturgical refrain—"for the mercy of God endures forever"—points in faith to the grounds of both creation and salva-tion. Faith trusts in that mercy as the unifying principle of cosmic order. All creatures that eat (136:25) participate in this mercy. Thanksgiving at table thus brings the community to stand within ordered cosmos, in the company of "all flesh."

This consideration of texts with cosmological import could continue. The myth of the Canaanite storm god making the fruitful land hovers behind some biblical passages (for example, Ps. 104); only now that creator is YHWH, the God of Israel who covenants with the people as holy wit-nesses. The transnational wisdom movement gets connected to the idea of God's creative word, and Lady Wisdom, the great Wise Woman, then appears as God's architect and builder in making the cosmos, the mythological house of seven pillars (for example, Prov. 9:1; compare Bar. 3:32-34). Only now this wisdom exactly corresponds to Torah, to the wisdom of the law given to Israel and so appearing on earth (Prov. 9:4-6; Bar. 3:36-37). Fragments of yet other mythological cosmologies appear throughout the Bible (compare Gen. 6:1-4; Rev. 12:7-13), but they are integrated within the great intention of the story: to bear witness to the judgment and mercy of God holding all things. Time and again diverse cosmologies are received into the biblical tradition. Then, by the addition of a few elements,[34] by the juxtaposition of

---

33. Christians using this psalm may well remember other fish given away in the wilderness as food (Mark 6:38; 8:7; compare John 21:9). Indeed, in the ancient church, a fish, the sign of chaos tamed to be life-giving food, was often a eucharistic symbol. And, for Christians, the encounter with the resurrection is an encounter with God's new creation, the making of order for all things through the conquest of death itself. Still, the situations of chaotic need continue. And the prayer of lament will thus continue to arise that the God who made summer and winter and all the luminaries, the God who raised Jesus from the dead, would once again make life-giving order.

34. Note that Psalm 29, for example, could be regarded as a Canaanite song except for the name YHWH and the final verse, 29:11. Those additions reorient the meaning of the psalm.

a contrary text, by a *mimesis* and reversal of values, by a tear or a hole, these cosmologies are reaimed, reoriented. And time and again, this reorientation has a liturgical expression—the sabbath, thanksgiving at table, lament and beseeching, embracing Torah, use of the broken myth as a psalm or a prayer—inviting the people to stand in the reordered cosmos before the holy God.

The New Testament carries this general biblical pattern of reinterpretation yet further, with christological and trinitarian purpose. When the reinterpretation has to do with cosmology, a liturgical expression frequently lies close at hand. Thus, two of the most important cosmological texts of the New Testament—John 1:1-18 and Colossians 1:15-20—involve reworkings of prior material. The Johannine prologue uses the Jewish wisdom tradition together with the Greek logos-speculation to speak of the cosmic meaning of Jesus Christ. Further, the opening words of the book ("In the beginning") probably intentionally mimic and reinterpret the opening words of the first creation story of Genesis. Colossians makes use of many "likely stories," not least of all the *Timaeus*.[35] And most scholars agree, both texts are hymns, fragments from the liturgical life of early churches.

Similarly, old Jewish or proto-Gnostic son-of-man speculation stands behind the vision in Revelation 1. Only now it is the Crucified-Risen One who holds the seven stars—those old astronomical pillars of the universe, the seven *planeta*—in his hand (1:16). Christ stands at the center of the cosmic order, and the churches echo and present this cosmic order (1:20) insofar as their meetings—their liturgies—are filled with the seven spirits from before the throne of God (1:4). This vision constitutes a radical reuse of apocalyptic speculation about the structure of the cosmos around a mysterious semidivine figure. Now the whole vision can be taken as an articulation of the meaning of Sunday or Lord's day assembly (1:10), even for a lonely exile remembering the assemblies, in touch with the assemblies only by letter. Sunday assembly means the encounter with the cosmos-holding Risen One, the communion of the churches with each other, the cosmic significance of the churches, the judgment of the churches on the basis of their fidelity to this vision.[36]

---

35. Eduard Lohse, *Colossians and Philemon*, Hermeneia (Minneapolis: Fortress, 1971), 41–61. The *Timaeus* regarded the sphere of the cosmos itself as the visible image of the invisible God (92c). The *Timaeus* regarded the cosmos as a living body (31b). Colossians supplies Christ and the church in these places.

36. Lathrop, *Holy People*, 26.

Jewish apocalyptic also stands behind Paul's eschatological reflections on the world in Romans 8:15-27. Only now this apocalyptic language has been turned to speak of what it means for the assembly to pray in the Spirit and in Christ, in the midst of a world filled with suffering.

Many different cosmologies fill the pages of the Bible. They do not necessarily cohere or agree. No single, comprehensive biblical cosmology can be found. No "doctrine of creation" can be presented as biblically founded if it also utilizes a closed system and supposedly perpetual "orders of creation." No detailed eschatology can be asserted to be revealed if it is essentially about something other than the encounter with the Spirit now, here. What can be found, widespread in the cosmic accounts of the Bible, is the critique and reversal in these accounts, the hole in any perfect cosmic sphere. For the Scriptures, none of the various candidates for a central cosmic principle can be adequate—not the perfect sphere, not the ruling planets, not the conquering god, not the dominant role of humanity, not the end of time, not the Logos, not the Son of Man, not the tree of life. But the cosmologies suggested by all of these can be received if they are turned, if their terms are reused to speak of the living God, if the community encounters that living God through all the gaping holes in their cosmological fabric. For Christians, that encounter is with the triune God, with the Spirit and Voice presenting Jesus through the tear in the heavens, with the day of the resurrection as an eighth day, with the Crucified One as Logos or as tree of life or as Son of Man, holding all things into mercy, known and tasted in the power of the Spirit. For Christians, that encounter with the triune God takes a communal, liturgical form.

One should be careful in making this assertion about a "hole" in cosmologies. The assertion could be taken to mean that one cannot speak of God when one is discussing any worldview, except as the "God of the gaps,"[37] the God projected by us to fill in any place where our ignorance has not yet allowed us to go. On the contrary, the God who comes through these biblical holes holds the entire cosmos in mercy, allows diversities of cosmic descriptions, but is guarantor of none of them. The God who comes through these holes is not a God beyond the spheres, but one known in our midst, on the ground, amid all the conditions of the world. The God who comes through these holes is the God of the burning bush. Precisely because

---

37. This term is usually traced to Dietrich Bonhoeffer's letter from prison dated May 25, 1944. See *Letters and Papers from Prison* (London: SCM, 1953), 102–4. Bonhoeffer's unfinished reflections remain a useful challenge to any Christian reflection.

of that encounter, "the place on which you are standing is holy ground" (Exod. 3:5). It is God and God's beloved, real world that are holy, not our theories of world coherence.

There are commonalities among the diverse biblical cosmologies as they are held under critique. They generally assert that the earth itself and all the "luminaries" are good and beloved by God; that this life is the theater of sin and grace, death and life; that history matters and moves in a direction; that the structures of things, including the stars, had a beginning and may have an end; and that all creatures—animate and inanimate—stand before God. But the actual order and description of these things differ. It is as if our cosmologies are among our human cultural treasures, "the glory and the honor of the nations" (Rev. 21:26). These treasures, in their rich diversity, are welcome to be carried into the city that finds its center in God and the Lamb. At the same time, they will be sifted, judged: "nothing unclean will enter it" (Rev. 21:27). The great diversity of the cosmologies of the Bible invites Christians to a new openness toward diverse world descriptions and, in our time, toward a vigorous pursuit of scientific cosmology. But the critique of the Bible—and the judgment at the gates of the city—also invite us to a critical stance toward these cosmologies and their consequent ethics. Only one is holy.

The Liturgy Is Biblical

The primary biblical work on cosmology involves continuous reorientation. Several of the major biblical examples of such reorientation have concrete liturgical expression: word, bread, cup, baptism in Mark; sabbath for Genesis 1; Sunday assembly for Revelation 1; confession and forgiveness for Genesis 2 and following; then prayer, songs and psalms, laments and thanksgivings at the table. Also in the manner of its cosmological work—of its worldmaking—the liturgy is biblical.[38]

Take the account of Jacob's dream of the ladder as a final example, following the reinterpretive trajectory of this story through several biblical texts. According to the Genesis narrative (Gen. 28:11-22), when Jacob put his head upon the stone at Bethel, he dreamed that the place where he lay was filled with God and the signs of God. A stairway or ramp—a Mesopotamian ziggurat, most likely—extended between earth and heaven. On it, the angels of God were ascending and descending, making Bethel the

---

38. For other ways in which the liturgy of Christians may be said to "be biblical," see Lathrop, *Holy Things,* chapter 1, and *Holy People,* chapter 1.

very center of a kind of commerce with the divine. Jacob could see this commerce, this series of exchanges that, according to many religions, takes place invisibly at temples and holy shrines. Bethel, in the classic role of the temple, was a place for perceiving the structure of the cosmos, a navel of the world, the cosmic omphalos.[39]

But the imagery of the narrative is also unlike the expectations of many shrines. God, whom we would expect to find at the top of the ramp, housed in the hut that was closest to heaven and receiving the intermediary angels, stands "beside" Jacob (28:13), promising presence and blessing without intermediary. The angels have become indicators of the importance and holiness of the place, not commerce-bearers. The structure of this cosmos differs from our expectations. When Jacob wakens, he proclaims, "How awesome is this place! This is none other than the house of God, and this is the gate of heaven" (28:17). Such awe belongs conventionally to holy places. Here, however, the awe is heightened because of the surprising character of this God: "Surely YHWH"—not just any deity—"is in this place; and I did not know it!" (28:16).

Of course, the story functioned once as the foundational cult narrative of a particular Israelite shrine, the "house" or temple at Bethel. This cult center, which may have had a Canaanite prehistory, played an important role in many Old Testament stories, being associated with Abraham (Gen. 12:8), Jacob, Deborah (Judg. 4:5), Samuel (1 Sam. 7:16), and finally the northern kingdom of Jeroboam (1 Kings 12:29-33). It was to Bethel that Amos came (Amos 7:13) to proclaim again a surprising view of God and of worship: "Even though you offer me your burnt offerings and grain offerings, I will not accept them. . . . Take away from me the noise of your songs . . . . But let justice roll down like waters" (Amos 5:22-24).

The surprising proclamation of Amos stands next to the surprise already present in the narrative of Jacob's dream: God is not captured in our cult, not manipulated by our cult conceptions, not resident at the top of our ladder of sacred exchange, not the guarantor of our own cosmology. Rather, God is far more awesome than we thought, present in promise to the littlest and most wretched ones, and transforming our holy places to be places of the encounter with God's presence, promise, and justice in ways we had not expected.

---

39. For the cosmic significance of temples, one might also consider the heavenly model after which the tabernacle was to be patterned (Exod. 25:40) and the long tradition of speculation about the meaning of the garments of Aaron (Exod. 28, 39).

But the surprise is not over. This story of Bethel, the "house of God," with its unexpected critical turns, hovers behind a passage found in John's Gospel. In the Johannine narrative of the gathering of the first disciples (John 1:35-51), Nathanael has already confessed that Jesus is "rabbi" and "son of God" and "king of Israel." Jesus responds to this series of holy titles with an even more astonishing assertion. "You will see greater things than these," he says. "You will see heaven opened and the angels of God ascending and descending upon the Son of man" (1:49-51). There is that opened sphere again, the hole in the system of the *Timaeus* in its Johannine form. There is that "son of man" again, reworked. And there is the echo of Jacob's dream, the hole in the cosmology of temples. For the Fourth Gospel, Jesus is himself Bethel. In him is the cosmological key, the gate of heaven, the awesome place, the holy exchanges, the very presence of God beside the poor and wretched. He is the one at the bottom of the ladder, overwhelming yet accessible to needy humanity. What humanity has longed for in shrines and temples is found in an utterly new way in him. From this new Bethel, new lines run out toward the structure of things.

The idea of Jesus as the holy place recurs in the Gospel of John, with ever new surprise and with continuing liturgical import: Jesus' body, crucified and risen, is the new Temple (2:19-22). The Father is to be worshiped, not on the Samaritan Mount Gerizim or the Jerusalem Temple Mount, but wherever the Spirit is poured out in the presence of the truth of the Son (John 4:19-26; compare 14:6). The water that is to flow from this Temple to water the wilderness is the Spirit and water from his heart (John 7:37-39). And all of this is said of the Crucified-Risen One, for he is that "house" or "dwelling place" (John 12:32; 14:3), the source of water and the Spirit (19:28-37; 20:22). Wherever the community gathers in this house, around this water, under this Spirit, it will have its conception of God, of cosmos, and of holy places radically transformed in a way that accords with the great biblical tradition of Bethel. The community will encounter the Holy Trinity, will be drawn into its very life, and will discover how this one God is "for us," standing with the wretched and needy, and drawing us all out of death into ways of justice and life.

Christian liturgy, at its best, has continued this tradition of Bethel. The liturgy has held Leviticus and Amos together, the enacting of sacred signs of God together with the prophetic denunciation of worship without justice. The liturgy has been a place where ordinary expectations of God have been invited into the surprise and transformation of grace, where our god-projections have been met by the judgment, the grace, and the life of the

Holy Trinity, where our attempts at exchange with the deity have been invited instead to become occasions to give ourselves to our neighbor. The liturgy has depended on the sense that the holy place occurs wherever the community gathers around the crucified and risen Christ, present in Word and Sacrament. The liturgy has seen the reading and preaching of the Scriptures and the celebration of the eucharist as Bethel-stones, as awesome places of the presence of the triune God who gathers all fearful Jacobs into promise and life. Indeed, these central matters that invite us into the broken cosmology of Bethel are themselves broken symbols, a universal word that is a specific story, an intimate meal to which all are welcome, a bath that makes us unclean with the unclean.[40] The liturgy has understood the angels as hovering about these "places" of Word and Sacrament, not as intermediaries but as markers of the cosmic centrality and holiness of the place. We indicate this presence by our song together with the angels in the *gloria in excelsis* of the word-service and in the *sanctus* at the table. The liturgy has welcomed participants into this Bethel-assembly by immersing them in the water and Spirit that come from the Crucified, by bringing them to the new birth of baptism. Because of the unexpected grace of the God of this Bethel—the way this God is present in the world, at the bottom of the ladder—the liturgy has turned its participants toward God's beloved world, oriented them in a cosmos held in mercy: in intercession for all things, in sending food and money to those in need, in sending the community itself to be the body-of-Christ for the world.

We may rightly ask ourselves if the liturgy we are celebrating in our Sunday assemblies is such a Bethel, such a "house of God."[41] The question will not only be an inquiry about how much awe is experienced in the meetings of our congregations. It will also be an inquiry about whether or not our conceptions of God and of cosmos are undergoing a transformation by the encounter with the surprising grace and truth of the Trinity. When our worship services have instead become conventional ways of "going to church," with our own identities and worldviews and commerce with the divine as the accented centers of the event, they may run the risk of being more like Mesopotamian ziggurats than like Jacob's surprising Bethel. The

---

40. On the central matters of Christian liturgy as "broken symbols," see Lathrop, *Holy Things,* chapter 4.

41. Further elaboration on this theme may be found in Gordon W. Lathrop, "How Awesome Is This Place: The *Lutheran Book of Worship* and the Encounter with God," in Ralph R. Van Loon, ed., *Encountering God: The Legacy of the Lutheran Book of Worship for the 21st Century* (Minneapolis: Kirk House, 1998), 40–51.

same may be true if our services are primarily romantic pageants of the ways we imagine the Middle Ages or "Bible times" to have been, or consumer gatherings for entertainment and for the sale of religion, dealt with as if it were a commodity, or sacred dramas reinforcing a single, hieratic ideology, as if in a time out of time.[42]

But the Word and Sacraments of Jesus Christ are surprisingly resilient. Allowed some presence in our assemblies, they will call us to the surprise of a reoriented cosmos. If we lay down our head on them, even a little, they will be Bethel-stones for us, full of the presence of the triune God and enabling a new view of the world. One of the medieval wooden churches of Norway, located in Uvdal in Numedal, has had, since shortly after the Reformation, these words painted on the wall, surrounding the whole assembly: "This is none other than the house of God, and this is the gate of heaven." It is a remarkable promise, pointing to the cosmic location of a little assembly before God's mercy.

One final biblical image will help. It is the image in which this book is wrapped. When, in the Revelation to John, the sixth seal has been opened and almost all of the apocalyptic terrors coming upon the earth have been revealed, a pause is called. An angel ascends from the rising of the sun, halting all the damage that may be coming to earth and sea and trees, until all the servants of God are marked with God's seal (Rev. 7:1-3). The marking angel calls to the wind-holding angels, "Do not damage the earth or the sea or the trees, until we have marked the servants of our God with a seal upon their foreheads." The surprising promise of the Revelation text seems to be that the well-being of the earth itself is tied to the well-being of the "sealed," those seemingly powerless ones in the structure of things who are held in God's treasuring hand. Earth, sea, and trees are spared for the sake of the continued marking of this assembly of God's servants, just as, in Abraham's argument, Sodom should be spared for the sake of the ten righteous ones (Gen. 18:32).

No Christian community ought easily claim that it is the source of the well-being of the earth. Nonetheless, by the grace of Jesus Christ, the liturgical community is a community around that "seal of the living God." The mark of God is made on the body of the baptized through baptism itself. The seal of God comes also, received again and again, in the word and in the Holy Communion, marking the community that hears and eats and drinks, turning us all into beggars and so into receivers of mercy. The assembly is at least

---

42. For a discussion of these and other enacted conceptions of the Christian assembly for worship, see Lathrop, *Holy People,* chapter 1.

one place where the innumerable multitude should begin to gather "before the throne and before the Lamb," and where the sealing should continue to be extended to "all tribes and peoples and languages" (Rev. 7:9). The Revelation then gives to that assembly a surprisingly cosmic location. And the voice of the angel invites the assembly of this seal to join in the spirit of the great, saving prohibition: "Do not damage the earth or the sea or the trees!" As the seal extends to more and more people, as we ourselves receive the seal in the liturgy, we are drawn into the care of the earth, the sea, and the trees, made to participate in the holding back of the destructive winds.

A hole in the heavens, a little community of the powerless as cosmic protection, a ziggurat upside down, Leviathan beloved of God, Leviathan given away to the Israelites in the desert, the cosmic tree as an annual bush, the cosmic omphalos of the temple as a crucified man, a bush aflame but not consumed, holy ground all around—these are symbols of cosmological reorientation in the Bible. What is the structure of this cosmos? The structures are many, depending upon the diverse treasures of diverse cultures. These treasures all are welcome to express the biblical worldview, as long as they also are ready to be inverted, broken, criticized, reoriented. And for current culture, such an urgency of critique makes the biblical cosmological reorientation remarkably consonant with experimental science in our time, though not with scientism, not with "science" held as a fully coherent, unbroken system. Only one is holy.

Sabbath, the eighth day, thanksgiving with all flesh at table, lament, the bath that assembles us with others, the bread that brings us to see, the word of the cross, the word of forgiveness, the seal of the living God—these are liturgical forms for the encounter with God, the encounter that is at the heart of the biblical reorientation to the cosmos. The place on which you are standing is holy ground.

Now we need to ask, in some detail, how our liturgies actually bear this responsibility and how we may sing and walk together on this holy ground.

reframe
Only One is holy

2

The Cardinal Directions:
Liturgical Reorientation

The Christian liturgy orients its participants in the world.[1] This orientation provides one primary and essential connection between worship and ethics, liturgy and daily life. Such orientation can be understood as far more compelling than mere lists of rules. Symbolic orientation in the world is also far more basic to what actually should go on in renewed liturgy than leaders simply prescribing actions that the people ought to follow. Many Christians who engaged in liturgical renewal throughout the twentieth century did so with explicit interest in the communal orientation to justice and to social action that they believed the newly strong symbols would give. Some have believed that the renewed, ecumenically rooted liturgy can indeed respond to Suzanne Langer's appeal for public symbols that hold and orient us in material and social realities, that propose to us a cosmology by which we may currently live.[2]

But what do we mean by orientation? Each of us, as we grow up in human cultures, learns to understand the patterns and structures of the world as we experience them together with others in our culture.[3] Among

1. Parts of this chapter were originally written as an homage of thanks for the work of Don E. Saliers and published in E. Byron Anderson and Bruce T. Morrill, eds., *Liturgy and the Moral Self* (Collegeville, Minn.: Liturgical Press, 1998), 41–53. The chapter continues to be an act of thanks to Saliers here. See, for example, his "Liturgy and Ethics: Some New Beginnings," *The Journal of Religious Ethics* 7, no. 2 (fall 1979): 175: "When worship occurs, people are characterized, given their life and their fundamental location and orientation in the world."

2. Suzanne Langer, *Philosophy in a New Key* (Cambridge: Harvard University Press, 1978), 288–89. It should be noted that Langer despaired of such symbols being provided by the churches. See above, introduction.

3. See, for example, Linda Schele and David Friedel, *A Forest of Kings: The Untold Story of the Ancient Maya* (New York: Morrow, 1990), 64: "As we grow to adulthood, every human

those structures are the ways that we know where we are and where we might be going. "Orientation," the skill of locating ourselves in relation to certain important points around us, belongs to the tools of our sense of world. This skill and its reference points are culturally determined. For the ancient Maya, for example, the cardinal directions—what we call north and south, east and west, zenith and nadir—were set by the observation of those places on the horizon where the sun was seen to rise and set, especially at the solstices, and where Venus appeared and disappeared through its cycles. Those "places" were, of course, directions as they were actually observed through the year from locations in Central America. But they were also places that had come to be given immense cultural weight. Each of these directions was associated with a color and a god or gods.[4] The directions seem to have been further associated with values: east with dawning and beginning, west with death and loss, north with mystery, south with warmth and life. To walk on the earth was to walk in relationship to these deities and colors and values. The central place, the place where the local Maya community lived, was associated with green. It was the place of the great tree-at-the-center, the world tree that binds together all the levels of the universe. Some Maya rituals, to this day, can be interpreted as the reassertion of the presence of this tree in the midst of the local community—through the presence of the tree-identified king in ancient ritual,[5] through the complex construction of a temporary ritual center in the modern practice of Maya ritual leaders and shamans.[6] For the Maya, as for us all, the establishment of place relates deeply to a knowledge of the directions.

The examples do not need to come from other cultures or other times. Two of us from North American culture might be flying on an airplane. One looks out the window and sees a very large canyon. Remembering the length of the flight so far and consulting the rough map in the back of the airline magazine, this passenger says, "We are above northern Arizona." "No,

being acquires a special way of seeing and understanding the world and the human community. This is a shared conception of reality, created by the members of a society living together over generations, through their language, their institutions and arts, their experiences, and their common work and play. We call this human phenomenon 'culture,' and it enables people to understand how and why the world around them works."

4. Important associations of color with direction occur among other Native Americans as well, for example, among the Zuni and the Navajo.

5. Schele and Friedel, *Ancient Maya*, 90–91.

6. David Friedel, Linda Schele, and Joy Parker, *Maya Cosmos* (New York: Morrow, 1993), 29–58.

we are not," says the other passenger, resolutely, not particularly interested in the window view. "I am in seat 10B on this airplane and you are in 10A!" Both are right, of course. And both are concealing something. The one who looks out the window has not acknowledged that it would be quite difficult—even deadly—to try to be in meaningful relationship with anything in northern Arizona right now. "Arizona" is partly a set of lines relatively recently drawn on a map by our culture, and the air traveler is now able to see something of the stunning contours of the land that are only suggested by the map. But Arizona is also, more really, a network of real relationships, a collection of cultures, an economy, in which our traveler is only a very marginal participant. The other traveler rightly focuses on the embodied moment, the present relationship. Still, being above the Grand Canyon, in its air currents and clouds, able to see a little of the habitat of its animals and the flow of its water, is not nothing. Even more, "seat 10B" is a cultural convention that enabled the peaceful loading of the plane in Los Angeles as it began its journey to Philadelphia. "Seat 10B" is a suspended but directed location now, from one city and toward the other.

Both travelers locate themselves by a kind of orientation, by a reference to other places—some of them culturally determined, some of them culturally valued—in order to establish their own place and their own direction. Both of them use maps: the one uses the map in the back of the magazine but also the remembered map of the continent; the other has interiorized a seat chart but also is living in a larger interiorized map that includes Los Angeles and Philadelphia and the way to get home once they get to Philadelphia. And both of them use *triangulation*. In orientation, that word—far from being the dangerous thing that it can be in current psychology—stands for the wonderful process of establishing one's location by reference to at least two other points. When triangulation is combined with a reliable map and compass, a traveler can find the way out of the woods. But another kind of triangulation might be just as important: one person next to another person before a place of need might help establish a moral location. In any case, our air passengers used the visible canyon and each other and the airports and the interior of the aircraft in their debate about location.

In what follows in this book, we will talk about maps, triangulation, and orientation as means to understand how it is that we walk upon the earth in this solar system. The use of these words will be only partly metaphoric. If we wish to discuss cosmology, it is really important to think about our actual location on this earth, together with the cultural and physical features that help us to have a location, and to think about how our physical location and our moral location coinhere, how where we are and what we are responsible for relate. And we all do live by maps—not just the roadmaps that help us get around these days, but also the interiorized maps that mark places of importance in our memory. Even the person lost in a city or the person simply staying at home makes use of triangulation: "This is 23rd and Main; which direction is 22nd?" Or "the children are playing in the back, by the hedge. I wonder if they hear that cardinal singing in the tree in front?" Some maps are more accurate and helpful than others, and cosmology must ask what makes them so.

But when we begin to say that liturgy orients us in the world, we have also ventured into the realm of metaphor. That is obviously the case when we talk about finding our way toward justice. And when we say that the resurrection of Jesus Christ is the dawn of the true sun on the darkness of the world and our assembly gathers to face toward that dawn, we are using the richest of the metaphors of orientation. But the metaphor carries within itself a suggestion about actual life on the earth. The sun and its rising matter; they are not cast aside in the symbol-making of Christianity. The sun and the moon—and Venus and the other planets and Orion and the other constellations, too—are beloved markers, and they themselves, Christian faith has said, are saved in the salvation of the true sun.

The Australian Aboriginal practice of making "songlines" may serve as an analogy. For some Aboriginal groups, the "songs"—the rituals known by the people—are ancient gifts of the ancestors, the very ancestors who were involved in making the features of the landscape in the Dreamtime. The songs helped to make the landscape, represent the landscape, are actually etched upon the landscape, though that etching may be seen only in the ritual. In any case, to sing the songs is to sing a map through the world. Christians also believe that the word that made the world is the very word around which they assemble and, graciously, the very word put in their mouths to sing. Also for Christians, this word actually etches its lines upon the landscape. This word gives a way to walk through the world.

In fact, the word "orientation," in cultures influenced by Christianity, originally indicated a liturgical practice. Such orientation involved locat-ing the assembly and its building or space so as to place it in the world, facing toward the east.[7] This practice intended to give the assembly a cosmic

---

7. Most commonly, the apse of the ancient basilica was directed toward the east. Sometimes, as in St. Peter's Basilica in Rome, the facade of the building was toward the east so that a presider, standing at the holy table in the midst of the people, would be facing the rising sun.

[handwritten note in top margin]

setting, interpreting the four directions, the lines toward the "ends of the earth" and toward the surrounding sky, as creations of God, and interpreting the east, the place of the sunrise, as standing metaphorically for God's time. To face east in prayer was to be in the world that God had made, on the earth, under the sun and moon and stars, before God, expecting the open and manifest coming of the day of God in the coming of the risen Jesus Christ. To be in the assembly toward the east was thus to bear witness in the world while waiting and yet already receiving that Coming One. Worship, by repeatedly inserting the gathering into these directions, thus "oriented" the community in both time and space and was intended to orient it, thereby, in a world of meaning and meaningful action.[8] This ancient orientation of the assembly or of the assembly's building depended upon the surrounding cultural awareness of the sun and of the sun's rising point on the horizon, important symbols in the late-classical Mediterranean area. In new cultural circumstances—in the Arctic, for example, with its weeks-long night—Christian communities might consider other ways to make sure that the assembly has a sense of being in God's world, in God's time.

Orientation has also been expressed much more personally in the history of Christian liturgy. The mid-fourth-century instructions to newly baptized adults, which have been preserved for us as the *Mystagogical Catecheses* of Cyril of Jerusalem, proposed that receiving communion itself was to be an "orientation" of the senses toward a world held in the extravagant mercy of God.

> After these things, you hear the cantor, in a sacred tone, inviting you to the communion of the holy mysteries and saying, "O taste and see that the Lord is good." . . . Come near, therefore, . . . making the left hand a throne for the right, as if it were about to receive the King, and having hollowed the palm, receive the body of Christ, answering with the Amen. After you have then, with certainty, sanctified your eyes by the touch of the holy body, eat. . . . Then, after your communion in the body of Christ, come near also to the cup of the blood. Not extending your hands but bowing and saying the Amen, in the manner of worship and reverence, be sanctified also by partaking in the blood of

8. "The concretization of the moral life requires a vision of a world, and the continuing exercise of recalling, sustaining and reentering that picture of the cosmos in which norms and practices have meaning and point" (Saliers, "Liturgy and Ethics," 174 [see also note 1 above on page 51]).

Christ. While the moisture is still on your lips, touch it with your hands and sanctify your eyes and your forehead and the rest of your means of perception.[9]

The Lord of all the universe, the one who is Lord by enacting the opposite of "kingship," by giving himself away in love, is now also "Lord" here, in the hands and heart of the communicant. The Christian macrocosmic orientation is reflected in the microcosm of this believer.

But this microcosm does not turn inward. The Christian individual is henceforth to experience the cosmos, through all of his or her means of connection to the world, through the actual senses, as covered with the very same gift that has been received in communion. Two of these senses have already been addressed: "O taste and see that the Lord is good," sings the cantor in inviting the people to communion, quoting Psalm 34 (and 1 Peter 2:3) and proposing that this meal might be healing to our sight, a sensual reorientation in the world. That such eating helps us to see—or, in other contexts, that reading and hearing can be a type of eating—these assertions are surprising metaphors for faith. But the metaphors carry within themselves a strong and intended further connotation: such faith is lively orientation in the cosmos. This liturgy makes us, each one, to be the son of Timaeus. If all things are henceforth seen, sensed, as covered with the gift of the cup, with the blood of the New Covenant, and if, henceforth, faith sees that the creating and redeeming God is good, the worldview and the ethic of Christians follow.

Amid the repeated exchanges of holy things and holy people, the very exchanges of Christian assembly, each participant is invited to a new relationship to the world, a new orientation in the world. The ancient orientation of the church building is one example of such liturgical exchanges. The piety of communion is another. But there are many more.

The Geography of the Liturgy

One way to consider such orientation of persons and assembly as the primary link between worship and world, liturgy and cosmos, is to apply a metaphor. We may discuss the *geography* of the liturgy. Worship is, of course, no topography lesson, no essay on the interdependence of landmass, living creatures, and weather, no exercise in map reading, route finding, "orienteering." But such a metaphor can surprise us into seeing the many indica-

9. Cyril of Jerusalem, *Mystagogical Catecheses*, 5:21–22.

56

tions of location, direction, time, and physical interdependence with which classic liturgy is filled. The metaphor may invite us to evaluate the importance of these indications for our basic orientation in the world that God has made. There are limitations to the metaphor. We need to see that liturgy is not writing and study, not any kind of "graphy." The liturgy may be more like binoculars, map, and compass together in the hands of a group that is walking in the field. Or it may be the group's seeing a distant peak, finding a nearby spring, and, with that help, reading the map and walking carefully and accurately in the world. Furthermore, Christian liturgy is capable of pointing beyond this planet, so if it has a "geography," that geography must be of the newer sort, with a section about the solar system, the galaxy, the local group of galaxies. Nonetheless, many human communal rituals do have a "geography," songlines that run out from the songs of the ritual across the land, dreams that see the land itself as it was or as it will be. Christian ritual has such lines as well, though it establishes its geography in particular and unique ways, ways that accord with Christian faith.

A good modern geographer knows that maps are interpretations and that mapmaking is an exercise in power.[10] If we ask about the "maps" that Christian worship may propose, we also need to ask about the power that is being exercised in the assembly and about the criticism of that power. Nonetheless, like all human beings, we need such communal interpretations of our surrounding space in order to live. Furthermore, a good modern geographer knows that time, and not just space, is involved in any understanding of location and in any map, and that location involves the interdependence of all the creatures nearby. Similarly, our "geography" will not be complete without a sense of liturgical orientation that connects to the past, to the future, to all the surrounding communities of creatures, even to the cosmic and geologic location of the earth itself. Geographers know that one place can be mapped in many different ways and not all maps tell the truth.[11] Our liturgical "geography" will need to ask about its own correspondence to the truth and its own relationship to the other maps, perhaps some of them false or misleading, by which we live.

For we all do live among and by many different geographies. We sit, of an evening, before the television set and its images of a sporting event, a

10. Compare Hugh Brody, *Maps and Dreams: Indians and the British Columbia Frontier* (Vancouver: Douglas & McIntyre, 1988).

11. Mark Monmonier, *How to Lie with Maps,* 2nd ed. (Chicago: University of Chicago Press, 1996).

political convention, the Academy Awards, even a distant war. Suddenly, we are in a geography: the playing field or the concert hall or the bombed city is the center; our living room is at the periphery. We get a good view of the center, we think, but we also know that we are having little effect upon that center, except as part of someone else's calculations of mass-marketing, mass-polling tallies, political support. We are marginal. So is our living room. The trees and animals and setting sun outside our window are out of scope entirely. Such is a common, contemporary, experienced geography in cultures where television plays a major role.

Or, by means of bridge or ferry, we drive up to the watery border between, say, Maine and New Brunswick, and, with the assent of the authorities, we cross into another world, another flag flying to mark its space. It is another economic world, or it is at least slightly so, with demarcated lines of commerce, currency, taxation, political authority. But it is not another world at all to cormorants, gulls, guillemots, osprey, seals, whales, even many of the human residents of these island, bayside, and riverside communities. Some of these animals, including the humans, find the border nearly as insignificant as those wandering herders, the Maasai, find the invisible line between Kenya and Tanzania. By which geography shall we live? Which tells the truth? The answers, while sometimes obvious, are never easy.

There are many other geography-making tools within our experience. Novels, films, concert halls, the news, the brief but repeated narratives of television advertisements, astrology columns, astronomy reports: all map our sense of the world, our lines of connection and meaning, of good and bad, of home and away-from-home. Cultural celebrations, multicultural hopes, and the "race" categories available on official forms map our sense of our neighbors and of the lines between us. Highway systems, train lines, and vast suburban malls create our sense of the city, move us through it, map it for us, neglecting decaying neighborhoods and older, less consumption-determined public spaces. These geographies imply patterns of action. These orientations in the world bring along an ethics. The sheer force of their presence and repetition in our lives may form us to think that such an ethics is inevitable, "natural," taken for granted.

Among these maps stands the Christian liturgy. One danger has been that we have neglected to see the ways in which the assembly for worship orients us in the world. A deeper danger is this: that the orientations we have allowed our religious rituals to give us have been almost exclusively interior orientations to the self, a map of the human heart without a macrocosm, without exterior references except to a World Away From Here, "heaven," we may call it. Such orientations have nothing much to do with mapping the community of life outside our window, and they leave largely unchallenged and untransformed the maps created by television, daily news, advertising narratives, highway systems, racial categories, and national boundaries.

It is not our business here to analyze extensively any of these other mapping systems. They all have their important uses. They also have their dangerous untruths. Television is a useful tool, though its "you-are-there" fiction can distort its users' sense of reality. But our concern is to ask whether heaven and the self are the only directions that authentic Christian liturgy knows. The assertion of this book is that the renewed Christian liturgy, the liturgy resulting from recent ecumenical study and ferment and influencing the books and the practice of many different North American churches, is full of lines that run out to the world, full of a communal orientation that is also a personal ethical formation.

What are those lines? What orientations occur in the liturgy? It would be a useful and important exercise for anyone who thinks about Christian worship to catalogue and analyze the ways in which "orientation" occurs in classic and renewed liturgy. Such a catalogue would include the texts and stories at the heart of the meeting, the intercessory prayers for all the world, the collection for the poor and for action in the world, the utterly basic shared meal with enough for everyone, the sense of baptismal "citizenship" in the city of God, the musical genre of the meeting, the architecture and arrangement of the meeting room, the timekeeping practices of the assembly's calendar, and the connections between this assembly and other such assemblies. This book presents a beginning catalogue of the most basic of these world-signifying ritual practices.

If an assembly for worship is making clear and strong use of even the simplest form of the ecumenical *ordo* for liturgy[12]—baptism, word, table, all amid a participating community—it has in its midst the tools of a geography. The liturgical assembly dwells in an enacted map. The narratives of the Scriptures can provide a sense of the world as being before God.[13] They can

---

12. See Lathrop, *Holy Things* (see above, intro. n. 2), chapters 2 and 3.

13. See Saliers, "Liturgy and Ethics," 175: "Christian moral intention and action is embedded in a form of life which is portrayed and shaped by the whole biblical story. Such a narrative understanding of the world found in Hebrew and Christian Scripture provides a way of placing human life *in conspectu dei,* before the face of God. Such narratives are not ethical systems or lists of rules and principles as such; rather they portray qualities of being-before-God which are focused upon features of God such as holiness, righteousness and lovingkindness."

provide each local place with a past and with a future, held in God's own hands. The stories, poetry, and letters, and the preaching that is informed by these texts, can bring to expression our experience of the world and set that experience in relationship—oriented—to God. The intercessory prayers may behold the actual world in the light of that narrative, holding it in hope and beseeching before God. The collection can be understood as not for God nor for us here, but as intended for the hungry and for action in the world, in response to the truth about God and the world. It can thus be part of a songline. The meal can locate the assembly within the economies necessary for eating. It can use local food.[14] Then, by its simple gesture of feeding everyone with limited food, when conjoined to the ancient Christian practice of giving most of the food and money away, the meal may make one feature of our geography unforgettable: people need to eat and many people are ill-fed.[15] When baptism—a belonging that is open to all, defying flags, boundaries, racial categories, and even religious purities—is remembered or enacted, it may help us redraw our experienced maps.[16]

Yet more tools for geographic orientation lie close at hand. The use of the ancient yet growing repertoire of Christian hymnody and of diverse ways to do the whole liturgical action musically can mean that the song of this assembly will link it to other moments in cultural history, other places in cultural geography. Thus, there may be created at least a slightly more complex view of the world, against any tendency among the participants to map the world too simply from a monocultural perspective.

If this assembly makes use of a space that has been arranged to support the central things of the liturgy, then the building itself can coordinate with the map proposed by the *ordo*. This correspondence can be there whether or not the building makes actual use of the old Christian practice of "orientation"—though that may be desirable, if the assembly understands the locating, mapping purpose of this ancient eastward positioning. The local assembly place will, however, also be oriented and orienting in other ways. At its best, it will be important, weighty, holy, not marginal to the supposed reality and magnitude of distant, televised events. Its holiness can come to expression by its ability to house a community, each member of which is welcomed in personal dignity, to center that community around the central matters of the *ordo*, and to do so with a sense of openness toward

---

14. Lathrop, *Holy People* (see above, intro. n. 2), 129.
15. On eucharist—word and meal, together—and cosmology, see below, chapter 5.
16. On baptism and cosmology, see below, chapter 4.

God's future, of accessibility to strangers and responsibility to the surrounding natural world. Here is a contemporary version of orientation: The house-for-the-church will need to be about being here on this earth in open community, not about going away from the earth, not about being an essentially unlocated self or about the self as the only location of reality. Such mapping of the world can be seen in the humblest of Christian buildings when they are accessible and when they are used well for the interactions of word, baptism, prayer, and meal in community.[17]

In its use of the *ordo*—perhaps even in its concrete use of hymnals and worship books—this assembly will be in communion with many other assemblies around the world. Those assemblies may show up in this local community's intercessions and thus on this community's horizon. That communion—thus, that geography—will be indicated also by the nature of the local leadership. The liturgical presiders of most Christian communities need to be recognized, at least by the topographically extensive communion or denomination of which the assembly is part. And the worldwide geography of the assemblies will also come to expression in the wording of prayers (for example, "for the well-being of the churches of God and for the unity of all, let us pray to the Lord"). Urgent longing for a greater communion, for Christian unity in witness and action, may be one of the characteristics of this community's prayer and thus of its proposed ethical map.

The very shape of liturgical prayer, of thanksgiving and beseeching intertwined,[18] will indicate a way that this community may walk upon the earth. Gratitude for the good things that surround us and lament for the actual situations of need both have a locating force. In its deepest structure, Christian prayer does not fly away from here.[19]

The timekeeping of the assembly will also point to our actual place on the earth. The prayers to mark the day and the night, the observation of the seasons as a grid on which to stretch a celebration of the diverse riches of the gospel, and the very acute awareness of the seasons will all place us in a relationship with the movement of this planet around its axis and around the sun, with continuing links to the much larger world beyond that orbit.[20]

Such are some of the principal lines that may run from the Christian liturgical assembly into the whole world, creating a sense of space and time,

17. On liturgical space and cosmology, see below, chapter 6.

18. Lathrop, *Holy Things,* 55–59.

19. For further reflection on thanksgiving and beseeching as themes in a liturgical spirituality, see below, chapter 3.

20. On liturgical timekeeping and cosmology, see below, chapter 6.

a location, a worldview-from-here, an ethos in which meaningful action may occur.[21]

We can also obscure the geography proposed to us by the assembly. We can reduce the use of Scripture in our gatherings to single verses functioning as ideological supports, not as rich narratives placing us and all the world before God. We can blunt the force of the intercessions, the collection, or the meal, so that they do not refer to the concrete needs of the world. We can reduce the frequency of the supper. We can understand baptism as establishing, not ending, ritual purity and the line between ourselves and others.[22] We can refuse to see the connections provided us by our song, our gathering space, our community linkages, our timekeeping. We can avoid doing justice in the actual conduct of the meeting, by our choice of leaders for the sake of their power according to other mapping systems, or by our refusal of hospitality.

But if we receive, unobscured, the regular and repeated gift of the basic elements of ecumenical Christian assembly, we will be receiving an orientation in the world. Even when they are obscured, these root elements of the mapmaking liturgy may break out of their hiddenness to indicate location and direction to some of the participants in the assembly. The Scripture, read even in fragments, may speak a liberating word about the truth of God and the world. The supper, even protected and minimized, may connect a communicant to the hunger of the world and to our common need before God. The very practice of prayer, regardless of its content, may indicate the orientation of the world.

Still, a healthy liturgical practice will try to allow these central orienting matters to stand forth in clarity. It will try to let the practice of the meeting itself at least approximate something of the justice and mercy that liturgy clearly hopes for in all the world. It is not that the goal of the meeting is ethical formation. The central matters of renewed liturgy are central for more fundamental reasons, because they are central to Christian identity, because they speak and bear Jesus Christ. But when these central matters—the *ordo* set out in a participating community—are allowed to stand forth in clarity, the result is inevitably an ethos, a topography, a map. The renewal of the liturgy in lucidity, simplicity, and focus around the central things is thus a matter of some urgency, not least because such a renewal will orient the community in God's world.

---

21. On the *ethos* of the liturgy, see especially Don E. Saliers, *Worship as Theology: Foretaste of Glory Divine* (Nashville: Abingdon, 1994).

22. See Lathrop, *Holy People,* 181–82.

This centered liturgy does not imply a narrow ethical or political agenda. How the liturgy has an ethical meaning—and how that meaning is to be acted out in the course of our lives—admits of quite different formulations. But the orientation in the world does give points of reference and directions of significance that will be shared by the resultant courses of ethics: that this is God's world, not ours; that we are fellow creatures, along with many others; that the care for the earth and its careful use for our needs are given to us all in common; that our creatureliness and our insertion in the community of creatures indicate limits on our existence; that none of the boundaries we draw between ourselves are ultimate; that all the boundaries must be judged before God. The cardinal directions in Christian liturgy are these: toward God, toward each other in the assembly, toward the needy, toward the earth.

Misdirections

Still, such lines of significance, such directions into the world, are not necessarily followed. Even fervent participants in a liturgy do not always act on its indications. Worse: we all are consummately skilled in self-deception about whether we are so acting. And worse yet: the lines into the world that we may sense as established by one or another of the centers of the liturgy may turn out to be false geography, in need of radical alteration.

The story of the Taiping Rebellion in mid-nineteenth-century China serves as sobering instruction to those who care about the connection of liturgy and ethics.[23] Hong Xiuquan and the other "kings" of Taiping knew much of the biblical story, read largely from Protestant tracts. These leaders were quite capable, in the manner of the best Easter Vigil, of applying the Exodus story to themselves. They had a "sabbath" liturgy too: they read the Bible and proclamations of the "kings"; they recited the Ten Commandments; they prayed and offered incense and flowers and food to God. They also baptized, thereby establishing, fiercely, the pure and disciplined ranks of the faithful with a kind of "catechumenate." They were not so good at putting the words about and from Jesus next to that baptism. They were not so good at the holes in the heavens, the reversals of the stories. And they had no Lord's Supper, no practice of reversal at the table. In fact, the "Heavenly King" and his court ate separately from the people and the men apart from the women.

---

23. See, most recently, Jonathan D. Spence, *God's Chinese Son: The Taiping Heavenly Kingdom of Hong Xiuquan* (New York: Norton, 1996).

But these leaders did discover in the biblical story, in their rituals, and in their own dreams a kind of map. It led from rural southern China, by way of violence, destruction, and ultimately the deaths of millions of people, to their establishment as a brief imperial court in the ancient city of Nanjing. (The court itself witnessed thousands of executions, commanded by the Heavenly Father, including the death of the East King, who was the mouth of the Father, the brother-in-law of Heaven, and the very presence of the Holy Spirit, and the further retaliatory deaths of the North King and the South King!) This empire proposed itself as coextensive with the realm of the Heavenly Father, the "elder brother" Jesus, and the heavenly younger brother, Hong Xiuquan himself. Such a "Christian" geography needs to be pondered seriously.

But such biblically justified mapmaking does not belong only to other times and other peoples. A biblical account of the "chosen people," for example, might be read in our assembly, with all the best liturgical sense that the texts read here should, indeed, be interpreted of us. The account may not be further corrected by any other reference to passages about the mission and responsibility of the "chosen," about the judgment and overthrow of the "chosen," about outsiders and strangers, about God among the strangers. Then the liturgical use of the language about the "chosen" can participate—and has so participated—in establishing a geography marked by the uncriticized exercise of our own power, marked by boundaries in need of judgment. But, just as with the Taiping leaders, to our own consciousness there is no God available to do the judging, for to us God is none other than the one who has chosen us.

Or, the force of the water-washing that is baptism may be taken quite seriously. Indeed, in good liturgical form, a great deal of water may be used, and we may be brought to see that a massive purification is taking place here, just as in Taiping. Then we may consider ourselves to be the purified. And does that not clearly draw a line, a map, a topography, in which the unpurified are somewhere else?

Or the holiness of our space for worship may be intensified. Holiness, God, is then considered to be here, in the center of our room. As a result, the resultant map of the world may well have very large spaces for the profane. Is that the map of the world we think Christian liturgy proposes?

Draw a line that includes us and excludes many others, and Jesus Christ is always on the other side of the line.[24] At least that is so if we are speaking

---

24. This remarkable dictum comes from the systematic theologian Duane Priebe of Wartburg Theological Seminary, Dubuque, Iowa.

of the biblical, historic Christ who eats with sinners and outsiders, who is made a curse and sin itself for us, who justifies the ungodly, who is himself the hole in any system.

The reference to Jesus Christ is the principal contribution of healthy Christian liturgy to Christian ethical mapmaking. Talk about the "chosen people" in Christian liturgical use can never be directly applied to "us." The Christian assembly uses such language with great respect for its history of use among the Jews, for the Jewish moral seriousness about the burdens that the language brings, and for the contemporary Jewish interest in seeing the language transformed in its reference. But among Christians, such talk, even biblical talk, must be run through Christ, through his stance with the little ones and the outsiders, through his cross, indeed, through the Crucified One, the one made to be among criminals and the unclean. For Christians, this outsider is paradoxically the one "chosen" by God, on whom the Spirit rests, from whom the Spirit pours.

The experience of the centered holiness of the liturgical building must always be discovering the disorienting, eccentric reference at the heart of the meeting. The one around whom we gather when we actually use the building, the one who is present for us in the hearing of the Scriptures and the celebration of the sacraments, is himself always also away from here, identified with those who are outside our circle, outside all circles, disassembled. In him, the Spirit blows where it will. In him, every place, even and especially the most god-forsaken, is before God.

And baptism must never be seen as simply "purification." Indeed, the words that accompany the washing, the words that make it a "sacrament," will make of the washing a participation in the cross of Christ and thereby an end to ideals of ritual purity. Baptism by water and the word, rather, is an immersion in identification with all the needy ones of the world. Such identification makes of the church that is created by baptism a paradoxical society, a centered society of the open door, the Spirit-formed "body" of the one in whom God is reconciling all things, a community carrying its own contradiction.

Reorientation

Healthy Christian liturgy, for this christological and trinitarian reason, is full of juxtapositions. Texts are put next to texts, in tension, even in disagreement, and that whole is put next to an oral proclamation of Jesus Christ.[25]

25. See Gail Ramshaw, "The Gift of Three Readings," *Worship* 73, no. 1 (January 1999): 2–12.

The meal follows the word service. Thanksgiving is conjoined with lament, song with silence, people with leaders. The water-washing always follows or precedes a lengthy immersion in the word that is about Jesus. "Direction" is thus found in the liturgy by means of a kind of triangulation: this mountain peak actually seen near this spring, read in relationship to map and compass, yields an accurate reading of direction. Only by the use of at least two things may we avoid being immediately misled. These liturgical pairs lead to a "third" thing: to prayers before God for the world, to mission and service in the world. That third thing can be seen as a lively expression of the geography established by the juxtapositions of the liturgy.

One can say that Christian liturgy, at its best, receives our senses of direction, our maps, our geographies, our cosmos, and radically reorients them.[26] Such reorientation is the most important form of liturgical map-making, the liturgical way of enacting the reversals of the Bible. We may come expecting centered holiness, and we are given a direction away from here. We may come looking for God-in-the-distance, and we are given God-in-our-midst. We may come for us, and we are given them. We may come for them, and we are given ourselves, our selves truly, in community, before God, not cut off from them. We come to a cultic event, and the cult gives us the radical critique of cult.[27] We bring religious expectations to "chosen people" in the Scriptures, "holiness" in our architecture, "purity" in our baptisms, and find these geographic designations profoundly revalued. We come to be ourselves "saved," and we hear, "Do not damage the earth and the sea and the trees."

These reorientations correspond exactly to the central and identifying faith of the church in Jesus Christ, to his parables, to his cross and resurrection, to his contradiction and reorientation of words like "lord," "messiah," "salvation," and "holiness." These geographic reorientations correspond exactly to the church's trinitarian faith. They arise in an assembly that is enlivened here by that Spirit that blows over the face of all deeps. They occur in an assembly around the presence here of that Crucified and Risen One who holds all the stars and all the needy in his hands. These reorientations thus position the assembly before the face of the God who is more

---

26. "Neither the achievement of moral ideals per se nor the adoption of a view of life adequately accounts for the shape of the Christian moral life. An actual reorientation of sensibility and intentional acts is involved, as well as a new self-understanding and a "world-picture." Saliers, "Liturgy and Ethics," 179.

27. "The prophetic relativizing of the *cultus* is always contained within the very narrative and the Word by which the Church prays, proclaims and enacts," ibid., 188.

than our own projections. These reorientations belong to the geography of trinitarian faith, constantly redirecting our own experienced worldviews toward the new set of cardinal directions.

Cyril teaches Jerusalem's neophytes—and us as well—that communion itself has given us a map. This map includes its own critique of all mapmaking power by referring to the one who is Lord by being no lord at all. This is thus a reoriented map. This map locates us in time as well as space, inviting us to wait confidently amid all things for the healing of all things, and to run out, in all our actions, toward the coming of that healing. This map is given in juxtapositions: Christ's healing of our eyes with food, Christ's food next to his words about the food, this little food next to all the hungry world next to all of the cosmos. O taste and see. The place on which you are standing is holy ground.

In what follows, we will first seek to see how the lines that run out to the cosmos from the central matters of Christian liturgy may mark the actual ways that Christians walk in the world. Then we will turn to consider in closer detail how baptism, eucharist, and Christian space and timekeeping reorient the whole assembly.

3

Walking on the Holy Ground: Liturgical Spirituality

Orientation enables walking in a certain direction. If Christian liturgy orients its participants in the world, then the lines of its significance run out into that world, ready to be followed—toward the cardinal directions, along the songlines on the ground, into patterns of meaningful connection. Maps and triangulation lead to accurate travel. Worldview has its ethos, cosmology its ethics, liturgy its spirituality. That is to say, in ways both metaphoric and abstract, when one holds or is held by an understanding of "cosmos," one is held also into patterns of behavior that ought to make sense in such an ordered world. If we wish to explore a liturgical cosmology, then a discussion of liturgical spirituality that reflects that cosmology is part of the exploration.

But what if the principal means of "mapping" emerges as what we have called "reorientation"? What if the focus of our cosmology is paradox: a hole in the perfect heavenly sphere, an annual bush as the cosmic tree, a blind person who sees, the ordinary ground spread out before the only-holy-one as holy ground? Does this worldview still have an ethos? Or does it yield only confusion and inaction? Are the directions for our walking clear?

We have said here that the primary liturgical forms of the Christian community echo and restate the broken cosmologies of the Bible. We could argue further that each of the most central matters of the Christian assembly best propose such broken cosmologies when they are practiced as "broken symbols." Christians gather, through a bath that associates them with the unbathed, around a set of narratives that confound the inevitability of narratives and around a feast that makes them hungrier—hungrier with the hunger of others, with the longing for God and for public justice. In each of these actions, they give thanks with a thanksgiving that is also always conjoined with lament or beseeching. In this assembly, they thus gather around a center that refers away from here, in a community that betrays its identity if it becomes a closed circle, to a holiness that always involves the giving away of mercy. Yet, in order for the symbols to be broken, they must be set out in strength. We have nothing else than such symbols if we wish to speak of God and of the order of God's cosmos. So let the symbols be made stronger, larger, more open.[1] We gather through a great bath to a great book and a beautiful feast, all redolent with the rich hopes of washing water, authentic speech, festive food. With these things, we gather to a magnificent implied cosmic order. But text next to text in tension, text next to bath, text next to meal invites us into the deepest level of meaning here: a broken cosmology that corresponds to the biblical uses of cosmology, a broken symbol that corresponds to Jesus Christ.

Does such a liturgy have a "spirituality"? The word "spirituality" can be very unclear, more mystifying than helpful. Let the word stand here for the ethos that goes with a religious worldview, the "walking" that goes with a religious orientation. If liturgy proposes a worldview, then let spirituality stand for "living on the basis of and within the scope of" that worldview.[2] Let the word "spirituality" evoke "a lived experience, a disciplined life of prayer and action" that manifests that worldview.[3] Let the word stand for the connection of liturgy and life, for the experienced resonance of communal celebration in the ordinary life of individual members of the community. Does a liturgy that finds its center in broken symbols and enacted paradoxes have a spirituality?

Yes. By all means. However, the character of this spirituality will be like that of these liturgical symbols—broken, welcome as a discipline and practice, but always referring beyond itself, never sufficient. Such a spirituality cannot be a timeless description of individual religious achievement. It will continually fail if it categorizes others as "unspiritual." It will find its source rather in that encounter with the triune God that reverses or revalues all ideas of the spiritual and welcomes the holiness of the ground. If spirituality

---

1. This theme was of one of the major accents of the pastoral liturgical writing of Robert Hovda. See, for example, his *Strong, Loving and Wise: Presiding in Liturgy* (Washington, D.C.: The Liturgical Conference, 1976), 80–82.

2. Alister E. McGrath, *Christian Spirituality: An Introduction* (Oxford: Blackwell, 1999), 2.

3. Don E. Saliers, "Spirituality," in D. Musser and J. Price, eds., *A New Handbook of Christian Theology* (Nashville: Abingdon, 1992), 460.

is supposed to involve the human spirit reaching for the timeless verities and intelligible truths of Plato's perfect heavenly sphere, away from the ordinary stuff of the earth, then this liturgical spirituality will be a kind of anti-spirituality. Indeed, one important, classic description of Christian spirituality points out that

> Christian faith has its beginnings in an experience of profound contra-dictoriness, an experience which so questioned the religious categories of its time that the resulting reorganization of religious language was a centuries-long task ... a task which every generation has to undertake again. And if "spirituality" can be given any coherent meaning, perhaps it is to be understood in terms of this task: each believer making his or her own that engagement with the questioning at the heart of the faith which is so evident in the classical documents of Christian belief.[4]

And that "questioning" lives not only in the "classical documents" but in those documents come alive in a faithful use of the central symbols of the liturgical assembly, in the practice of the liturgy as a biblical event. The ethos that goes with this worldview, then, the walking on the ground that goes with this communal reorientation, will involve the invitation for each participant in the assembly to embrace the broken symbols as constant sources for the questions of faith in the heart of daily, ordinary life. Liturgical spirituality will involve the continual and personal reorientation in the world by each assembly participant, using the materials that the assembly makes available for this reorientation. What follows here will explore what this assertion might mean.

Ordinary Holiness: Liturgy and Life

Consider, first, the relationship between another sort of ritual worldview and its ethos. Go, as we said we would, to one of the indigenous accounts of the land and of walking on the land. Among the Navajo people of the

---

4. Rowan Williams, *Christian Spirituality* (Atlanta: John Knox, 1979), 1. Williams, whose book was published in England under the title *The Wound of Knowledge,* continues: "This is *not,* it must be said, to recommend any of the currently fashionable varieties of relativism or to romanticize a wistful 'half-belief.' The questioning involved here is not our interrogation of the data, but its interrogation of us. It is the intractable *strangeness* of the ground of belief that must constantly be allowed to challenge the fixed assumptions of religiosity; it is a *given,* whose question to each succeeding age is fundamentally one and the same. . . . By affirming that all 'meaning,' every assertion about the significance of life and reality, must be judged by reference to a brief succession of contingent events in Palestine, Christianity—almost without realizing it—closed off the path to 'timeless truth.'"

North American southwest, a singer—a *hataałii*—might commonly sing, during a ceremony for the restoration of someone who is sick, in the name of that sick person, something like this:

> Before me it will be beauty as I live on,
> Behind me it will be beauty as I live on,
> Below me it will be beauty as I live on,
> Above me it will be beauty as I live on.
> Beauty has been restored.
> Beauty has been restored.
> Beauty has been restored.
> Beauty has been restored.[5]

The sheer ritual repetition, of course, intends to effect what it says, to put the powerful word to work, to enable the reemergence of the sick into the beauty of the earth. Simply to read these words, to imagine something of their force if they were to be sung over me when I was sick—or in need of some other sort of restoration or protection—is to experience something of that power. The Navajo are known for their devotion to natural beauty. Calling the beauty of the earth to surround the sick, the singer also evokes the more general Navajo ethos of "walking in beauty." In this very song, for example, the *hataałii* also chants:

> Earth's feet have become my feet;
>> by means of these I shall live on.
> Earth's legs have become my legs;
>> by means of these I shall live on.
> . . . There are mountains encircling it and
>> beauty extends up their slopes;
>> by means of these it will be beauty as I shall live on.[6]

One might take this ritual song and the ethos it implies very much at face value. Many of the non-Navajo observers of this practice do so. Perhaps some of the practitioners do as well. Say it like this: Illness and alienation are not beautiful. The earth and the ceremony and song that reflect the earth are. By surrounding the sick person with this ceremony, soaking the alien-

---

5. From the Blessingway Chant, quoted in Gary Witherspoon, *Language and Art in the Navajo Universe* (Ann Arbor: University of Michigan Press, 1977), 26–27. Here the word *hózhó* has been translated as "beauty."
6. Ibid.

ated person in these words, restoration is achieved. The restored one is called upon to "walk in beauty" with those very feet that have been identified with the feet of the earth. It seems like a simple and beautiful idea.

The only problem is that *hózhó*, the word that has been translated here as "beauty," is not a simple word.[7] It does indeed mean "beauty," but it also means a whole environment marked by the constant presence of duality in tension and the constant movement toward the creative, life-giving harmony of all dualities. This aesthetic term has ethical significance, and that significance is hard to put into a single English word.[8] *Hózhó* carries the heart of Navajo religion along with it. The term needs to be seen against the background of the central stories of *Diné bahane'*, the basic cosmological account of the Navajo, an account evoked in almost all of the ritual songs of this people. These stories narrate the origin and meaning of the directions, of the present world into which people have emerged, of the sacred mountains, of the sun and moon and stars, and of the Navajo themselves and their clans and social order. The stories make extensive use of duality,[9] and that duality comes to an important expression especially in the accounts of First Man and First Woman. According to these accounts, for example, the very disharmony between First Man and First Woman, their argument based on each one's estimate of his or her own personal self-sufficiency, brought about the birth of those Monsters that are constantly threatening all life.[10] Duality is dangerous, precarious, threatening. On the other hand, this very disharmony was reversed—and *hózhó* itself was given a narrative image—when Changing Woman (who is the Holy Person who stands for the Earth) said to the Sun, in what may be the most central speech of *Diné bahane'*:

> Remember, as different as we are, you and I, we are of one spirit. As dissimilar as we are, you and I, we are of equal worth. As unlike as you and I are, there must always be solidarity between the two of us. Unlike each other as you and I are, there can be no harmony *[hózhó]* in the universe as long as there is no harmony between us.[11]

7. See ibid., 23–34.

8. Clyde Kluckhohn, "The Philosophy of the Navajo Indians," in F. Northrop, ed., *Ideological Differences and World Order* (New Haven: Yale, 1949), 369.

9. Paul G. Zolbrod, *Diné bahane': The Navajo Creation Story* (Albuquerque: University of New Mexico Press, 1984), 353 n. 15.

10. Ibid., 58–62, 97.

11. Ibid., 275.

Thus, an orientation toward both equality and harmony is spoken by the earth to the sun, by the woman to the man. This "precarious but necessary balance"—this kinship and solidarity even—this vision of profound difference reconciled in beauty, now becomes the ethical imperative that arises from the ritual cosmology. "Beauty" both exists and is to be continually achieved between the woman and the man, between the earth and the sun, but also between the human beings and the animals, the *Diné* (the Navajo as "the people") and the Holy People, indeed, "between all the disparate elements of the universe."[12] Part of the maintenance of *hózhó* is communal, artistic, and ritual: singing, weaving, storytelling, sandpainting, house building, constantly referring to and drawing on the cosmological myth.[13] The ritual then spills over into the way one walks through daily, ordinary life. Such "beauty" is not a simple idea.

If we proceed with respect, acknowledging that this brief reference does not begin to do justice to the complexity and depth of Navajo thought, we might nonetheless find here a helpful analogy to Christian liturgical spirituality. Christians who have cared about the recovery of what has been called "Celtic spirituality," for example, may see the analogy already in the traditional Irish hymn called "St. Patrick's Breastplate." In this hymn, it is not "beauty" with which the threatened and needy one is verbally drenched, but Christ. The classic English translation sings:

> Christ be with me, Christ within me,
> Christ behind me, Christ before me,
> Christ beside me, Christ to win me,
> Christ to comfort and restore me,
> Christ beneath me, Christ above me,
> Christ in quiet, Christ in danger,
> Christ in hearts of all that love me,
> Christ in mouth of friend and stranger.[14]

The first-person speech is analogous to the first person of the Navajo chant, only here one imagines not a ritually knowledgeable singer identifying with

12. Ibid., 405 n. 82.
13. Ibid., 351 n. 11.
14. The words, attributed to St. Patrick when he was under threat, in the Cecil Frances Alexander translation, are found in many hymnals, for example, *The Hymnal 1982* (New York: Church Hymnal Corporation, 1985), hymn 370. The words quoted here are found there as stanza 6.

the endangered person in the midst of a long communal ceremony, but a communal hymn, perhaps sung as part of a baptismal remembrance, in which the shared words are available to be applied to each individual. Communal liturgy is made available for personal spirituality. Then, like the Navajo chant, there is also added to this powerful, repetitive evocation the further verbal invoking of the beauty and power of the cosmos itself:

> I bind unto myself today the virtues of the starlit heaven,
> the glorious sun's life-giving ray, the whiteness of the moon at even,
> the flashing of the lightning free, the whirling wind's tempestuous shocks,
> the stable earth, the deep salt sea, around the old eternal rocks.[15]

We might take this song, as well, at face value. Many singers of the song do so. Say it this way: "Christ" here is the name of divinity or of the holy power of divinity, available, addressable, and nearby. This God is further seen as the creator of all things, of the cosmos itself, so it follows that any singer may rightly evoke the power of those things as protection. The cosmos is not alien, not inimical, but allied with the friends of God. I might sing the song quite alone, for myself, forgetting its communal origin. Walking through the cosmos, I can call upon both the unbroken power of God and the unbroken power of the created cosmos for protection. It seems like a relatively straightforward, unbroken, and beautiful religious idea.

Except that the word "Christ" is also not a simple word. If what is meant is "Jesus Christ"—and the context makes clear that this is indeed the intention—then the name points to a tension-laden duality, just as with *hózhó*. Only now, the duality is not the mythic and structural tension of male and female, earth and sky, human and animal, animate and inanimate, continually being balanced and harmonized in ritual and ethics. The tension is rather historic, particular, and unresolvable, arising from the very heart of Christian faith. The word "Christ" wraps the paradoxes of that faith around all the circumstances of ordinary life, making those paradoxes the source of spirituality.

That name—Jesus Christ—carries within itself both the hope for ordered cosmos and the "hole in the cosmos" of which we have been speaking. The name involves an important religious category, a category used to imagine the hope for social order, being radically upended as it is applied to a crucified man. Furthermore, when used in this way, the name inevitably

15. Ibid., stanza 4.

carries within itself a further great upending of any talk about deity or holiness, an upending that comes to expression in language about the "Trinity":
God, indeed, but God in a way we had not expected. The name carries
along also all those who are identified with Christ, the liturgical assembly
but also the world's outsiders. The "I" of the hymn is necessarily surrounded
by the great multitude "in Christ," just as the very idea of "hymn" implies
community. And the name comes to expression in those central liturgical
symbols that faith sees as being full of the presence of Jesus Christ, existing
now in the midst of the world: broken symbols, when they are used faithfully;
full-hearted thanksgivings that are also fully honest beseechings. Because of all
of this, the name and its implied connections are interwoven with all the
occasions of ordinary life. Walking in the world as "Christians," surrounded by
all the dualities that this name holds together, involves being gifted, as one
walks with fresh harmony where there have been old tensions—between
men and women, earth and sky, animate and inanimate, for example—but
also, newly and importantly, between outsider and insider, us and them, disorder and chaos, life and death. "Christ" is not a simple word. It arises from the
heart of Christian religion, expresses profound, double-sided liturgical meaning, and is then available to accompany and reinterpret daily life.

Say this all a little more slowly: The Christian communal confession,
"Jesus [is] Christ," can be taken to be the central broken symbol of Christian worship. All the other liturgical symbols reflect it. The confession makes
use of the word "Christ," carrying as it does the ancient longing for the
perfect king, the perfect royal "son" of the divine, the perfect bringer of
public justice on the earth. We must make use of some such language of
religious hope, especially if we wish to speak of what God is doing in the
midst of the actual conditions of the real world. Yet this language is deeply
inadequate, finally fails, and needs to be criticized and reversed. So here is
the tension-laden duality: it is Jesus who is confessed to be this king. He
does not reign, has no crown, no court, no kingdom, no anointing except
"beforehand for . . . burial" (Mark 14:8). He has been killed, executed in a
manner that left him not only exposed and powerless but also ritually
unclean, a pollution on the land. Yet, faith says, in this cross are life and
health for all things, more than any king's reign would ever bring. In this
cross, God has come so deeply into our wretchedness that henceforth all
falling into wretchedness is falling into God and God's mercy, not away
from God.[16] And this Crucified One is "risen." With the resurrection,

16. Hans Urs von Balthazar, *Heart of the World* (San Francisco: Ignatius, 1979), 43.

thanksgiving and the sense of the goodness of the earth itself are being continually restored. Faith understands this resurrection to mean that the Crucified One is still present, still continually giving himself away. This presence
is his "reign," a reign that extends far wider than any "kingdom" ever did.
Here are that "profound contradictoriness" and that "reorganization of religious language" at the heart of Christian faith and spirituality. Say it this way,
in Martin Luther's provocative use of the contradictory religious language
of Christianity: "apart from this man there is no God."[17]

The assembly may then make analogous confessions, further echoing
the paradoxical assertion, "This human being is God." The finite does contain the infinite. The earth itself is the locus of salvation. And in the assembly, this word we read and sing and speak is the mercy of God in Christ.
This prayer is the assembly being in Christ before God. This bread is the
body of Christ; this cup, the blood of Christ; this water, immersion in
Christ's death that we too might live; this mission, the body of Christ being
given away in the world. Such is the duality, the tension in the word
"Christ." And this duality has strong implications for daily living: We are
invited to treasure the goodness of the earth and to exercise solidarity with
those who suffer. We are invited to avoid any closed religious or cosmological system.

The trinitarian resonance of the name is also liturgical and also has
implications for spirituality. Indeed, this trinitarian resonance may be seen
as one of the principal ways that talk about Jesus Christ is itself saved from
becoming a closed religious system. If the community confesses Jesus Christ,
it does so because of the Spirit of God. Christians believe that the Spirit
poured out from the resurrection of Jesus—the Spirit that has come on
earth through the hole in the heavens, to say it with Mark (1:10); the Spirit
that blows where it wills, to say it with John (3:8)—has become the Spirit
of this meeting and thereby has brought us to faith. More: if the community
confesses Jesus Christ, it confess that God has identified with all of the
wretched of the earth and that, in Christ, God has begun to knit up all the

---

17. Luther's assertion is an existentially powerful confession of faith, based upon the
"communication of attributes" in Chalcedonian Christology: "But now, since he is a man
who is supernaturally one person with God, and apart from this man there is no God, it must
follow . . . that everything is full of Christ through and through, even according to his
humanity" Martin Luther, "Confession Concerning Christ's Supper," in Robert H. Fischer,
ed., *Luther's Works,* vol. 37 (Philadelphia: Muhlenberg, 1961), 218. German text in *D. Martin
Luthers Werke* (Weimar: 1909), 26:332, henceforth cited as *WA* ("ausser diesem menschen
kein Gott ist . . . und alles durch und durch vol Christus sei auch nach der menscheit").

dualities and divisions throughout the cosmos itself, beginning with the division between God and suffering. More: if the community confesses Jesus Christ, then it stands with this man, in thanksgiving and prayer, before the face of the ancient and eternal God in whose name he has come. These three, then, are confessed: God the Spirit of the meeting; God with the poor and separated, including the ones away from here; God before whom we and all the cosmos stand. Yet there are not three Gods, but one God, God's own self as a flowing mutuality of love. There is not one eternal monad, one absolute ideal against which to measure all human life, but three distinct persons in communion, inviting human life itself to model such communion. Neither God the Spirit of the meeting nor God with the wretched nor God the creator of all things is dominant. But all three, in a dance of mutuality that breaks open even these central Christian religious concepts—the spirited assembly, the care for the poor, creation itself—continually encounter us as the One Holy. That the old Celtic hymn intends something like this meaning of "Christ" is also clear in the hymn itself:

> I bind unto myself the Name, the strong Name of the Trinity,
> by invocation of the same, the Three in One, the One in Three.
> Of whom all nature hath creation, eternal Father, Spirit, Word:
> praise to the Lord of my salvation, salvation is of Christ the Lord.[18]

So the name "Christ" carries the name of the Trinity. There follow at least these implications: Human life is invited to delight in diversity, yet to rejoice in communion and to refuse the practice of domination.[19] More: Our dependence on the Spirit, our need to continually come to faith again, marks all of our days, giving us no grounds for spiritual arrogance against our neighbor. More: God and God's holiness are encountered amid ordi-

---

18. *Hymnal 1982,* hymn 370, stanza 7; compare stanza 1. The other stanzas of the hymn also invoke the saving events of Jesus' life and death (stanza 2); the whole company of angels, prophets and saints (stanza 3); the cosmos itself (stanza 4, see above); and power, wisdom, might, eye, ear, hand, shield, and word of God (stanza 5) as all involved in the "strong name of the Trinity" and in the name "Christ." See further below. Note: When Christians invoke "Christ," they invoke also all those who are "in him." This idea echoes in stanza 3: "I bind unto myself today . . . confessors' faith, apostles' word, the patriarchs' prayers, the prophets' scrolls. . . ." Of course, one ought to remember that "apostles" and "prophets" were themselves sinners and outsiders, whose "faith," "prayers," and "scrolls" all testified to God's healing mercy.

19. Catherine Mowry LaCugna, *God for Us: The Trinity and Christian Life* (San Francisco: Harper, 1991), 377–411.

nary life, on the ground before the Trinity as if before the burning bush, wherever the Spirit will blow, in solidarity with the wretched with whom the earth is filled, yet in praise-full connection to all the actual circumstances of God's created cosmos.

It matters that all of this meaning of "the strong name" comes to expression in a *hymn*. The Christian community sings this invocation, making it available to each individual believer. The name in which the Chris-tian assembly gathers is the triune name and the "soul" of its liturgy can be said to be the doctrine of the Trinity.[20] The liturgy is a bodily form of this dogma, and the assembly doing this liturgy can be called "the assembly of God"[21] or "Jesus Christ existing as community"[22] or "the communion of the Holy Spirit,"[23] all these names meaning the same thing. More: the name of Jesus Christ and the presence of the triune God need to be seen as coming to expression explicitly in Scripture reading and preaching, in baptism and the word of forgiveness, and in the Holy Communion—those actions that give the assembly a center. What does "Jesus Christ" mean? Receive this meal if you wish to know. What does the "name" of the Trinity mean? Listen to this communal Scripture reading next to this bath if you wish to know. When you sing this name, invoking it to be before and behind you, there comes all about you the whole reality of God with the wretched and poor, God with the assembly, God knitting up the broken world. There come the assembly itself and all the little ones who belong to Christ. There come the Scripture and baptism and the Holy Communion and the word of forgiveness. All of these are "Christ," engaging all of the circumstances of life. And the place on which you stand is holy ground.

Then see what that "name"—wrapped around you, washed over you, above you and below you, given for you to hear and eat and drink—means for your daily living. Indeed, you may see that meaning also if you never sing "St. Patrick's Breastplate" or have never even heard of the hymn. We have only been using the hymn as an image and example of the way liturgy, in its tensions, intertwines the Christian paradox with life. You may see that meaning also if you have never reflected with conceptual, critical intelligence

---

20. See Lathrop, *Holy Things* (see above, intro. n. 2), 138. Compare Regin Prenter, "Liturgie et dogme," *Revue d'histoire et de philosophie religieuses* 38 (1958): 115–28: "La liturgie est la forme corporelle du dogme et le dogme est l'âme de la liturgie."

21. Lathrop, *Holy People* (see above, intro. n. 2), 21–48.

22. Dietrich Bonhoeffer, *Sanctorum Communio*. See Eberhard Bethge, *Dietrich Bonhoeffer* (New York: Harper & Row, 1977), 58–59.

23. Compare 2 Corinthians 13:13.

about the implications of "Jesus Christ" or the "strong name of the Trinity." If you are a participant in Christian liturgy, this "name" and all that it entails are already wrapped about you, calling you to a way to walk in the world.

What way? The "name" that is at the heart of Christian liturgy calls you to walk on the ground, under the sky, next to your neighbor and all creatures, in mutuality and communion, honest about the goodness of all things, honest about the need of all things, in thanksgiving and beseeching. One of the clearest lines that runs out onto the earth from virtually every liturgical interaction of the faithful Christian assembly and from the tensions in the word "Christ" itself is the line of thanksgiving and beseeching.

Thanksgiving and Beseeching: Reorientation of the Self

One way to sum up the central tensions of Christian liturgy is to recall that every basic act of the assembly is marked by both praise and lament, thanksgiving and beseeching.[24] In a classic Christian Sunday liturgy, the proclamation of the promises of the Scriptures is followed by the honest enunciations of the needs of the world in the intercessions. The thanksgiving prayer at the table cries out also for the hungry world. The praise of God over the water of baptism still begs for the coming of the Spirit. And put the other way around, the sermon articulates the truth about our need before also announcing the truth of God's mercy, inviting us to faith. The Lord's Prayer contributes old eschatological language, crying out for the reign of God, before also confidently asking for what the community already possesses: bread and forgiveness as the presence of that reign.[25] Christian prayer "may be the angry protestation before God that the world is nothing like it was supposed to be," yet it will also be "the wondering expression of gratitude for the paradoxical beauty of things."[26] Such is the prayer that Christians do "through Jesus Christ" or "in the name of Jesus Christ." The very tensions of thanksgiving and beseeching correspond to the "name."

These tensions give us a way to live. They propose an orientation in the world, an ethos, though not concrete answers to every question. "Thanksgiving and beseeching" may be used as one important way to sum up liturgical

---

24. Lathrop, *Holy Things,* 55–59.

25. Lathrop, *Holy People,* 76–78.

26. Graham Hughes, *The Place of Prayer: Leading the Prayers of Worship* (North Parramatta, Australia: UTC Publications, 1998), 3.

spirituality, a way to walk in the world that flows from the central things of Christian liturgy.[27]

According to one passage in Paul, as God's grace "extends to more and more people," it does so that it "may increase thanksgiving, to the glory of God" (2 Cor. 4:15). One purpose for the gospel itself can be said to be the increase of thanksgiving. In any case, participants in the astonishing grace of that assembly, which is focused on word, bath, and table, are invited to live their lives with thanksgiving.

Start with such an ordinary thing as meals. The tables of those who have gathered around the assembly's table may reflect that central table by being themselves places of praise, articulated in table prayers but also present in a sheer delight at the beauty and goodness and variety of food and of company around the food. A liturgical spirituality will care about common meals, about their peace and protection, about good food, about the local bread and the local drink, about the ecological network that supports the food and drink, about the cultural gifts of the festive table, about the focal practices of preparing and setting out food together,[28] about—for example, to draw on some particular cultures—candles and linens, plates and dishes, even crystal and silver, but also about the holiness of more simple meals, and always about mutual serving (the "manners" taught to children and still needed by adults, also in their relationships with the children), about receiving each guest with honor, about the art of conversation over food. All of this comes to expression in the simple prayer of thanksgiving. "O God," such a prayer seems to say, "all food comes from you, given to us to share, and we are before you here as on holy ground. Because of you, how good and holy is the food, this richness and diversity of your earth! How good and holy you have counted us that we may eat this food! Praise to you."

But being on such holy ground also invites us to put off our shoes in humility. The table prayers in classic Christian use usually go on: "Keep us mindful of the needs of others" or "May all the world be clothed and fed." It is as if we say also, "We beg you, merciful God, provide such food for the hungry and such company for the lonely. Make us bearers of that food and that common life. And hear us as we acknowledge here, in deep respect, the

---

27. The interweaving of thanking, praising, lamenting, and beseeching in Christian liturgy and in the ethos it establishes have been explored with special intelligence and sensitivity in Don E. Saliers, *Worship as Theology: Foretaste of Glory Divine* (Nashville: Abingdon, 1994), 85–136.

28. See Richard R. Gaillardetz, *Transforming Our Days: Spirituality, Community, and Liturgy in a Technological Culture* (New York: Crossroad, 2000).

animals and plants that have died that we might live." Thanksgiving turns to beseeching. The circle of this beautiful meal is not large enough. Outside of our family, our community, our guest list—or simply outside those who can be there—there is a massively hungry world and those who cannot be there. Were we to be content with thanksgiving, it would be as if we were saying that God approves of the arrangement whereby we have such food and others do not, as if God were glad to be praised for this arrangement, as if praise were a way to bribe God to keep up the arrangement. Thanksgiving can be taken as uncritical support for the status quo.

But the encounter with the triune God always creates a hole in any status quo. The Spirit may gather us into this prayer at table, but the Spirit also blows where it will. Jesus Christ eats and drinks—is even accused of liking to eat and drink a lot, of being a "glutton and a drunkard" (Matt. 11:19; Luke 7:34)—but he also hungers and thirsts, identified with those outside of any nourishing circle. God makes and loves all things, including the animals that may have been killed for this meal, including the people who are hungry this night. The beseeching that expresses faith in such a God is not intended as a salve to our wounded conscience, a sop in the general direction of the truth, but as a genuine prayer to a God who acts, as a hole in our thanksgiving, an intentional diminishment of our joy when our joy is for ourselves alone, and as a line into the world that we ourselves may follow.

Authentic liturgical spirituality, liturgical spirituality formed around the paradoxes of the broken symbols, intends to make of a life that follows thanksgiving also a life that follows beseeching. It belongs to the table practice of such a spirituality that those who pray and eat at table also support the local food pantry, sometimes fast in order to share the hunger of the world, give money to reliable agencies that act in situations of need, work for justice in food distribution, inquire about the damage to ecological networks that their eating may be doing, labor to restore such networks, be themselves the "food" of company to their neighbor, find "food" themselves in the dignity of their hungry neighbor, open their own doors in hospitality, and honor the life that they take in order to eat—by knowledge, by humility, by gratitude to the animals and plants, by wasting as little as they can.

Thanksgiving turns to beseeching. Yet all is not beseeching either. Were we to take strange fascination with lament alone, with discontent in the things that are before us on our table, and with the imagination that we ourselves know best what order would be true justice in the world, this lament would be its own kind of lie. It would be ingratitude, a refusal of the actual goodness of this food, a refusal of the glad truth of our dependence upon this food, a refusal of the knowledge that there are indeed other tables in the world and other generosities besides our own. The Spirit blows where it will. Jesus Christ sets out a feast now. And God is God. Beseeching turns again to thanksgiving, and the encounter with the Holy Trinity also blows a hole in our lament. Humility and modesty belong to a liturgical spirituality. So does the *cantus firmus* of praise. The great seventeenth-century priest and poet, George Herbert, knew this hole in his own discontent:

> Ah my dear angrie Lord,
> Since thou dost love, yet strike;
> Cast down, yet help afford;
> Sure I will do the like.
> I will complain, yet praise;
> I will bewail, approve:
> And all my sowre-sweet dayes
> I will lament, and love.[29]

The argument might be made that Herbert learned this duality, this lived paradox, at the holy table in the liturgy, being what he called "a priest to the temple," and that his poem is a piece of liturgical spirituality.

The gospel brings us to thanksgiving. The gospel also brings us to "supplications, prayers, intercessions . . . for everyone" (1 Tim. 2:1), not just thanksgivings. Both assertions are true. This thanksgiving and beseeching are constantly modeled in the classic Christian liturgy. The pair, together, sets out a way we may see the world, a way that arises out of the cosmology of the holy ground and reflects the trinitarian soul of the liturgy. The pair also gives us a way to walk in the world, and not just with our food.

Given the centrality of the eucharist in Christian Sunday liturgy, what we do with our food may indeed be a primary pattern flowing from a liturgical orientation in the world. Nonetheless, what we do with our food can be seen to be very like what we do with all of our days. The liturgy invites us to walk through our days in thanksgiving. Classic Jewish spirituality can teach Christians many things in this regard. The days of the observant Jew may be marked with countless "blessings." That is, the *berakah* form of prayer, the blessing of God as being the source of every gift, also has its primary model in the prayers that frame a formal meal, the prayers

---

29. George Herbert, "Bitter-sweet," in C. A. Patrides, *The English Poems of George Herbert* (London: Dent, 1974), 176–77.

said when those at table begin to use the holy food. Yet, this model is echoed in other forms to be used throughout the day: on waking, on washing hands, on smelling something fragrant, on hearing thunder, on seeing beautiful trees or animals, and on and on. Here is the blessing on seeing beautiful trees or animals:

> Blessed are you, O Lord our God, Sovereign of the universe,
> who has such as these in your world.[30]

That is all. Such a prayer greets the beautiful creature and rejoices in its beauty, acknowledging God as the source of this goodness. Here, the only "use" of the creature is the sight itself. Like the creatures who are celebrated in God's speech to Job (38:39—39:30), the encountered tree or animal is God's, for God's delight, a delight we are permitted to glimpse, while letting the creature still be free and quite other than we are. So, similarly, Gerard Manley Hopkins answers his own question, "How meet beauty?"—a question he now asks of meeting people, not trees and animals—with these lines: "Merely meet it; own, / Home at heart, heaven's sweet gift; then leave, let that alone."[31] I cannot "have" such beauty for myself; it must remain a mystery, beyond me. Walking through our days in thanksgiving will be like this: encountering the goodness of "heaven's sweet gift" all over the actual earth; using with deep respect only what we need and only what is truly available to us; seeing much that is way beyond our use; doing what we can to let all the other creatures be free; renouncing domination.

"Home at heart," says Hopkins beautifully of one who gives such thanksgivings. In an interesting turn of phrase, sometimes people who are so "home at heart" are called "grounded." They stand firmly upon the earth, finding their center of gravity within themselves and not in an anxious search outside of themselves. The self is at home. In a time marked by advertising and other means intended to stimulate desire artificially, such a virtue may be difficult to develop and maintain. It is a virtue, such personal integrity, such centered location. But such a virtue, if it is described as being "centered within oneself" and if it is the only virtue, may also be self-delusion. There are good and

---

30. Altered from *The Authorized Daily Prayer Book* (London: Eyre & Spottiswoode, 1962), 388. Compare William W. Simpson, *Jewish Prayer and Worship: An Introduction for Christians* (London: SCM, 1965), 102.

31. Gerard Manley Hopkins, "To What Serves Mortal Beauty?" in W. H. Gardner, ed., *Gerard Manley Hopkins: A Selection of His Poems and Prose* (Harmondsworth: Penguin, 1953), 58.

legitimate desires, hungers, longings. These, too, are part of the actual cosmos. We are contingent beings, hungry animals, dependent for life on what is outside of ourselves in food and community. The pattern of thanksgiving and beseeching invites us to acknowledge that contingency but to reorient its reference toward a wider world. The world itself is a wounded and needy place. The "grounded" person, formed by the liturgy, will be standing on holy ground, before God, together with the community, home at heart in thanksgiving but also not home at heart in lament and beseeching. Both.

Because the liturgy also invites us to walk through our days in beseeching. *Kyrie eleison* is a cry in the church, as we name the many needs of the world; it is also a word from the midst of life. The piety of the "Jesus Prayer," originating in Eastern monastic and then Russian lay spirituality, has widely circulated in some circles, recommending that a Christian interiorly pray, all of the time, united with the breath and the heartbeat, this prayer: "Lord Jesus Christ, Son of God, have mercy on me, a sinner." It might be wiser, given the nature of the strong name and of the liturgy that celebrates that name, to reorient the prayer: "Holy One, Holy Three, have mercy on this man I am meeting, this woman I am passing, on this child I am holding, on this city I am visiting, on these distant people about whom I am reading, on these woods through which I am walking, on that wild animal hiding from me, on this creek and the creatures that drink from it, on those stars beyond my reach or knowing," and on and on. "And upon me, a sinner." Our actions may learn to follow the prayer. Not that we will solve the problems and aching needs of all that we meet. That is exactly the point. Rather, "beseeching" forms us in being willing to inhabit the need of the others, to be together a needy "us" with the cosmos itself. Out of such a prayer of the heart there may at least arise a habit of mutual mercy. The prayer for forgiveness will be real as well: in spite of all the longings to the contrary, we will indeed use more than we need, forget the mystery of the other, seek to be rid of the others, even need, sometimes, God help us, to exercise domination. "O God," we may sometimes rightly pray, "save the world from me."

Still, to let ourselves be at home only in beseeching can also delude us. We have a seemingly endless capacity to feel wounded and to imagine, thereby, some other person or group or circumstance outside of ourselves as the source of our wounding: my father, my mother, my childhood circumstances, the rich people, that other race, that other nation, the infidels, and on and on. We each can come to define the "self" as none other than that wounded one, over against the others. We can let a life of beseeching be misunderstood as a life based on our own hurt. We can even turn our religion into a massive cosmic system over against those "others," constantly reinforcing our own sense of injury. While we are indeed sinned against, we are also the sinners, involved also in corporate sin, in need of forgiveness. For the Christian, thanksgiving arises in part because of the presence of that forgiveness now, mediated in the assembly. And thanksgiving invites us again to find our self-definition also as gifted ones, not just wounded and needy ones, so that out of such strength we might find that our need is the common need, the wider cosmic want. In thanksgiving and then beseeching, beseeching and then thanksgiving, we turn and turn again, resisting the sense that we have been personally "transformed" once-for-all-time or that we have found the perfect cosmic schema whereby to order our lives.

Such grounding in thanksgiving and beseeching is enabled by communal liturgical practice. These particular songlines, these lines into the world, run out from the common Christian liturgical inheritance, from Sunday assembly, Scripture reading, preaching, prayer, table, and from the bath that introduces us to this practice. They also run out from the daily prayer that the churches may exercise to echo the Sunday assembly, from the festal year the churches observe, even from the buildings the churches may build to house the assembly. Part Two of this present book will consider more deeply again how the central matters of the liturgy may shape an ethos for the community in the world, how the practice of baptism may relate to the boundaries we make, how word and table may relate to the care of the earth, and how daily prayer, festal time, and liturgical house building may relate to contemporary astronomy.

But there is one more thing that may be said here about how the thanksgiving and beseeching that arise from central liturgical practice may be seen as surrounding our daily life. They are exercised in communal prayer on the occasions of crisis and passage through which each life moves.[32]

Such prayers at occasions of change in personal condition or status are frequently called "blessings." In spite of an occasional reference in the Bible to a "blessing" as a transfer of power, a kind of *mana,* the core biblical tradition understands blessing as good words before God: the acknowledgment in thanksgiving that God is the source of every good, including the current one being celebrated; then the bold beseeching of God's fidelity and gifts in this particular case, which is also a case of need. The most basic biblical

---

32. For a further discussion on the meanings of these rites of crisis and passage as they are related to baptism, see below, chapter 4.

model is found in the encounter of Melchizedek and Abram over bread and wine (Gen. 14:19-20), not the patriarchal handing on of power and privilege in Genesis 27.[33] Judaism has faithfully continued that biblical tradition by the construction of the genre *berakah*. Christianity, though sometimes tempted to blessing as transfer of power or as "consecration," has continued the biblical and Jewish tradition in the great pattern of *eucharistia*. Both Jewish and Christian blessings are marked by the double strand of thanksgiving and beseeching. A thing or person is "blessed" by gathering that thing or person verbally into the story of God and holding that thing or person verbally under the freedom of God for the future.

The core "blessing" of Christianity is the *eucharistia* at the table of the Lord. There, thanks is given for God's promise, manifest especially in Jesus and Jesus' gift, and the Spirit is besought to make use of this bread and wine and this community and to remember the hungry everywhere. The prayer itself is a vigorous exercise in trinitarian theology alive in the assembly. This meal is thus "sanctified," not by any transfer of power, but by the word of God (not anything we recite, but what God has promised) and by prayer (1 Tim. 4:4-5). Many other things and people are "blessed" in the church, in analogy to this table prayer. It is as if there are concentric circles of meaning around this central instance of Christian blessing. So we give thanks at our own tables, blessing God over our good food, experiencing our meals as blessed, as little images of the Lord's Supper and of the eschatological banquet, being formed ourselves to care for the hungry. So we give thanks over the water of baptism (the prayer at the font is a blessing), over the light of the candle of the Easter Vigil or of Evening Prayer, over candidates for ordination (the ordination prayer is a blessing), over people who are affirming baptism, and also over oil and ashes.

We need more such blessings throughout our lives. When Christians celebrate rites of passage, such a prayer is frequently at the heart of the Christian additions to what is otherwise a culturally determined ritual. So we may pray at marriages (the nuptial blessing is an act of thanksgiving and beseeching) but also at births or at the moving into a new house or at retirement or in illness. We may also pray over fishing boats or airplanes, over tools and art works, over fields for farming or over land reserved as a wildlife refuge. In each case, a faithful blessing will give thanks to God, the source of all that is good *(eucharistia),* through Jesus Christ who stands with all who

33. There, of course, the biblical point is that God subverts the system, working with the youngest and the excluded one, the one who is a thief at that!

need God's goodness and mercy *(anamnesis),* and will acknowledge, none-theless, the free Spirit of God, beseeching that Spirit *(epiclesis)* to make use of these things, this moment, these people, our brokenness, beseeching God to remember all who may lack such good things. The thanksgiving should be honest about the goodness of the earth and its structures. The beseeching should insist on remembering those who are outside such goodness, blow-ing a hole in any status quo.

As the nuptial blessing demonstrates, Christians also give thanks and beseech God over sexual relationships. Here may be an especially important instance, in our times, where thanksgiving and beseeching will help us to walk carefully in the earth. We will do best if we realize that Christian min-istry here has always been accepting of the current social practice, receiving that practice like the local way of making bread, the local way of living with the good mystery and potent danger of sexuality, as long as the ministers could also ask several critical questions and could engage in the beseeching. Christians did not make up marriage or marriage rites. They did pray for the couple, in thanksgiving and beseeching. They did so, first of all, at the home, amid the cultural wedding rites. In Western Europe, Christians later began to bring their recent marriage past the church building, where the blessing occurred at the door. Subsequently—at first in only a few cases and then in many more—the blessing occurred in the church itself, near the altar or the font. But before this prayer, the Christian leaders also asked critically if both parties, not just the man, entered this union with free con-sent and if they both intended lifelong fidelity, that is, if this union was weighty, even transcendent, and socially important. The long use of the cri-tique of these questions—and of the beseeching—may have helped to move Western marriages away from being a property arrangement, with the woman as chattel. In any case, it set, at the heart of the Christian wedding celebration, a "hole" in any ideology of perfect marriage.

There seem to be some historic examples of similar prayers over same-sex friendships.[34] If our culture is beginning to explore the social impor-tance of faithful gay and lesbian relationships, and, what is more, if baptized Christians are experiencing the goodness of God in these relationships, prayers that give thanks for God's goodness, remember Jesus Christ, and beseech God's Spirit in such relationships—that they may be hospitable and caring in a needy and lonely world—are certainly called for. So are the old critical questions that correspond to the beseechings. Here might be some

---

34. John Boswell, *Same-Sex Unions in Premodern Europe* (New York: Vintage, 1995).

such questions: Have you freely agreed to do this? Are you promising life-long fidelity? Will your fidelity be marked not only by sexual monogamy but also by care for the other? Will your hearth be a place of hospitality? In a church more centered on eucharist and more prodigal with all of its prayers of blessing, such a prayer might be no big thing—the rite may or may not be regarded as a "marriage," depending on the social context—and yet the prayer may be an important sign of the gospel. If such relationships are becoming one of the "local ways of making bread," then here is the thanksgiving and beseeching over the table.[35] And thanksgiving and beseeching are, together, not just a pattern of prayer but a way that a Christian in any cultural arrangement may live with the mystery of sex.

Still, while arguing for more blessings, it might be important for us to remember that, in the Gospel of Mark, the only things that Jesus blesses are bread and children (Mark 6:41; 10:16), signs of his death and of his identification with marginality and powerlessness. But then we should note the reversal, the "resurrection." In Christian faith, both bread and the marginalized one have been made into great signs of life. Beseeching is intertwined with thanksgiving and vice versa: such is "blessing."

This grounding in thanksgiving and beseeching, in praise and humility, is available not only to the learned or the critical. "Liturgical spirituality" marks many people who would not know what the words mean, not know how to describe the phenomenon. Rather, they live a thanksgiving before God that they have learned in the community, standing upright and grounded before God. But they also live a humility, an openness to the need of others, a longing for a far wider wholeness, that makes it clear that their "grounding" is not in themselves.

When a community gives thanks in strength, around such strong symbols as bread and wine, water and word—or at the daily table or in the midst of the passages of life—the self of the individual participant can be drawn into the praise. If the thanksgiving is articulated authentically, before the biblical God, with strong metaphors that draw on the biblical tradition alive in the present time, the self can already experience a reorientation—toward life as praise. But if the thanksgiving then turns to beseeching, the self may follow, experiencing a continual rebirth as a "we" with all the needy

35. In many cases, the wisest pastoral decision for such a "blessing" may suggest that the prayer take the form of a house blessing (including a blessing of the bedroom!) in the home of a long-committed gay or lesbian couple. On the other hand, several models for a full blessing prayer over the couple, in the gathered assembly, intertwining thanksgiving and beseeching throughout the prayer, are also being developed.

cosmos, as the "I-that-I-are."[36] Liturgical spirituality involves an ongoing reorientation of the self within the reorientations of biblical and liturgical cosmology.

Amid Yet Other Ritual Cosmologies

Liturgical spirituality might be articulated in many other ways. One could take any one of several concrete themes—especially the paired themes—important to the communal assembly, finding the resonances of that theme in daily life. Word and silence, community and margin, creation and forgiveness, law and gospel, strong central symbols and open door, feast and everyday: all of these matter in the liturgy and could be used to describe the life that follows the cosmic reorientations of the assembly. This book will look further, in the chapters that follow now, at some of the ways that lives might flow from baptismal politics, eucharistic economy, festival time-keeping, and liturgical space making. But however described, a biblically faithful liturgical spirituality will always be one that seeks to live out the paradoxes alive in the liturgical sources, one that walks on the earth under the hole in any perfect sphere.

It should be no surprise, then, that such a spirituality will be resistant to fundamentalisms and legalisms of any sort. Only one is holy, and that Holy One is not us, not our ideological structure of belief, not our reading of the laws, not our beautiful, unbroken cosmic spiritualities. The trinitarian encounter with that Holy One always destabilizes any of our perfect systems. Liturgy can be used to shore up such systems, and we will need to consider further how the encounter with the Holy One sometimes leads to the criticism of liturgy itself.[37]

But it should also be no surprise that such a liturgical spirituality will find parallels of great interest in other places where ritual cosmologies are both welcomed and criticized. Some expressions of Zen Buddhism might be an example. The self-undermining character of some South American Indian ritual and storytelling could be another.[38] The popular devotional poetry of some forms of Śaivite Hinduism could be yet another.

One such devotional *vacana,* preserved in Kannada and attributed to the tenth-century C.E. reform figure, Devara Dasimayya, alludes to the impor-

---

36. Gail Ramshaw, *Under the Tree of Life: The Religion of a Feminist Christian* (New York: Continuum, 1998), 18–19.
37. See below, chapter 7.
38. See Lathrop, *Holy Things,* 209.

tant ritual times and to one especially central ritual place. Then the poem turns the ritual references inside out:

> To the utterly at-one with Śiva
> there's no dawn,
> no new moon,
> no noonday,
> nor equinoxes,
> nor sunsets,
> nor full moons;
> his front yard
> is the true Benares,
> O Ramanatha.[39]

"The true Benares," the true holy city, the true site for bathing in the holy river, lighting the sacred fire, building the sacred funeral pyre is "his front yard." If such an assertion went paired with the devotee nonetheless still keeping the prayers at dawn and at sunset, it could be of considerable interest to anyone who was looking for a way faithfully to live out of paradox. The *vacana* celebrates the cosmic as well as the religious significance of the front yard. Christians who consider what Mark has done with the *Timaeus* should be interested in what this little devotional poem might be doing with the whole, stratified Hindu ritual system.

A similar critical reversal of ritual practice can be found in an earlier work from the same Bhakti movement, a remarkable Tamil verse from the seventh century C.E. This verse is attributed to Tirumular and found in his *Tirumantiram*:

> Offerings to the God
> Pictured in temples
> Never will reach
> The God in humans.
> Offerings to the humans
> Surely will reach
> The God in temples.[40]

39. A. K. Ramanujan, *Speaking of Śiva* (Baltimore: Penguin, 1973), 105. "Ramanatha" here is "Rama's Lord." Thus Śiva is spoken of as the God of gods, the God beyond all gods.

40. Mu. Varadarajan, *A History of Tamil Literature* (Delhi: Sahitya Akademi, 1988), 99. Varadarajan also gives a prose translation of the same verse: "Our offerings to the temple deities never reach God, who resides in the hearts of walking temples, i.e., human beings.

This "economics" of the Bhakti movement will be of great interest to Christians who reflect upon the economic proposals of the eucharist and upon a liturgical spirituality centered in the shared table. Also, for such Christian teachers as Ambrose and Chrysostom, almsgiving is the true sacrifice, and feeding the poor puts food into the mouth of God.[41] Neither Tirumular nor Chrysostom do away with "temples," but a significant hole is torn in their rites. Temples themselves are frequently constructed as if their architecture images the shape of the cosmos. This critique of the temple also functions as a critique of its cosmology.

While we have already looked a little at the *Diné bahane'*, interested in the tension present in its idea of "beauty" or "harmony," we might look further at the whole Navajo system. To the extent that Coyote plays a role there, upsetting any perfect balance—like the clowns who function similarly in the ritual practice of Pueblo peoples—we may find something very like the Hindu poems. Furthermore, the very fact that Changing Woman upbraids the Sun, that this female earth addresses a male sky with a speech about equality and solidarity, is itself an important shaking of the status quo, also among the Navajo themselves. As well, while it is not for us to say, one might presume that someone has been doing with *Diné bahane'* what the hole in the heavens does to the *Timaeus*. After all, popular Navajo practice is sometimes especially marked by a dualism that places a person who is considered a "witch" utterly outside the realm of salvageable human life. This practice seems to acknowledge, wisely, that there are people whose acts are evil, hurting the very fabric of social life. But is this system ever applied unjustly? And is the evildoer really beyond rescue or repentance? These categories, which seem so closed to an outsider, do reflect parts of the cosmogonic myths of the *Diné bahane'*. Furthermore, while the healing chants are beautiful, what is to be done with the person who, after endless songs, is not restored, not healed? Must one find fault with the intention or purity of the sick person? Or with the ritual of the singer? Doubtless, the holes in the system that are needed here have already been perceived, are already being enacted, if only in the lives of wise and compassionate Navajo people. To some extent, the very minority status of the cosmology of this people of the earth may already give that cosmology an experienced hole in its scheme. Furthermore, *Diné bahane'* itself may also stand as a helpful

Whereas our offerings to human beings will reach God who resides in the temple as well." I am grateful to Kamala Suntharalingam for this reference.

41. See Lathrop, *Holy Things,* 148.

counterview—a "hole"—to the worldview of the dominant North American culture.

Similar questions might be asked of any religious system. Christians have turned the very materials of the Bible and of their liturgical history into tools for systems that have *systematically* excluded and even killed the other: the Catholic, if you are a Protestant; the Protestant, if you are a Catholic; the Muslim or the Jew if you are either. One thinks of the old stories of inquisitions and pogroms and the Holocaust. One thinks also of more recent "ethnic cleansings" in the Balkans and the endless murders in Northern Ireland. Where is the hole in this system?

Many people are longing for the hole to be found—and lived and taught—in what is perceived as the perfect system of the Koran, the system that is seen by some to divide the world fiercely into faithful and infidel, public men and private women, us and them. Again, it is not for us to do this work. But it is for us to ask. We live in the same world, on the same earth, under the same sky.

Wherever some whisper of living by paradox survives, there we may find a cosmology that may refresh us. Diverse cosmologies are not the enemy of the Bible or of a biblically formed liturgical spirituality. Their very existence may help us relativize any cosmology, while at the same time inviting us to rejoice in the great variety of treasures among the nations. What the Bible and the biblically formed liturgy propose to us is a life formed out of the critique of all finally ordered systems, a life before the Only Holy One, on the holy ground.

The spirituality that arises from Christian liturgy, thus, should enable the Christian to be both at home and not at home in many places. The second- or third-century *Epistle to Diognetus* already knew this:

> For [the Christians] do not inhabit cities in some place of their own, nor do they use their own strange dialect, nor live their own sort of life . . . . Rather, living in Greek or Barbarian cities, according to the lot of each, and following the local customs, in clothing and dwelling places and the rest of life, they demonstrate the amazing and confessedly paradoxical character of the make up of their own citizenship. They are at home in their own countries, but as sojourners. They participate in all things as citizens and they endure all things as foreigners. Every country is their homeland and every homeland is a foreign country.[42]

42. *Epistle to Diognetus* 5:4–5. Greek text in Kirsopp Lake, *The Apostolic Fathers, vol.* 2 (London: Heinemann, 1959), 358–60.

The point of this ancient Christian wisdom ought not be taken to be that "heaven is their home." Rather, all customs and all places are before the God of the "strong name," being both saved and criticized. The Christians are invited to be at home in thanksgiving and, at the same time, to be foreigners in beseeching, to be at home in the confident service of world citizens, yet to be foreigners in humility about what we can do and in constant identification with outsiders and "others" everywhere. For we have no cosmos but this wounded one, before God, under God's mercy.

A liturgical spirituality will be marked by strong habits of prayer: in the Sunday assembly, at the daily table, at morning and evening every day, at the festivals, at occasions of passage in human life. With strong and basic symbols of prayer as the stones—with icons and candles, with a beautiful shared loaf to begin a family meal, with a wreath then a tree then a star then shared fasting then eggs and flowers to mark the passage of the year—such a spirituality may build something like Solomon's Temple in the lives of the observant, something like Solomon's bronze "sea," in which the observant may be daily immersed. Such a spirituality may be enriched with images from surrounding pieties and surrounding worldviews. But, then, if it is a Christian spirituality, formed from biblical sources alive in the liturgy, it will also know the central paradox about all such prayer, a paradox George Herbert addresses to God:

> All Solomon's sea of brasse and world of stone
> Is not so dear to thee as one good grone.[43]

Life in the temple and amid the groans—both—such are the marks of liturgical spirituality.

In Hippolytus of Rome's early third-century book, *The Refutation of All Heresies,* several of the fragments of the pre-Socratic philosopher Heraclitus have been preserved. These fragments are among the great articulations of paradox in the Western world, but they were not written down by Hippolytus because he liked them. On the contrary: for Hippolytus, who desired to present a consistent and rational view of Christian faith and of the cosmos, the very Christians he sought to condemn could best be regarded as disciples of Heraclitus rather than of Christ. While treasuring some of the gifts Hippolytus has given us, we may rightly wonder at the justice of his condemnations and may wish he had embraced the very paradoxes he so vehemently

---

43. George Herbert, "Sion," in Patrides, *English Poems,* 120.

rejected, paradoxes profoundly appropriate to faith in the Holy Trinity made known in Jesus Christ.[44] Still, there in his text is Heraclitus saying:

> Fire is both want and fullness.[45]
> Coming upon all things, it will judge and sentence them.[46]

The fire of the burning bush does indeed judge all things, the universe itself and all coherent accounts of that universe. But Christian faith trusts that its sentence consists, finally, in an all-restoring mercy, the bush and the ground themselves unharmed. This fire joins the universal need in the life and death of Jesus. This fire pours out the endless fullness in the presence of the Spirit. Liturgical spirituality walks in the way of need and fullness, on the holy ground.

44. For more on the pastoral implications of Hippolytus's refusal of ambiguity and yet on the survival of paradox in his liturgical work, if we may regard the *Apostolic Tradition* as from him, see Lathrop, *Holy Things,* 177–79.

45. Fragment 65. *Refutation of All Heresies,* 9:10,7. Greek text in T. M. Robinson, *Heraclitus* (Toronto: University of Toronto Press, 1991), 42.

46. Fragment 66. *Refutation of All Heresies,* 9:10,8. Greek text in ibid., 44.

PART TWO

Maps
Liturgical Ethics

O WISDOM,
COMING FORTH FROM THE MOUTH OF THE MOST HIGH,
REACHING FROM END TO END,
STRONGLY AND DELIGHTFULLY ORDERING ALL THINGS,
COME
AND TEACH US THE WAY OF GOOD SENSE.

—*Magnificat antiphon,*
December 17

4

Baptism and the Cosmic Map

B egin again, considering such maps as there may be of the place where we stand and of its connections to other places. These maps may lead us to "cosmos."

"All maps are imperfect; this is the sadness of maps."[1] Thus the cosmologist Timothy Ferris remarks, as he observes how the exercise of mathematics itself might be considered to be a kind of mapmaking and how the general theory of relativity might be taken as a map of the universe. Maps are imperfect, notes Ferris, because they inevitably carry less information than does the actual terrain they represent and because, in order to represent that terrain, they distort.[2] Both in the actual pages of an atlas and in the use of "map" as metaphor, the map is not the territory.[3] The widely known example is a map of the whole earth in which the spherical globe is represented by one or another projection upon a flat sheet of paper, Greenland or Siberia or Antarctica often swelling to exaggerated, impossible proportions. But the examples could be multiplied, also for the things—theories or

1. Ferris, *Whole Shebang* (see above, intro. n. 6), 70.
2. Ibid., 71–72.
3. This assertion, usually attributed first of all to A. Korzybski, has become a generally accepted dictum in cartography. See Alfred Korzybski, *Science and Sanity* (Lancaster: International Non-Aristotelian Library, 1941), 58. Using this dictum as a title, Jonathan Z. Smith reflects upon the tensions among the diverse ways that human cultures and religions can be seen to map the cosmos, resisting the hegemony especially of what he calls the "locative map," with its imperial and early urban associations, as the only mapping system known to religious studies. "We need to reflect on and play with the necessary incongruity of our maps before we set out on a voyage of discovery to chart the worlds of other men. . . . 'Map is not territory'—but maps are all we possess" (Jonathan Z. Smith, *Map Is Not Territory* [Leiden: Brill, 1978], 309).

charts or cultural patterns or symbol systems or rituals—we metaphorically call "maps."

Maps are sad for yet further reasons. They can lie.[4] They can be tools of domination. And they can do this while presenting themselves as conventional but objective images of reality. That is, for any actual map, any actual cartographic product, somebody has decided what information to include, what to exclude, and how to represent what is included. Those decisions can be made on the basis of a certain set of values—say, the commercial value of the land—and can intentionally or unintentionally exclude other values. The very act of mapping is an exercise of power, and the intentional exclusion of information can be a kind of powerful, though invisible, lying. Something similar may be said of our metaphorical maps: a cultural construct, a ritual practice—such as who gets to eat with whom and in what order—can "map" a society powerfully, making whole classes of people invisible and ordering things to the benefit of an elite. "This is simply how we do things" can be the standard explanation. "Think nothing of it."

But maps are also wonderfully useful and imaginally expansive. This is the joy of maps. They actually can assist you in getting from one place to another, both physically—as in roadmaps—and mentally—as in scientific taxonomies and mathematical formulae—even if, in consequence, you do rush right by many things that the maps have excluded. And sitting at home of an evening with a map spread across your lap, you might imagine or remember that path, that road, that village, that temple, sometimes beginning to include in your experience places you have never been or places you have long forgotten. The world atlas is such a map. So is a hiking map of Hornstrandir in the Westfjords of Iceland or a rail and subway map of Tokyo. So is a star chart for an August night at forty-five degrees latitude. Then there are the metaphorical maps: A tree graph representing the interrelationships and differences of Native American languages may be called a map. So may the human genome, a chart of genetic connections and developments among differing species, or the periodic chart of the elements. "Maps are graphic representations that facilitate a spatial understanding of things, concepts, conditions, processes, or events in the human world."[5] Maps show connections through space or connections that can be spatially conceived, as well as boundaries or obstacles to those connections.

4. See above, chapter 2, notes 10, 11.
5. J. B. Harley and D. Woodward, eds., *The History of Cartography*, vol. 1 (Chicago: University of Chicago Press, 1987), xvi.

A Navajo sandpainting or an ancient petroglyph may also be such a graphic representation, such a chart of boundaries and connections. So may an Aboriginal Australian bark painting of the spirit beings who make and mark the land. So may a ritual meal or a ritual dance. Maps not only represent the "territory" they are interpreting—whether that territory is an actual piece of land or a body of research connections or a structure of social relationships—they also represent the culture that has made this to be a territory. In a certain sense, map is territory.[6] That is, maps are cultural artifacts conveying the values and meanings of a culture as it orients itself in the cosmos, in its own version of an ordered world. To the very large extent that "territory" is also a cultural construct, a map of such territory can represent the value and meaning of the territory and thus be that territory to the map's users. In any case, time and again a culture represents its cosmology and the public symbols that hold its cosmology together by maps.[7] At the same time, many cultures also represent graphically in these same maps something of the order of their society.

Such cultural meaning does not release the map from failure. All maps are imperfect, even potentially powerful tools for lying. All maps carry human hope for ordered knowledge and an ordered world. Both assertions are true. When considering their relationship to cosmology, one must speak of both the sadness and the joy of maps.

Ritual Mapping

When human ritual has engaged in mapping the cosmos, it has sometimes been said to have done so in at least two ways.[8] Jonathan Z. Smith has

---

6. David Turnbull, *Maps Are Territories: Science Is an Atlas* (Chicago: University of Chicago Press, 1993). See also Hugh Brody, *Maps and Dreams: Indians and the British Columbia Frontier* (Vancouver: Douglas & McIntyre, 1988), and Mark Warhus, *Another America: Native American Maps and the History of Our Land* (New York: St. Martin's Press, 1997).

7. The connections of cosmology, social structure, and maps have been powerfully demonstrated by the exhibition *Beginnings* at the Library of Congress. See www.loc.gov/ exhibits/world.

8. For what follows, see Jonathan Z. Smith, "The Influence of Symbols upon Social Change: A Place on Which to Stand," in James D. Shaughnessy, ed., *The Roots of Ritual* (Grand Rapids: Eerdmans, 1973), 121–43. Smith, however, is not given to easy explanatory dualisms; the use of these terms must also be carefully nuanced, with attention especially to particular ritual circumstances. Smith can also argue that beginning with cosmology is exactly the wrong way to proceed when one considers ritual, though cosmological implications will always still arise from the ritual use of place. See his *To Take Place: Toward a Theory in Ritual* (Chicago: University of Chicago Press, 1987). In the 1973 article, Smith speaks of "locative" cultures, myths, and rituals, but the term "liberative" is my own.

argued that when "cosmos" has been primarily achieved for human society by myths and stories of order and enclosure, walling off the threat of chaos, and when the best human being is regarded as the wise person who knows how to keep his or her place within the limits, then the ritual practice will frequently be "locative." That is, the patterns of the ritual will echo and reinforce the lines that organize both the cosmos and our society, celebrating the important—even central—location of this particular place within that structure and giving yet greater weight to the importance of each of us "keeping our place": imagine a coronation or the rituals of feudal submission or the dedication of a sacred building. The ritual map of such a cosmos will especially show the borders, intimating what is dangerous beyond: "here be dragons." To this way of understanding the world belong the rituals of ancient Near Eastern city-states, for example, and the myth of the "hero-that-failed," like Gilgamesh or Orpheus, the hero who has learned the impossibility of escape and the wisdom of limits. Mary Douglas's "positional" cultures and their rituals should also be considered here.[9]

On the other hand, when the vastness of the cosmos is not seen as threatening but rather as an opportunity for expansion or for liberation from the local oppressive structures, when the ideal human being is the one who escapes and takes others along, then the ritual practice will frequently be "liberative." That is, the ritual will tell of a place beyond the oppressive structures and will enact and assist a journey—perhaps an ascension—out of here: imagine rituals of ecstasy or the initiation into a mystery religion. The ritual map of the cosmos will demonstrate the boundaries that oppress—for some classical forms of religion, that was the very cycles of the planets themselves—but will especially show the doorways through those boundaries. To this latter way of seeing the world belong the rituals of ancient gnosticism, for example, and the myth of the "hero-that-succeeded," like various saviors or redeemers, the hero who knows the escape routes and shares that knowledge with other initiates. Our own North American cultures, their fascination with liberty, with "away-from-here," and with modern versions of gnostic rituals should also be included here, at least in part of their concerns.

Says Smith: "The question of the character of the place on which one stands is *the* fundamental symbolic and social question. Once an individual or culture has expressed its vision of its place, a whole language of symbols

9. See above, introduction.

and social structures will follow."[10] The character of the local place, together with the ways it connects to other places, comes to expression in our rituals. Our rituals thus have important social ethical significance as they may give one or another value to the place on which we stand.

This book seeks to apply the metaphor "maps" to Christian ritual practice for three principal, interlocking reasons. The first reason draws upon these reflections from the history of religions: the use of this metaphor helps us freely to acknowledge that all human rituals do indeed organize—"map"—the cosmos in one way or another, beginning with the place where we stand,[11] and that Christian rituals share this characteristic. Indeed, Christian rituals are made up of cultural materials with a long prehistory, and that prehistory includes ways in which the world was organized by the purity rites, meal rituals, communal narratives, liturgical uses of space and time, and other ritual matters that came to be reworked in Christian practice.[12] We will need, then, to consider further how the resultant Christian rituals relate to the locative and the liberative conceptions of ritual mapping.

The second, related reason is explicitly about the metaphor: to call our central rituals "maps" enables us to remember more clearly, imagine more powerfully, that Christian liturgy does imply space, not just personal event. Or, rather, the way personal and communal events occur in Christian liturgy must be seen also to involve "representations that facilitate a spatial understanding of things." That will be true, of course, simply because one thing put next to another in a public ritual sequence implies a space and so a cosmos.[13] But we need to explore more explicitly what the Christian liturgy has to say about that space, and so, whether the meanings of that liturgy can be seen to be in dialogue with other forms of cosmological public symbolism, other kinds of maps, other sorts of global organization.

The third reason has to do with ethics: what happens with our maps, what takes place in the dialogue, how we enact our understanding of the place where we stand and of the places beyond matters for our living. Maps can connect us imaginally and really with a whole world. So, specifically, can Christian rituals. How do we enhance and follow those connections in a time so much in need of authentic cosmology in all of its senses? To pursue the liberative or locative question even further, how might our liturgies

10. Smith, "The Influence of Symbols," 137.
11. In addition to Smith, see Rappaport, *Ritual and Religion* (see above, intro. n. 3), 209–15.
12. See Lathrop, *Holy People* (see above, intro. n. 2), chapters 7 and 8.
13. Rappaport, *Ritual and Religion,* 209 and following.

reflect the importance and goodness of the local place in the network of places without simply reinforcing the status quo? On the other hand, how might they reflect liberation but not necessarily escape? Furthermore, maps can lie, can be tools of uncriticized power, can subtly distort the world to our advantage. So, specifically, can Christian rituals. How do we avoid or minimize the lies, criticize the power?

In what follows, we will pursue these questions in considering the most central of Christian ritual practices: the washing that joins us to the Christian community, the assembly gathering for "word and table," and the ways that this assembly locates itself in space and time. These central matters of Christian identity propose maps of the cosmos, in dialogue with the other maps by which we live. Such cosmological proposals are, then, not only the interest of one or two Christian hymns or an occasional Christian prayer. Nor are they the concern of only a certain kind of spirituality, depending upon your taste for such things. One way or another, cosmology is alive in baptism and eucharist, in the keeping of Sunday and the liturgical year, even in the arrangement of the church building, and this cosmology needs to be allowed to stand forth in greater clarity. The practice of baptism and its experienced meaning can be in dialogue with all of our public symbolisms. The practice of word and table can join in very specific ways with those who speak for the care for the earth. The assembly use of space and time can be seen to draw a map that is aware of the cosmological frontiers of current astrophysics.

But do we really need such ritual maps? According to the *Popul Vuh*, the Mayan account of the creation and ordering of both the cosmos and Mayan society,[14] when human beings were first successfully created,[15] they could see everything, everywhere. "Their sight passed through trees, through rocks, through lakes, through seas, through mountains, through plains. . . . They understood everything perfectly, they sighted the four sides, the four corners in the sky, on the earth. . . . "[16] Obviously, seeing everything perfectly,

14. Like the *Diné bahane'*, the *Popul Vuh* combines a cosmogonic narrative with an account of the history and structure of the society of the people.

15. In the *Popul Vuh*, before the successful creation of humans from corn, there were three earlier attempts that resulted in (1) the animals generally, (2) a disintegrating earth-creature, and (3) the monkeys, none of whom were capable of the words of praise and the sacrifices that the gods desired.

16. Dennis Tedlock, trans., *Popul Vuh: The Mayan Book of the Dawn of Life* (New York: Simon & Schuster, 1996), 147. As with other Native American peoples, the "four corners" are very likely the points on the horizon of the rising and the setting sun at the summer and winter solstices (p. 210).

they did not need maps. But, according to the story, this sight was taken from them by their creators, the gods. Now it is the "council book," the *Popul Vuh* itself, and especially its oral and ritual performances, that restore something of this original vision of "the four sides, the four corners," "in the sky, on the earth."[17]

The Mayan myth can be instructive to us. Not that we should think that human beings could ever see everything everywhere or that Christians would think that such seeing would be very helpful to creatures like us who could not possibly respond with all-embracing compassion. There is an appropriate, limited beauty in our ability to see only what is before us and to see farther only with exceptional instrumental help. From a Christian point of view, we are invited to love and respond to what is actually before us, not long to see through it to something else, something bigger. Nonetheless, ritual recovery of cosmological knowledge, the possibility of coming to see the "corners" and the "sides"—the structure and connections of things—through communally engaged symbols: this is a rich and widespread human theme, useful also to us, alive also in our rituals, balancing the many other ways we know and construct our world.

In the Western Middle Ages, the *mappamundi*—the name given to various charts of the known world and of its unknown edges, charts that came to play their own role in evoking quests into that unknown—drew some of its features from Christian ritual practice. For example, these maps generally organized the world around Jerusalem, echoing the centrality of the image of that city to the shaping of many Western buildings for Christian liturgy or to the development of the Christian liturgical year as a kind of Jerusalem-through-time that could be available everywhere.[18] Furthermore, the usual T-O shape of these maps made use of the ritual *tau* or cross mark to represent the pattern of the principal waters of the world and thus saw the world itself as marked with the cross.[19] That old map, of course, has to be radically redrawn, reflecting the current status of human knowledge, but we need to ask if current Christian ritual can similarly help in setting out structures of meaning within what we know of the connections and boundaries of the world.

17. Ibid., 63–64, 192; compare 29.
18. Smith, *To Take Place,* 94–95.
19. For a T-O map, see Turnbull, *Maps Are Territories,* 42.

Baptismal Ordo *and Cosmology*

The most powerful of the Christian cosmological maps is the one set out in the baptismal process. That process may be for us an enacted *mappamundi,* even something like the performance of our "council book." But this ritual map engages us most powerfully precisely because it includes both boundaries and doors, location and liberation, because it expresses both the sadness and joy of maps, imperfection yet enacted connection.

If the ecumenically renewed baptismal *ordo* is celebrated in strength and clarity,[20] it will be full of some obvious cosmological references. In the thanksgiving over the water at the heart of the rite, for example, many Christian communities praise God for the goodness of the water. From the midst of our watery earth, aware of our need for water simply to live, we give thanks, believing that God has made the water and used the water again and again to save or to recreate:

> At the beginning your Spirit was at work,
> brooding over the waters of creation's birth,
> bringing forth life in all its fullness.
> Through the gift of water
> you nourish and sustain all living things.
> Glory to you forever and ever.[21]

"The waters of creation's birth": there is an understanding of cosmos. This understanding depends upon the image in the first Genesis creation account of all things being originally a "deep," a great collection of "waters" (Gen. 1:2), and of these waters being first separated to make space for the "dome" called "Sky," and then gathered together, delimited into seas, to make space for the dry land called "Earth" (Gen. 1:6-10). The power of the image need not be destroyed by our scientific knowledge that water is very rare in the universe, that there is no "dome," and that our planet also moves through and is itself part of what we used to call "sky." If anything, this knowledge helps us to see more acutely how precious the water is—absent now, mostly leaked away, from what we know of Mars and of our moon, probably circling the sun in the relatively rare comets (were collisions with

---

20. The earlier books of this trilogy have reflected upon that *ordo.* See Lathrop, *Holy Things,* 59–68, and *Holy People,* 133–48.

21. "Thanksgiving over the Water," *Book of Common Worship* (Louisville: Westminster John Knox Press, 1993), 422.

comets one source of earth's great waters?), perhaps present in abundance in Neptune, Uranus, the subsurface of Mars, the atmosphere of Saturn's moon Titan, and some great nebulae beyond our solar system—though at temperatures and in conditions hostile to life as we know it—but gathered together in fecundity in our seas and rivers, rainstorms and glaciers. Then "creation," by this image, has intended such fecundity from the beginning, and the "birth" of all things is seen to parallel all mammalian births, "water" sustaining the growing life and then breaking out to herald the emergence of the newborn.

Such an image tends toward being terracentric and even anthropocentric, privileging our watery home and the life it makes possible as the center of an ordered cosmos, at least as we might behold it. The myth behind the words seems to be a locative myth: the world is an island or a bubble within the dangerous but now ordered waters, the waters within this bubble being tamed to fruitfulness. But not quite: the prayer gives thanks to *God*. Beyond the ordered waters, through the waters, it is God—not the water or the pictured order—who gives a center to the cosmos implied here. How God might hold into order the vast waterless places of all the universe—the chaos not of water but of fire and dark matter and space itself, the fiery infernos and stellar furnaces, the black holes, the seeming voids—is not said, but the very act of thanksgiving opens to its possibility, beyond our knowing. Nonetheless, it is through water that we and all of our fellow waterborn creatures have been included in this vast array. At the edge of this precious, life-generating water we stand and give thanks.

Such a thanksgiving, in these or similar words, is said over the waters of baptism in most churches. But it is not only the various words of such a prayer that imply a cosmos. The recovery of such a "flood prayer" (as Martin Luther called it) in recent liturgical life has been paired with the even more important recovery of a significant pool of water for the baptizing. Where such a pool exists, its waters not only give a stronger center to the rite. They also provide a center to the world. Here is a womb for the birthing of new life, as ancient Christians would say. Here is a sea on the shores of which the church may be as a new city open to all the peoples. Here is a spring from which the whole earth may drink and be washed,[22]

---

22. The eleventh line of the fifth-century baptistry inscription at the Lateran basilica in Rome reads: *fons hic est vitae qui totem diluit orbem* ("this is the fountain of life which washes the whole orb"). This sixteen-line poem, often thought to have been written by Leo the Great, was divided into eight distichs and inscribed on the eight-sided architrave resting on pillars surrounding the octagonal font. See F. van der Meer and Christine Mohrmann, *Atlas of the Early Christian World* (London: Nelson, 1958), 129.

a tiny point in the scheme of things that nonetheless gives a center, a little pool of water that washes all the people.[23] If the Christian liturgy has a locative character, that is, if it tends to propose that the world is organized around a center, an omphalos, then that center is first of all the local Christian font, not distant Jerusalem or Rome. No wonder hundreds of third- to seventh-century fonts tended to be massive and significant pools, frequently built in their own octagonal buildings, with that single local font often giving a center to a city or village.[24] Today, with the font newly set out or built in the assembly place of the church, the very symbol of the waters greets us as we enter and begins to remind us that what goes on here is not only about human culture but also about cosmos.[25] The water comes here from elsewhere in the world's water system, from a river or lake or underground stream, ultimately from the rain itself. But then, what water does come here is gathered together in fecundity and force here. If the water is before us in abundance, it may awaken in us inchoate but powerful longings for both a cleaner earth and a widespread slaking of thirsts; it may give us a place for our reconceiving death and life within this watery world; it may give us a cosmic center.

But the prayer over the water and the use of the waters themselves are set within a process, an *ordo* of events used to welcome new members into the Christian community. This whole *ordo*, when celebrated in fullness, can also be seen to have cosmological resonance. Outlined simply, the process is this: (1) candidates for baptism are taught the faith and the ethics of the community and formed in the way of the community's prayer; (2) this teaching and formation then bring the candidates to the bath, and, in turn, (3) to the table, to participation in the life and mission of the community, and to remembrance of and action for the poor. The elements of this *ordo* have been unfolded with differing accents and richly various secondary symbols in the diverse churches of the world, being somewhat rearranged,

---

23. The last line of the inscription in the baptistry of the church of St. Thecla in Milan reads: *ut puncto exiguo culpa cadat populi* ("that at this little point the guilt of the people falls away"). For the text, see Peter Cramer, *Baptism and Change in the Early Middle Ages* (Cambridge: Cambridge University Press, 1993), 271.

24. S. Anita Stauffer, *On Baptismal Fonts: Ancient and Modern* (Bramcote: Grove, 1994), 17–44. Central baptistries tended to disappear in later architectural practice, being replaced by smaller fonts in parish churches and built over in large cathedral projects. In the eleventh and twelfth centuries, however, in Italy and Provence, there was a burst of baptistry building. These central buildings served again to focus a diverse city-state in the focal point of baptismal enactment. For one discussion, see Cramer, *Baptism and Change,* 267–90.

25. Lathrop, *Holy Things,* 94–95.

for example, when children are the candidates. But the cosmological accents remain. Teaching the faith involves, as its first and basic move, teaching that there is a world and not just chaos, that this world is created, and that human beings have a compassionate and caring role within that creation. Christian faith is, first of all, trusting the creator, trusting, therefore, that the world is not some trick. Formation in prayer, then, involves learning to stand within this world in thanksgiving. Then, at the edge of the water, four other primal elements often function to call our attention to this world center, this spring, this birthplace: a *fire* burns—that most widespread phenomenon of our universe, creative and destructive burning—here as a paschal candle giving light, evoking in a small way both the warmth and the danger of this new life; olive *oil* is poured out or marked upon those baptized, fruit of the life-giving trees of the temperate regions of the earth, evoking healing, festivity, and, here, the sacred office given to the baptized; new *clothing* is put upon the baptized, great white robes, as if those immersed here came forth a whole new sort of humanity, making a fully new beginning; and the whole community then leads these newly baptized ones to a *meal,* a sharing of the sources of life within the world, sustenance for this new humanity, for these new witnesses to the order of the cosmos.

Your assembly may not do it just this way. However you do it, though, the obvious cosmic resonance, the sense of a cosmic omphalos, should probably be heightened. In our time, there should at least be these things: a more striking pool of water, a stronger formation in creation faith, a profound recovery of thanksgiving, a strengthening of local community. Much of your assembly's life should involve the constant return to these things: gathering together as an assembly being a matter we learned and repeat in relationship to these waters; the alb our ministers wear being our common baptismal clothing; the eucharist we celebrate being the repeatable part of this life-altering event; our vocations in the world being the many ways we live out our "sacred office," our responsibility as "new humanity," as witnesses to the order of the cosmos. Baptism introduces us to life in a place.

Except, there are dangers here. Baptism may be seen as such a locative event that it ends up quite strongly supporting the status quo. If the baptized are the "new humanity," then the boundaries are clear. Beyond those boundaries are the "others," and our ritual map may then signal that among the others there is danger. The "cosmic order" may simply be the order around us, around our own familiar neighborhood, organized the way we want it, or around our ecclesial authorities and our obedience to them as we "keep our place." We may call what we do by the exalted title "vocation," but the "witness" we thereby give may be only to the closed structure of our own vision. If this pool is the center of the universe, the *axis mundi,* why would we need to care about any other place? Especially when, in the history of Christianity, baptismal identity came to be seen as coextensive with local or national citizenship, these dangers were very real. They continue to be real in those parts of Christianity that regard baptism with new rigor, as the introduction to a heavily boundaried, new, and total society.

Still we have not yet said all that there is to say about the *ordo* of baptism and the kind of map it draws. The Christian faith is not only about creation. It is also about salvation and about the community in the Spirit. Formation in prayer is also formation in beseeching, in crying out for help for the sake of the whole needy world. The immersion itself has always been understood to be a death: immersion into identification with the crucified Christ and so identification, in him, both with the wretched outsiders and with his resurrection to new life, beyond all oppression. Baptism introduces us to an assembly, but this assembly is not simply local. Rather, it is an assembly of assemblies or one worldwide assembly of those who are being made witnesses to God's salvation for all things. Baptism can also be seen as a liberative event, a resistance to local oppressions, mapping connections beyond "here" to a far wider world.

When the son of Timaeus follows Jesus toward a new way of understanding the cosmos, according to Mark, he follows him toward his death.[26] Perhaps the young man who flees away, without his garment, from the arresting soldiers—from the enforcers of the current order of this world— and then reappears clothed, as a witness to the resurrection, is to be identified as Bartimaeus. But whether he is or not, when the readers go along with Bartimaeus, they are nonetheless brought to this naked immersion in Jesus' death. Then, in case they have not yet gotten the point, they are sent back to the beginning of the Gospel, to the baptism of Jesus, to the revelation of the triune God's identification with the need of the world, to the hole in the perfect sphere of the heavens, to the journey from place to place. Christian baptisms recall and reenter this baptism of Jesus. The baptismal *ordo* takes place under that hole in the cosmic sphere. The ritual map of baptism cannot be simply locative.

Such themes in baptism also come to expression in the rite. Christian liturgical prayer—as well as other poetry associated with the rite—expresses the faith that the waters of baptism are available to wash the whole orb of

26. See above, chapter 1.

the world because they flow paradoxically from the death of Christ.[27] In the "flood prayer," for example, a paragraph like this inevitably occurs:

> He is the never-failing spring
> who has promised that all who thirst can come to the living water . . .
> By the baptism of his own death and resurrection
> he set us free from bondage to sin and death
> and opened to us the joy and freedom of everlasting life.
> As he suffered for us,
> the piercing of his side brought forth water and blood.
> Glory to you forever and ever.[28]

"Freedom from bondage," "slaking of thirst"—these are images of salvation, liberation. Such images multiply in the rite. The immersion itself is not only the local birth of a new humanity, it is also the death and resurrection of wretches who are at the end of their rope, the consummate washing of sinners, the illumination of the blind, the introduction to the Way, the creation of a worldwide communion. The baptismal *ordo,* then, can be taken as a journey, a movement toward a promised land. The anointing marks those who are beginning to arrive in the new place, and the meal gives a taste, a down payment on the fruitfulness of this new land.

These images of salvation should also be heightened in our practice. A whole variety of biblical metaphors for liberation—exodus from slavery, the arrival of jubilee, cancellation of debt, forgiveness of sin, resurrection from the dead, release from deafness and blindness, healing of paralysis, slaking of thirst, inclusion in the new company, refuge in the new city, initiation into the new age[29]—can all be unfolded in the church's teaching about baptism and in the prayers and readings of its rite. The preparation for baptism can be marked by secondary rites that celebrate some of these images: the signing

27. The twelfth line of the Lateran baptistry inscription completes the thought: *sumens de Christi vulnere principium* ("this is the fountain of life which washes the whole orb, *taking from Christ's wound its source*"). Van der Meer and Mohrmann, *Atlas,* 129.

28. *Book of Common Worship,* 423.

29. The earliest baptistry images so far discovered—those at the third-century house church of Dura Europas—reflect many of these themes. See Lathrop, *Holy People,* 82–83. The eight images painted in the tenth century on the octagonal walls above the font in the baptistry of Novara, Italy, represent the horrors arriving in the world at each of the seven angelic trumpet blasts (Rev. 8–11) and then, on the eighth side, the birth and ascension of the Child of the Woman (Rev. 12). Those born anew in this font are here born to participation in this liberation. The eighth day is the sign of the liberation from the seven. See Cramer, *Baptism and Change,* 279–80.

of the senses at the beginning of a catechumenate, for example, or the enrolling of names in a great book at the end. Catechumens can be "initiated" into the mystery of salvation. Baptism introduces us to a journey.

Only, here, too, there are dangers, the potential sadness of maps. When baptism only liberates, it can ignore the goodness or the real struggles of the place where we are. Especially when that land toward which we journey has been identified with heaven or with life after death, when the ritual death we undergo is seen as a dying of our relationship to the actual world[30] around us, when baptism has been dealt with like a mark that enables a soul to pass the cosmic gatekeepers as it gets out of here, once and for all, and when the authoritative keepers of the mysteries have been regarded as keepers of the keys to the doors for getting out of here, then the result of this "salvation" has been a quite thorough degradation of creation. If we practice such a ritual map, we may quite rightly be accused as coconspirators in the current ecological crisis. As a public symbol among the wealthy, such an understanding of baptism may help make our religion irrelevant to the things we actually do with the earth, the only unhappy exception being that we sometimes do live as if we truly are people who have the right to transcend any limits, consuming anything we want, claiming any "new" territory (new, that is, to us) as our own. There is an ugly but currently common meaning for the worldview of "globalization." "Life without boundaries" or "boundariless," proclaim some current advertisements, lying or at least hiding the truth, acting as if there really could be life without boundaries. On the other hand, among some non-Western peoples, the escape may be from the current conditions of local culture, using baptism as a way to approach and to identify with Western society and economy. And among the poor of any place, such an understanding of baptism as a public symbol may be part of the much discussed opiate, anesthetizing the wretched to current suffering because of the coming great escape.

But the faith celebrated in baptism is a faith in both creation and salvation—and in the Spirit who forms a community that holds both in tension. The prayer in which baptism forms us is both thanksgiving and beseeching. The Spirit of God enlivens our praise and groans within us. And Jesus Christ, with whom baptism identifies us, is both the hero-that-failed and the hero-that-succeeded. Or neither. That is, the Crucified-Risen One is forever the

30. "World," in this liberative understanding, building upon the language of late-Jewish apocalyptic, has been construed as a collection of false values, as part of the unholy three, "the world, the flesh, and the devil." Still, the word for such a construal is still "world," "cosmos," and the paradox of John 3:16 is easily forgotten: "God so loved the world. . . ."

failure, in his death, and forever the transcendence and transfiguration of limits in his resurrection. The Spirit poured out from his death is the wisdom of life within limits. The Spirit breathed from his resurrection is the way beyond oppression and the fear of death. Yet there is one Spirit: "in the one Spirit we were all baptized into one body . . . and we were all made to drink of the one Spirit" (1 Cor. 12:13). Baptism in the power of this Spirit is locative and liberative, boundary and door. Both.

The joyful ritual map of baptism is capable of containing within itself the failure and sadness of maps. Neither the locative nor the liberative map alone suffices to tell the truth about the cosmos as it is held in the mercy of the triune God. Baptism ought not be used to support the status quo; neither should it present a world-denying way for getting out of here. This place where we stand is, indeed, a little place, dwarfed and marginalized and threatened in the vast chaos of things; yet this place is beloved, dear, central even. This place where we stand thus matters immensely, yet it is connected to all places. Oppressive structures do truly surround us, yet they are not eternal; they should be challenged and changed. This book is written, of course, amid the privileges of Northern and Western life and has no right to say that escape—even symbolic escape—is not sometimes a creative alternative to pain and sorrow, torture and hopelessness. Yet the ancient practice of the Christians, including especially poor Christians, has been to trust that it is the structures of terror and oppression that are most unreal in God's real world, and then to cast very real, very local networks of mutual support and shared food—assembly as witness—in the face of such oppression. Such a practice expresses baptismal meaning, both liberative and locative. Further, vastness does indeed threaten, yet held in the hands of God, this vastness is also open, beckoning, new, interesting even. And we do truly die, yet we do not need to organize our whole world around our fear of death as the primary principle. We may find the place and span of our limits to be the very place of transfiguring grace and echoing song. Allowed always to say both things, the public symbol of baptism can constantly challenge whatever public organization of space may mark our current culture.

Baptism will exercise such a challenge, not because Christians love to be contrary, but because baptism is always a washing into the community of the triune God, into the single mystery of the death and resurrection of Jesus Christ, under the tearing of the heavens, the end of any perfectly consequent cosmology. On one level, of course, baptism begins by persons simply wishing to join the church or, with somewhat more complexity, wishing to change their lives. Or it begins by parents wishing to protect and pray for their children. This practice does not seem, in the first place, to be a proclamation about location or cosmos or map. In baptism, Christians believe that they stand on holy ground before the only Holy One, not on sacred ideology before their own current conception of the organization of space. Yet because of the "holy ground" that is inevitably entailed in standing before God, baptism does have implications for cosmology. It does draw a ritual map of the world. Baptism holds together both locative and liberative conceptions of the cosmos because of its theology, because of the God the liturgy itself proclaims as active in these waters. So baptism corresponds to Jesus Christ, hero-that-failed, hero-that-succeeded, both, neither. In the power of the Spirit, baptism forms the community to exist as Jesus Christ before the face of the one, holy, eternal Majesty. These themes are present in baptism, even when our practice does not clearly express them, even when our practice diminishes them. To our great surprise, these themes—this enacted theology—will sometimes break out of hiddenness and embrace us and the place where we stand into meaning.

Nonetheless, as much as we can, our baptismal practice ought indeed heighten the sense of the locative: this birth-giving pool of water, these primary symbols, set out *here,* in this community, strengthening our sense of the importance of life within this place. And, at the same time, our baptismal practice should also heighten the sense of the liberative: these images for salvation brought forth in clarity, a strong way for us to identify with people in need, with a worldwide assembly of witness, and with a vast world that is also *away from here,* beyond our boundaries. Both. And because this is baptism into the reality of the triune God and not just a general ritual affirmation of either location or liberation, then woven through the whole *ordo,* often by means of the tension-laden juxtaposition of both of these themes, there will need to be continual witness to the "hole in the heavens," the tear in any spatial system. The baptismal process enacts the most powerful of the Christian cosmological maps, because it embraces the hole in the maps, the inadequacy of any of the systems.

What do these reflections imply for actual practice? Here are a variety of concrete suggestions. You may think of yet more.

—Recover a strong, central baptismal pool. In fact, consider building one such font for all the Christian communities of a given place. Or consider using together an actual local river or lake. At the same time, work on the open door of the assemblies—open to the other assemblies, open to the outsiders, open to people away from here.

—Recover baptism as a process, both for adults and for those who surround and answer for an infant, and use this process for both locative and liberative formation.

—So teach and preach and practice that people are baptized into one real and responsible local community, but also into the universal church.

—As candidates for baptism learn creation-faith, make sure they read and think about Job 38–42 (as well as other biblical creation accounts), not just Genesis 1 and Genesis 2–3, about the independent value of the rest of creation, not just the centrality of our human drama. Yet invite them to think about the seriousness of the drama of sin and death as well. "You are earth, to earth you shall return": such is the locative wisdom of Genesis 3:19 and probably the best form of the words to use in the liturgy of Ash Wednesday, at the start of the great baptismal remembrance that makes up Lent.

—As the candidates for baptism are formed in prayer, help them learn lament and beseeching as well as thanksgiving, thanksgiving as well as lament and beseeching.

—As they learn these patterns of prayer, join with them in praying for other species of life than merely our own, in commending to God the diversity and well-being of these species, in thanking God for their existence. Perhaps even mountains and rivers and seas—even solar systems and galaxies—could enter our prayers. Baptism must not be about saving us from this company, but with this company. Yet learn together again the prayer for needy humanity as well.

—As the candidates learn the life of compassion, help that compassion to flow toward the present community but also toward those outside of our circle, toward those outside but also toward the present community. Consider also acts of ecological responsibility together with acts of human solidarity and charity as part of what is learned in the baptismal process.

—As the candidates learn the liturgical use and biblical reading of your community, consider helping them to learn those same uses in at least one other community with which your community is not in full communion.

—As the community gives thanks and beseeches God over the water, consider shaping the prayer so that the vastness of the universe and both the marginality and the preciousness of our watery planet are recalled.

—As the baptismal candidates enter the water, consider helping them to reflect on the relationship of clothes to social status, indicating that taking off some of their clothes does indeed indicate their letting go of status structures ("As many of you as were baptized into Christ have clothed yourselves with Christ. There is no longer Jew or Greek, there is no longer slave or free, there is no longer male or female"; Gal. 3:27-28). But reflect with them that taking off their shoes also indicates their letting go of absolute ownership of the land ("Remove the sandals from your feet, for the place on which you are standing is holy ground"; Exod. 3:5).

—As these candidates are actually baptized, use words that help us all to understand that God is a flowing, communal reality, holding all things in mercy, under the hole in the heavens, not a patriarchal monarchy, with the authority inherited along a masculine line of succession. While the words from Matthew 28:19 will be used in most of the churches, they may be introduced and surrounded by other words that expand and deepen the understanding of the Trinity and connect this linguistic usage to Jesus' baptism in the Jordan and to the revelation there of the sphere-breaking mercy that is saving all things. "I baptize you in the name of the Father and of the Son and of the Holy Spirit, Eternal Majesty, Incarnate Word, Abiding Comforter, one God."[31] This difference in being-before-God makes the greatest difference in the ritual map drawn by the rite: the universe is not a hierarchy organized underneath a single authority; it is a vast, diverse richness held in embracing love.

—Then let the baptized come to the meal, a local meal that enacts a longing for the whole world to be fed.

—And let all the baptized meet together, at least every Sunday, rejoicing in the local assembly as an identity place in a vast world, but also remembering the poor, indeed, all of creation beyond this circle, signing the hope for a wider well-being.

To even begin to do such things, the local assembly must be practicing its baptisms as a process, as a catechumenate for adults and their sponsors, for children and their parents and godparents. The recovery of such a process is an important place to begin in allowing the public meaning of baptism to come to clearer expression, and the churches have been widely involved in

31. For other examples, see Gail Ramshaw, "In the Name: Toward Alternate Baptismal Idioms," *Ecumenical Review* 54 (2002), 343-52.

this recovery.[32] Even so, such a burden as is outlined here is too great for a single process. Such a baptism takes our lifetime to do. Learning that we have been made part of a new humanity in this holy bath, we must also begin to learn our connections and identifications with others. Learning the lines of connection to all the earth, we must also learn the sweet importance of this local place. But then we are face-to-face with yet another of the paradoxes or ambiguities of baptism. A once-for-all event, baptism takes a whole lifetime to unfold. The members of the church are invited always to be newcomers with the newcomers, learners with the learners, beggars with the beggars, yet also always hosts and keepers of the bread at this center. Such a practice, holding the many meanings of baptism together with all that this implies for the place on which we stand in connection with other places, requires a lifelong catechumenate.

Baptismal Politics

From the beginning, Christian baptism has held more than one thing together in lively tension. Baptism takes place once, yet it is for all of our life. It is for living, yet it is also done in the face of dying. It happens to individuals, celebrates individual persons, yet it constitutes a community, is an event for the community. Baptism is an utter gift of grace, a thing that can never be earned or learned. Yet it calls for conversion, discipleship, teaching the faith, lifelong learning. It happens in a single great bath. Yet it rightly unfolds in a ritual process, an *ordo*. It has occurred through twenty centuries in many different places, with all the waters of the world: in Mediterranean pools and baptistries, in the African surf, even with North American hospital eyedroppers. Yet there is only "one baptism" (Eph. 4:5). In its utter grace, baptism is for infants but also for adults. In its realism about death and its good news about hope in Christ, baptism is for adults but also for infants. Indeed, we baptize infants as if they were adults, addressing them and according them great dignity, and adults as if they were infants, washing them and drying them off and holding them with tender care. Side by side with all of these ambiguities, there is the paradox of the place on which we stand: baptism constitutes a strong local community, yet it also identifies us with outsiders and with places away from here.

32. In addition to denominational materials on the catechumenate, the Christian initiation of adults, and the ministry of sponsors with children, see also Thomas F. Best and Dagmar Heller, *Becoming a Christian: The Ecumenical Implications of Our Common Baptism* (Geneva: World Council of Churches, 1999).

The paradoxes and ambiguities of baptism constitute the great public strength of this symbol. That is, by means of these interwoven, even conflicting, themes, the practice of baptism is capable of enabling a critical dialogue with the diverse regnant worldviews of our cultures, the public systems for the organization of space, our practical maps. If our society, for example, has a sense of the commercial opportunities present for us in the limitless space around us, regardless of the lives of other people or other creatures that may actually fill those "empty" spaces, baptism may critically introduce us to the great wisdom of life within limits.[33] On the other hand, if our society is afraid or closed to what is beyond our boundaries, then baptism may identify us with all outsiders, making us to be as citizens of each foreign place, siblings with each foreign people. It is not so much that baptism actually speaks a political word or enunciates a political agenda. But the polity of our society, its understanding of our identities in relationship with each other, inevitably entails an organization of space, a conception of the place on which we stand, a cosmology. Our politics—the organization of our πόλις, our city, our "country," and the roles we each play within it—carries along a conception of "world." Then, when the great bath of the assembly draws us in to stand before and be surrounded by God, the place where we stand is reconceived as holy ground, and all our polities, all our cosmologies, are under critique.

The presence of these ambiguities also carries a danger, however: baptism may be made to mean anything.[34] Baptism may be used rather to reinforce than to question a regnant social view. This danger arises especially, as we have seen, if only the locative or only the liberative aspects of baptism are brought to expression. But if the incongruities and tensions in baptismal practice are heightened and not resolved, and if the source of these incongruities is recalled, then such a shifting ideological use of Christian initiation will be more difficult. Indeed, as Smith says, "Ritual gains force where incongruency is perceived and thought about."[35] In the case of Christian

33. In his remarkable book, *The Other Side of Eden: Hunters, Farmers, and the Shaping of the World* (New York: North Point, 2000), Hugh Brody has been able to argue that hunter-gatherer cultures, for example, the Inuit, are the truly local peoples, associated with a single great landscape for thousands of years and only very gradually moving to new hunting grounds, while the agricultural peoples have been the true nomads, hungry for new land and pushing aside and making invisible the claims of the hunter-gatherers. The dominant North American culture today is the result of a relatively recent migration of agriculturalists.

34. Cramer, *Baptism and Change,* is partly a series of essays about the pivoting meanings of baptism in differing social circumstances.

35. Smith, *To Take Place,* 109–10.

baptism, that "thought"—that liturgical theology—must come again to Jesus Christ.

The paradoxes and ambiguities of baptism exist because baptism is anchored in Jesus Christ. We believe that his death is our life. His once-for-all coming gives a universal meaning to the world. In him, the wiping away of all tears and the doing of all justice—the promises of God's day—have already begun, yet they are still coming. In the Spirit that flows from him, all the diverse created things are held together, and all persons—infants and adults, men and women, rich and poor, those from the North and those from the South, hunters and farmers—stand before God in great dignity. Jesus Christ and the faith that is through him are utter gift, yet that gift takes a lifetime to learn. The word enlivened by his Spirit addresses each one; that same word forms the church. The Crucified and Risen One is at the center of our meetings as church, yet he identifies essentially with all outsiders, with those who cannot join our assemblies. Thus, the bath that is enacted in the name of Jesus Christ, in the triune name, is as he is, is as the triune God is, holding opposites together in mercy and grace. And the place on which we stand—this place and all the places to which it is connected—is holy ground.

Our difficulties with baptism have often arisen when we have lost these christological and liturgical tensions. We have met this effect before, as we have considered baptism and ecumenism.[36] Some Christians have seen only the conversion and teaching in baptism and forgotten the grace. Some have seen only the grace and forgotten the lifelong catechumenate. Some have seen an individual's rite. Some have found a communal identity. So difficulties also arise for baptism and cosmology as the incongruities in its understandings of space have been flattened or resolved. Renewal in the present time will be stronger as we restore the interwoven themes of baptism: strong single washing event, strong continual meaning for daily living; formation for this congregation, linkage to all the churches; then, also, location and liberation; boundary and door.

The political consequences of baptismal meaning might be especially clear as we consider the incongruities—the hole—in baptismal boundaries. A strong baptismal practice—a significant pool, a restored catechumenate, the importance of baptism and its remembrance to congregational life, the ethics learned in the baptismal process, the idea of the lifelong learning of baptismal meaning—will establish strong boundaries. That is, it will matter

36. Lathrop, *Holy People,* 115, 147.

a great deal to the congregation that someone is baptized, and it will be seen to matter. The baptized constitute church. Period. Furthermore, the locative force of baptism will come to the fore: this place, this congregation, this boundaried assembly will all be underscored. The present book joins other books and other teachers in urging such a renewal of strong baptismal practice and meaning. Indeed, in postmodern times, it will become increasingly important that the church knows itself to be a specific group, with a specifically demarcated task in the world. Let the boundaries be clear.

And broken. To be baptized is always to be identified with the one who himself identifies with the outsiders and the marginalized. In the New Testament accounts of the origin of baptism, we can see that a purity rite, intended to prepare a strongly demarcated people for coming of the day of God, has been broken and remade into the constitution of a people together with the Crucified-Risen One, who himself identifies with the least and the little ones. The boundaries of purity have been turned inside out: this is the bath that makes you unclean with the unclean; this is the distinguishing mark that makes you like the others: utterly in need of the mercy of God.[37] In the present time, we might say the matter in yet other terms: here are boundaries transvalued; here is the locative event that unites you with those who long for an end to oppressive centers, the insider event that identifies you with the outsider, the assembly event that associates you with the disassembled— because of Jesus Christ, because of the Holy Trinity, because of the hole in the perfect sphere, because of the holy ground. Only one is holy.

From this baptismal politics arises the assertion of the *Epistle to Diognetus* about the global citizenship of Christians: "They are at home in their own countries, but as sojourners. They participate in all things as citizens and they endure all things as foreigners. Every country is their homeland and every homeland is a foreign country."[38] From this politics arises an understanding of care for the poor, the outsiders, or the homeless that is not at all "charity," but common life and common cause. From this politics, this baptismal identity, arises the call to Christian resistance against such versions of absolutizing nationalistic or tribal or familial identity as divide the world: for the Christian, there must be no "best country." From this politics arises the possibility that Christians, home at heart, may come to be in respectful dialogue with people of other religions and cultures, other ways to organize space. Yet baptism, if it is maintained with the rich tension of its diverse

37. For this argument, see ibid., 161–82.
38. See above, chapter 3, note 42.

themes, finally has no political agenda. It is rather a ritual hole in agendas, a grounds for dialogue with polities, cultures, and patterns of commerce—especially when they take themselves too seriously.

The political consequences of baptismal practice may also come to clarity in considering how Christians might celebrate rites of passage in the light of their great bath.[39] That is, the statuses people assume and their relative value in a society make up a large part of their polity. Furthermore, these statuses are very often related to an organization of space, a map of the place on which we stand. People of higher status, for example, sometimes have clearer access to the center of our organized space and less to do with its margins. It belongs to a book about the cosmological meaning of Christian liturgy also to consider the rites of passage.

So does the greatest Christian "rite of passage"—that use of water we have been considering that proclaims the transfer of the community "from the power of darkness . . . into the kingdom of God's beloved Son, in whom we have redemption, the forgiveness of sins" (Col. 1:13-14)—have any echo in all the other rites of passage in which Christians, like all other human beings, mark the changing conditions of their lives? How shall we celebrate these rites—especially the transitions of those who are marrying and giving birth, of those who are ill, of those who are dying or mourning the dead—in such a way that we show forth both the dignity of local cultures and the dignity of our baptismal identity in Christ?

It is important to note that some anthropologists and scholars of human ritual have also discovered an *ordo* of sorts that they believe marks virtually all human passage rites.[40] Borrowing their terminology from a journey, from a passage through a territory, they believe we are able to discover these things about such rites: These "passages" from one "status" to another—from "unmarried" to "married," for example, or from "alive" to "dead"—are marked by three consecutive stages: *separation* (indications of the departure from one status), *transition* or the "liminal" phase (a period of belonging to neither one status nor another), and *reaggregation* or incorporation (a social and communal welcoming and recognizing of the new status). In each phase, there may be symbolic rites that recapitulate the whole process. The liminal phase is frequently marked by the demonstration and communication to the "passengers" of the deepest values and most important symbols

---

39. For what follows, see further the essays and the "Chicago Statement" in S. Anita Stauffer, ed., *Baptism, Rites of Passage, and Culture* (Geneva: Lutheran World Federation, 1998).

40. See especially the classic study by Arnold van Gennep, *The Rites of Passage* (Chicago: University of Chicago Press, 1960).

of the community. According to this understanding, the rites of passage are thus deeply immersed in a culture and are a primary means of passing on the values of a culture. Sometimes this dangerous "betwixt and between" stage is also very carefully protected and marked by the presence of *communitas* values, the leveling of status distinctions as they are known in the ordinary workings of a society.[41] The final stage of the rite, incorporation into the community in the new status into which one has moved, is frequently signed and accomplished by a communal meal.

In a certain sense, we may already discover this schema in what we have said of the baptismal *ordo*. Welcome to the catechumenate is a rite of separation, a beginning of the journey. The catechumenate itself is the liminal phase, with the catechumens learning the deepest values and symbols of the Chris-tian community. The actual rite of baptism recapitulates the process of becoming a Christian and incorporates that Christian into the community. The meal of the eucharist demonstrates and seals that incorporation. Many Christian communities call this entire process by the name "Christian initiation."

But there are important ways in which baptism itself breaks out of this schema. For one thing, for Christians the rite is never really over. We need to be, as we have said, lifelong catechumens. We baptize children and adults, and we continue to teach and learn with them all. Indeed, it is not just that baptism itself recapitulates the process of becoming a Christian; rather, the rite recapitulates the whole of Christian life. Furthermore, the rite introduces us to a new "status" only in a paradoxical way. With baptism we are, indeed, made members of the church, Christians in the company of Christians. Yet insofar as this is baptism into Christ, we are joined to the one who identifies himself with all humanity. This rite is finally not about distinguishing a few "passengers," but about continually refounding us all in the one baptism that unites us with all of needy humanity. If anything, the rite marks the passage or journey of the entire world out of "the old age" into "the new." Furthermore, Christians are encouraged to live *communitas* values all the time, not just when they are in a specific period called "catechumenate." The gospel is for the married and the unmarried, the children and the adults, the men and the women, the gay and the straight, the employed and the unemployed, the rulers and the ruled, the sick and the temporarily able-bodied, the living and the dead. Mysteries and symbols are certainly shown to those who are becoming Christians, but so are they constantly shown to us all. The principal "mystery" shown us is the gospel of the death

41. For this point, see Victor Turner, *The Ritual Process* (Chicago: Aldine, 1969).

and resurrection of Christ, proclaimed in Word and Sacrament so that we are continually reinserted into the mission of the triune God. At its best, the Christian congregation in which baptism takes place is not itself a *culture,* not a full organization of roles necessary for community survival, not an ethnic reality that passes on its status structures as it helps its people negotiate life's changes.[42] It is rather an ongoing dialogue with cultures. "Initiation" may be the wrong name.

These ways in which the baptismal process is both like and radically unlike a rite of passage can be helpful to us as we also consider the Christian use of such rites to mark life transitions. Christians are also participants in cultures. They also marry, give birth, take office, get ill, die—and engage in hundreds of other status changes that are recognized and marked in their diverse cultures. While these transitions and their celebrations are not the most basic rites of Christianity, not inherently Christian, they are culturally and politically important, beloved to Christians who love the earth that God has made, and powerfully significant to the vulnerable people who are undergoing the passages and transitions. They are important occasions for the proclamation of the mercy of God that holds all of human life and culture into hope and meaning. It is not surprising that Christians have thus sought to celebrate these transitions within the congregation or turned to the congregation and its ministers for help, prayer, and blessing while negotiating the change.

Christian communities should have two basic concerns when a congregation becomes the base in which such rites are enacted. They should, first of all, seek to make the rite itself a healthy rite of passage, fully utilizing all the stages of transition and carrying the best created gifts and values of the culture of which it is an expression. The ancient Christian interest that the parties to a marriage should both freely assent to the contract, that people who are sick should not be stigmatized and isolated, that funerals should express both honest sorrow and grounded hope—these are examples of such concern. We may be able to extend these ancient concerns by articulating the goodness of communal rejoicing, the importance of stages in transition, the value of communally expressed sorrow, and the beauty of many traditional symbols for change. In working with a passage rite, then, those who care about Christian liturgy might ask if it is marked by the presence of the

---

42. Thomas Schattauer, in "The Cultural Pattern of Christian Worship," R. R. van Loon, ed., *Encountering God: The Legacy of the Lutheran Book of Worship for the 21st Century* (Minneapolis: Kirk House, 1998), 167–69, helpfully discusses how the church, especially in its symbolic interactions, is *like* a culture, while not being a culture.

clear human schema for status transition, by a locally rich expression of that schema, by a resistance to any absolutizing of the status structures expressed in the rites, and perhaps also by an illumination of the meaning of "the human" by borrowing expressions from other cultures.

But in the midst of these transitions, the Christian communities should also seek to proclaim the gospel of Christ as the source of meaning amid all changes and crises. They should seek to set out something of the meaning of baptism, something of the ways in which the baptismal *ordo* breaks out of the schema of the rite of passage, something of the truth that baptismal identity in Christ is far more basic than any of the statuses that are the subject of the passage rites. This second task may be immensely difficult, given the powerful focus on the "status" itself in any rite of passage or in the experience of pervasive or chronic illness. How can we engage in this task?

Here are some beginning suggestions: To the extent that is possible, let the rite of passage take place in the midst of the congregation, perhaps even in the Sunday assembly.[43] Let the congregation's proclamation of the word of God be among the principal "mysteries" passed on to the passengers in the liminal phase. Let the prayers for the persons in passage be "blessings," constituted by fulsome thanksgiving and honest beseeching. Let the eucharist, with the entire community welcome to the communion, be the principal meal of the reaggregation phase. Carry signs of baptismal remembrance into the rites of passage: The oil of baptism may be used to anoint the sick. Part of the marriage rite may take place at the font. Anointing oil might also be used in marriage. Crowns or wreaths or a canopy, placed on or over the couple (as in the Eastern Orthodox or the classical Swedish Lutheran rites), may be taken as baptismal symbols. Clothe the dead in a baptismal alb. Place the body by the font and under a pall, interpreted as a baptismal sign, and light the great paschal candle of Easter and of baptism by the body. In any case, in the midst of the rites of passage, demonstrate love for the people in transition, honor for the various statuses of their transition, but also a profound sense that all such statuses are of only secondary, not ultimate, value. The great marriage, for example, is the marriage of God with the earth, and, in baptism, the wedding garment of Christ's righteousness is being put on women and men, children and adults, the married and the unmarried, gay and straight, the childbearing and the childless—in equal and abundant

43. In the nineteenth and early twentieth centuries, Swedish congregations—especially rural congregations—not uncommonly celebrated all weddings in the Sunday assembly and carried out all burials from the Sunday assembly.

measure. Nothing done in our wedding rites—or in any of our other celebrations of transition—should obscure this gift. Women must not be dealt with as property, being "given away" or "taken." Married people should have no higher nor lower status in the Christian community than other people. The family must not be deified, made the most basic value. We are the baptized, in mission in the world, and that identity relativizes all others, critically engaging our politics.

After baptism took place, Justin's community continually reminded each other of "these things."[44] As we recover the *ordo* of baptism in its strength, as we seek to discover anew the cosmological resonance of this bath, we, too, will need continually to return to baptism and its meaning. There are many ways to do so. Every Sunday's gathering of the Christian assembly is the first and most important of these reminders, the eucharist itself being the repeatable part of our common baptism. Every baptism celebrated in each congregation brings us back to the one baptism we all share. In the proclamation of the forgiveness of sins, in the ministry of reconciliation, we come back to the power of baptism. The annual Lent and Easter, especially as we recover the catechumenal significance of Lent and as we use Easter as the primary time for baptizing, will pull us all back to baptism. Our labor to strengthen the center of our assemblies while at the same time opening wide the doors—for welcoming others in and for going out to other places ourselves—will arise from and recall the diverse, unharmonized spatial themes of baptism. But not least among these reminders will be the setting out of our baptismal vocation in Christ in the midst of our celebration of the various stages of human life that are experienced and marked in our cultures.

Such are the politics of baptism. Such is the public symbolism of the baptismal process, in critical dialogue with the other ways we have to order our societies, to value the place on which we stand, and to organize our understandings of cosmos. We have said that "cosmology," in part, should be understood as any culture's sense of orientation in the universe, especially as that orientation is expressed in that culture's public symbols. For anyone among the Christians—and for any of the various distinct and mixed cultures with which those Christians live—baptism is certainly not the only public symbol. But it is one that, practiced in renewed strength, is capable of reorienting our cosmologies toward the cardinal directions of a world held in God's mercy.

44. 1 *Apology* 66. See Lathrop, *Holy Things,* 63–64.

Now, we turn to the first of the ways of continually reminding each other of this great bath. We turn to the Sunday assembly, the eucharist, and its critical dialogue with our map of this blue planet.

5

Eucharist and Earth-Care

The burning bush is not consumed. The place on which Moses stands is holy ground. Such is the ancient story. When the burning, all-holy God comes, a simple location in the earth, a simple living thing—a bush—suffices for the meeting place. That unpretentious place then becomes the center of a cosmos, a world now held into the possibility of order by the attention of God ("I know their sufferings," Exod. 3:7), by the passionate action of God to save from injustice ("I have come . . . to deliver," 3:8), by God's very name ("I AM WHO I AM," 3:14), and by the call to assemble because of that name ("Go and assemble the elders of Israel," 3:16). But the bush, the place of the meeting, the place of the fire, itself remains intact, not used up, unharmed, the object—we might even say—of miraculous and protective care. And more than the bush is protected: all around there stretches that holy ground.

If the Christian assembly gathers in the presence of this same God, the God celebrated in this story, does that assembly similarly deal so gently with the earth as God does with the bush? Does the assembly carry itself so harmlessly to the location of its meeting? Do we take off our shoes? The question is deeper yet: does that assembly invite us to see the place on which we meet—and the earth all around the meeting—as holy ground? Do the stories we tell, the meals we eat, the rituals we keep, engage us in caring for the earth with which we live? Or not? Do they rather support us in the contrary practice, in our own unlimited use of what lies around us, without concern for the consequence? With these inquiries, we come to the most obviously urgent of the cosmological questions before us. As we took up the task of liturgical cosmology, we could not ignore the accusation that Christian stories and Christian rituals have had their part in weaving the ideology behind the current ecological crisis. As we asked about the various conceptions of cosmology with which the Christian liturgy must engage, we needed to include that construal of world order that explicitly aims at the care of the earth. Now we must turn to these questions directly. We must do as we said we would: set eucharistic practice in dialogue with cosmology-as-ecology.

There may have been some initial help in considering baptism. The water for this central bath comes from the resources of this blue planet, the pool of water here amid the assembly being for us something like the burning bush. Also from the earth itself are the attendant fire and oil and, most especially, the food of that meal toward which baptism leads. The faith confessed at baptism begins with creation, with trust in the creator, thus, with the goodness of the world. Christians who are baptized into this faith must assume that the stewardship of the good earth is part of their concern and that a genuine ecological crisis calls for their response. Furthermore, the prayer learned at baptism begins with thanksgiving, concrete thanksgiving over concrete things. Thanksgiving, thus, is a kind of steady exercise of creation faith, and it marks a way to walk on the earth itself.[1] So the catechumens—and all of us, as lifelong catechumens—might be learning ecological responsibility along with response to the poor as part of baptismal ethics. These are at least possibilities in baptismal practice that might break out into important meaning for a Christian response to ecological need. Or, to describe the matter again in the more abstract terms drawn from ritual studies, we may say that the locative character of the rite tempers any tendency to escape from here, inviting the baptized to see the goodness and importance of each local place, including the importance of the interrelated web of species and habitat conditions in each place. But the liberative themes of this same bath can similarly temper the force of the local status quo, inviting the community to engage critically with misused local authority, including authority misused in relationship to the land, and connecting this local community to all the needy everywhere in the earth, also as these others are needy in the poverty of their environment.

Perhaps this sketch of the ecological implications of baptismal practice is right. Still, these environmental meanings will have been only rarely articulated in actual congregations. They may stand here as an invitation to

1. See above, chapter 3.

catechists and pastors to help the baptized reflect yet further on the implications of the great Christian bath. But it may also be that this outline of such implications is marked by what Huck Finn would call "some stretchers." They sound good. It might be nice if they were really so. But let us go on with the story, with the continued assembly of these baptized ones, seeing whether these baptismal implications actually prove to be true. What about church every Sunday when the baptized gather? Can we consider that most central of Christian rituals, the Sunday eucharist, the complex of texts and songs, prayers and the meal that the ecumenical liturgical consensus proposes as constituting the Sunday gathering? Does the eucharist really help? It will not do to be satisfied with stretchers, to say we are setting out symbols that matter for the current ecological crisis and to believe we are actually doing this simply because we say so.

Does Christian Sunday liturgy mean something important for the care of the earth?

In order to consider this question, we need to think again about how Christian liturgy means anything at all. Further, we need to consider how it might include us in that meaning. We have elsewhere argued that the liturgy uses juxtaposition—one thing put next to another, "one part against another across a silence"—as its most basic tool of meaning.[2] From this point of view, the shape or *ordo* of any liturgy is the sum of the major juxtapositions with which that particular liturgy is filled. Participating in a liturgy, we move through its *ordo,* become part of those juxtapositions, and so are gathered into the primary meanings of the liturgical action. In order to consider the relationship of the eucharist to the care of the earth, we need once again to consider the *ordo* of this ancient service of word and table. The assertion here will be that this *ordo* does not so much articulate a specific ecological agenda as that, simply by doing its explicitly Christian work, this *ordo* does constantly, repeatedly, form its participants in a worldview that includes a love for the conditions of the flesh, implicitly a love for the earth itself. So what is that shape or *ordo* and how can it have such a meaning?

2. The quotation is from John Ciardi, *How Does A Poem Mean?* (Boston: Houghton Mifflin, 1959), 995. For this idea applied to liturgical meaning, see above, chapter 2, and below, chapter 7, as well as Lathrop, *Holy Things* (see above, intro. n. 2), 82. For the relationship of *ordo* to world order—and specifically to care for the earth—see also *Holy Things,* 214–17. For liturgy and "meaning," generally, the most thorough exploration is found in Graham Hughes, *Worship as Meaning: A Liturgical Theology for Late Modernity* (Cambridge: Cambridge University Press, forthcoming), where the idea of the "hole," so frequently mentioned here, is also discussed.

Eucharistic Ordo and the Love of the Earth

Take an approach that may at first seem indirection, digression. In order to consider the shape of Christian worship and its meanings, consider first the shape of a principal source of the central texts read in the liturgy. Consider the shape of the Gospel books themselves. For example, look again at the odd conclusion of the Gospel of Mark and its structural implications. Widespread scholarly consensus now concedes that Mark 16:8, with its astonishing last words, "they said nothing to anyone, for they were afraid," does indeed form that conclusion. It is no wonder, with such an ending, that the manuscript tradition gave us several other ways to go on, alleviating this embarrassment. But we now think the great, authoritative Vaticanus and Sinaiticus—not to mention Clement of Alexandria, Origin, Eusebius, Jerome, and several important and early old Latin, old Syriac, old Georgian, and old Armenian witnesses—were right.[3] The book ends here. Why?

One way to answer that question is as we have already proposed: that such an ending inevitably creates an intended cyclic reading of the book.[4] The readers of the book and those who hear it read in a Christian gathering know that Jesus is risen. In spite of the silence and fear of the women, the word has somehow come to the community gathered around the book. In fact, the book itself, as a whole, is such a word. To resolve the puzzle of the ending as it is read in an assembly, the readers and hearers go back to read again. Soon they hear, "Now after John was arrested, Jesus came to Galilee, proclaiming the good news of God" (1:14). The people gathered together in this reading are back in "Galilee,"[5] the very place to which the young man who was seated at the tomb sent the community: "there you will see him, just as he told you" (16:7); the very place promised by Jesus himself: "after I am raised up, I will go before you to Galilee" (14:28). The risen Christ is encountered in the actual text of the book and in the proclamation and engagement that arises from the book. The Gospel book is as its title declares: ἀρχὴ τοῦ εὐαγγελίου, both beginning and ground of the gospel of Jesus Christ. The Gospel book, read in the assembly, is itself the resurrection appearance.

---

3. Bruce M. Metzger, *The Text of the New Testament* (London: Oxford University Press, 1964), 226.

4. See above, chapter 1.

5. Compare Willi Marxsen, *Der Evangelist Markus* (Göttingen:Vandenhoeck & Ruprecht, 1959), 59–61.

From such a reading of Mark, we can say that the liturgical tradition of making acclamations around the reading of the Gospel in the assembly—"Alleluia" and "Glory to you, O Lord" and "Praise to you, O Christ"—accords with the purpose of the book itself. From such a reading of Mark, we can say that Martin Luther was articulating the very intention of at least this evangelist and not just his own idiosyncratic idea when he wrote "A Brief Instruction on What to Look for and Expect in the Gospels." Take, for example, this passage:

> When you open the book containing the gospels and read or hear how Christ comes here or there, or how someone is brought to him, you should therein perceive the sermon or the gospel through which he is coming to you, or you are being brought to him. For the preaching of the gospel is nothing else than Christ coming to us, or we being brought to him. When you see how he works, however, and how he helps everyone to whom he comes or who is brought to him, then rest assured that faith is accomplishing this in you and that he is offering your soul exactly the same sort of help and favor through the gospel.[6]

"When you see how he works," writes Luther. But, then, how does the risen Jesus "work" in these texts? In exactly what ways might the actions or sayings of Jesus in the texts give word to what is happening to the present hearers? In the earliest Christian communities, stories of Jesus and the sayings of Jesus seem to have circulated orally—and perhaps in some written collections, as well—until they were gathered together into the Gospels, in which books they then had ongoing communal life. But the Gospels need not have taken the form or shape we find so familiar. Scholars have recently been reflecting again on the diversity of the forms of "gospel" books as they circulated in the first centuries. Among these scholars, John Dominic Crossan has helpfully provided a typology of the books that might be called "gospels."[7] For Crossan, two of the four types he provides are most important. They are the "discourse gospels" and the "biographical gospels."

The discourse gospels—one may take the widely known Gospel of Thomas as prototypical, but there are others—have no "stories of Jesus." In fact, these gospels evidence no interest in history and no historical anchor. They are all postresurrection revelations, collections of sayings generally

---

6. E. Theodore Bachman, ed., *Luther's Works,* vol. 35 (Philadelphia: Muhlenberg, 1960), 121.

7. John Dominic Crossan, *The Birth of Christianity* (San Francisco: HarperCollins, 1998), 36-38.

understood as revealed to individuals. If a community is reading the book, then, the accent will, nonetheless, be falling on the individuals in that community as they hear about the revealed techniques for their own individual salvation. The content of the books is largely knowledge of technique, of *askesis,* to enable the self to escape the fleshly conditions of life into salvational fulfillment. As Crossan says, the trajectory of these "gospel" books is toward "sarcophobic" Christianity, toward the kind of Christian practice that later will be called "gnosticism." The figure of "Jesus" projected here "works" to enable escape from the conditions of the "flesh."

But the very existence of these discourse gospels helps us to see with greater clarity the characteristics of the gospel books called by Crossan "biographical." These are the four books we know as the canonical Gospels. Here there is a fierce interest in history, in stories of Jesus, in the community around Jesus, in the death of Jesus, and in the encounter with his resurrection. Sayings of Jesus are present in these books as well, but they are pulled into the story, united with the narrative of the history of the one who comes to the cross. The sayings are made part of the gospel. These books also tell of individuals who encounter Christ, including individuals who encounter the Risen One. But such individuals are always gathered again into the community, sent again to the assembly, as Mary Magdalene is so sent, apostle to the apostles, in John 20:17–18. For Crossan, the trajectory of these books is toward "sarcophilic" Christianity, toward a community that loves and honors the "flesh," the conditions of the created world within which it lives. For these Gospel books, just as for the story in Exodus 3, the activity of God takes place in the midst of the actual places and circumstances of this world. As these books were read in assembly, the community would have heard stories read to proclaim the work of the risen Christ in its midst, exactly as Mark's Gospel seems to have intended. In these books, the risen Christ is perceived to be none other than the historical Jesus of the stories, indeed, the historically crucified Jesus, encounterable now. Stories, even stories of the same event, could be told with differing accents precisely because the intention of the telling was to announce the work of the historic Crucified-Risen One in the present community.

It is not only the ending of Mark that gives evidence of this intention of the "biographical" or canonical Gospels. The very collection of stories and sayings in the four books is arranged in such a way that the individual pericopes are made to lean forward toward the account of Jesus' passion and resurrection. These books are, in a sense, "passion narratives with extended introductions," as Martin Kähler said.[8] Or, rather, they are passion and resurrection accounts with long and now communally important introductions. The narrative strategies of the "messianic secret" in Mark and of the "book of signs" in the Fourth Gospel, for example, make clear that it is the Crucified-Risen One, the one "whose hour is come," the one who is now revealed to faith, who makes the new wine of the gospel flow in the "wedding feast" of the present church, replacing the old religious water of purity laws (John 2:1-11), or who now heals and forgives in the actual house church assembly (Mark 1:40—2:12). The Markan church, sent back to the story by its ending, is in on the secret, is made to be an assembly around Jesus, and encounters the Risen One in the stories themselves. For the Johannine church, these things—the texts of the Fourth Gospel itself—"are written so that you [plural] may come to believe that Jesus is the Messiah, the Son of God, and that through believing you [plural] may have life in his name" (John 20:31).

Community, history, interest in the death and resurrection of Jesus, engagement with the present world, the historical story as a form for speaking to present times and present conditions: these things are shared in common by the canonical Gospels in contrast with the discourse gospels. If we care about how the Christian assembly relates to care for the earth, then the canonical Gospel books, so centrally important to the reading in that assembly, matter intensely. Of course, these books also tell stories or use aphorisms full of the stuff of the earth—trees, birds, fish, sheep, meals, farms, vineyards, houses, lakes, sickness and healing, roads, wildernesses. Such a narrative commitment to materiality may be helpful to us as we awaken to the place where we live. But woven through all of these earthbound stories, these books share an even deeper commitment to the risen Christ present in actual assemblies in the midst of real history. It is this shared commitment that can continually form us and reorient us to a sarcophilic worldview.

But one other shared thing belongs uniquely to the canonical Gospels as well: a specific shape. Mark moves from the baptism of Jesus, to the collected stories and sayings of Jesus that "lean forward" toward the passion, to the meal (or meals) that show forth the meaning of the passion, to the passion itself, to the resurrection announcement that sends the reading community back to the beginning of the book again. Although the other three Gospels may add the Johannine prologue or the infancy narratives, passages

---

8. *The So-Called Historical Jesus and the Historic Biblical Christ* (Philadelphia: Fortress, 1964), 80 n. 11.

used to proclaim the origin of Jesus, they too follow exactly the same shape: baptism, narratives, meal and passion, resurrection and sending. Why? Why did the Markan form become normative?

"Biographical interest," we may say, echoing the label Crossan uses for these books. The flow of Jesus' life provided the structure for the collections and creations of each work. It may be so. But another possibility is this: the shape of the Gospels reflects the shape of the liturgy. Baptism and the remembrance of baptism as the community-forming event, an assembly around narratives and preaching, the meal-form encounter with the cross, the resurrection-based sending, the expectation of returning to proceed through this pattern again: such a list is, in exactly this order, recognizable to us as the emerging shape of the Christian Sunday meeting. Given the clear interest, arguable at least for both Mark and John, in the texts coming to expression in a Christian assembly around the Risen One, this latter proposal seems to be the stronger of the two. Did the Gospel books come to shape and perhaps even provide a kind of manual for the Christian practice?[9] Or did the Christian practice give shape to the Gospel books, which then, in turn, gave words and meaning to the practice? We do not know. Probably both. In any case, it can be argued that Sunday *ordo* and the shape of the canonical Gospels are, from the beginning, intertwined. In the communities of the sarcophilic Gospels, remembering Jesus and communal liturgical practice go together.[10]

It is no wonder, then, that the three Gospels written after Mark all add an image of the Christian assembly at the end of their books, as the locus of the appearance of the Risen One. Mark's Gospel as a whole already provides a schema for such a meeting. The other canonical Gospels make this assembly-locus explicit, gathering up and expressing the intention of their form of the gospel genre with this final image. In Luke, the *ordo* of the gathering is itself visible. Jesus is known, by the pilgrims to Emmaus, in the Scriptures read and preached and in the breaking of the bread. Then the little community explodes in mission: they return to the city of death with the news of life. Assembly is linked to assembly (24:13-35). John provides the note of the weekly ritual recurrence to the meeting for recognition,

9. Marianne Sawicki, *Seeing the Lord: Resurrection and Early Christian Practices* (Minneapolis: Fortress, 1994).

10. Marianne Sawicki, *Crossing Galilee: Architectures of Contact in the Occupied Land of Jesus* (Harrisburg: Trinity Press International, 2000), 160. As the practice of the "paleo-church," Sawicki argues for this: "Remembering Jesus occurs authentically in various places and practices, among which are liturgy, charity, teaching, and healing."

faith, and sending: "Eight days later, his disciples were again in the house" (20:26 RSV). And Matthew points to the communal responsibility for that baptism into the triune reality of God with which the whole Gospel *ordo* has begun, as the Son is baptized under the voice of the Father and the outpouring of the Spirit. At the same time, Matthew asserts the continual presence of the Risen One in this community of baptism: "I am with you always, to the close of the age" (28:20 RSV). There is no "ascension" here, only communal life in the midst of the world, under that hole in the heavens. Indeed, that community life in the light of the resurrection has already been adumbrated in Matthew 18, especially in 18:20: "For where two or three are gathered in my name, I am there among them."

But these final stories were not told in order to make the hearers wish they had been there too. Rather, in each case, the stories at the end of the Gospels characterize the actual continuing life of the assemblies that knew this book. Scripture and preaching, the meal and mission can be recognized as the pattern that was known in the Lukan churches (Acts 2:41-47; 20:7-12), a pattern we, too, have received. The Johannine churches met eight days later, to use the old and significant idiom for a week,[11] and eight days later, and eight days later, and we, too, have received that unbroken tradition of Sunday meeting. And the Matthean baptizing and teaching have continued to form the assemblies, including our own. Indeed, even Mark may have a reference to baptism at the end of the book, as part of the way in which the hearers were sent again to the "Galilee" of their own assembly. As we have seen, the young man who sends the community back to Galilee (Mark 16:5), back to the encounter with the Risen One in the assembly, could be interpreted as a *neophyte,* the naked man from the garden scene (Mark 14:51-52), perhaps even the son of Timaeus, now newly baptized in the death and resurrection of Christ, newly clothed, and newly aware of how the cosmos is valued and reconfigured when Jesus Christ is available to be seen "in Galilee." In a reversal, then, the latest, newest member of the community gives instruction to all the others about the resurrection and about the importance of the assembly,[12] and this instruction is explicitly not Neoplatonic or gnostic instruction about escape from the earth.

If something like this correspondence between gospel shape and assembly pattern is correct, then these four Gospels provide us with profound

---

11. On Sunday as the "eighth day," see below, chapter 6, and Lathrop, *Holy Things,* 36–43.

12. Compare Thomas Talley, *The Origins of the Liturgical Year* (New York: Pueblo, 1986), 207–9.

insight into the ἐκκλησία, the meeting around the Risen One. For an understanding of some of the earliest churches, we now have not just the name "assembly," ἐκκλησία, borrowed from the Hebrew scripture tradition and applied eschatologically.[13] We also have the great outlines of an *ordo*, widely shared in Christian circles and remarkably reflective of those central elements—word and meal—that could be discovered in the formative narratives of God's action in the assemblies at Sinai (Exod. 19–24), at the Water Gate (Neh. 8), and finally at Mt. Zion (Isa. 2, 25). By the time the Gospels were written, Christians were gathering on Sunday for word and meal and sending, and they understood that gathering as constituted by baptism. Such an outline ought not to be regarded, then, as the accidental development of later Christian history. The very dynamics of the *ordo* are available to us in the canonical Gospels. The "problem of the origin of the *ordo*," as Alexander Schmemann called one of his most basic questions,[14] needs to be discussed with New Testament evidence in hand.

We can say even more. This outline of the meeting represented the profound Christian idea—the "sarcophilic" Christian idea—that the actual history and death of Jesus have inaugurated the eschaton of God in this world. God's acting in justice and mercy for the healing of the created world could therefore be proclaimed in the gathered communities, in the power of the Spirit, by telling there the stories of Jesus and, reinterpreted through him, the very stories of Israel, and by eating there the eschatological feast of his gift. The assembly was thus a gathering through the Spirit, in the presence of the Risen One, before the face of the present God, an experience of what Christians would later call the "Trinity." This encounter with the eschaton, with what came to be called "the resurrection," was taking place in every local assembly, not in Jerusalem alone, or Rome alone, or some other "apostolic headquarters." The local meeting, imaged and reflected at the end of each Gospel book and by the shape of the Gospel book itself, was the holy place of eschatological assembly. "Where Jesus Christ is, there is the catholic church," the four Gospels can be taken as saying, as Ignatius of Antioch would express this same idea a few decades after their composition.[15] In each local place, the bath was remembered next to the words empowered by the Spirit next to the meal held as the taste of the end-time feast. These events, side by side, proclaimed the meaning of the death of

13. See Lathrop, *Holy People* (see above, intro. n. 2), chapter 1.
14. Schmemann, *Introduction* (see above, intro. n. 42), 40–71.
15. Ignatius, *To the Smyrnaeans*, 8:2.

Jesus and, thus, the meaning of all death and life, of the world itself, in the light of the judgment and mercy of God. These events enacted a sarcophilic cosmology. By gathering in this reality, again and again, eighth day after eighth day, the assemblies were formed as witnesses—to the one who went before them, to "all that I have commanded you," to the triune God, to the forgiveness of sins, to the presence of God's mercy in this world, therefore to a sarcophilic worldview.

Sunday after Sunday, if we have received this Gospel shape as the shape of our meetings, the son of Timaeus sends us back to that assembly that begins with baptism in local waters, under the hole in the perfect sphere of the heavens, the hole in any closed cosmology. Sunday after Sunday, we, too, are invited to encounter the life of the triune God embracing and holding the life of this world. Sunday after Sunday, the actual stories of this world are gathered up and reoriented by the parables and stories of Jesus and, thus, by all the reorienting stories of the Bible. Sunday after Sunday, a little meal is set out for all to eat, recapitulating the death and resurrection of Jesus, setting out the body and blood of Jesus for us to eat and live. Sunday after Sunday, our own worldviews are reconstituted, and we are made witnesses to the triune God's engaged care for the beloved, wounded earth. Of course, this repeated *ordo* is also full of concrete things from the earth: real people, actual languages, concrete communal stories and folk tales, diverse cultural music, a real place, water and fire, and, as Irenaeus of Lyons never tired of pointing out in his resistance to second-century gnostic interpretations of Christianity,[16] real bread and wine. Just as with the canonical Gospels, the central materials of this very material meeting are not disembodied ideas and spiritualities devoid of earthly connection. But it is finally the *ordo* itself that reorients us, again and again, toward the real earth where we live, reconceived as "world" held in the love of the triune God. Through the movement of the *ordo,* we are brought to experience and trust this "paschal mystery": because of Jesus, God is present with life-giving mercy in the midst of our very death, in the heart of that fear that drives so many of us to want to control and ultimately to escape the conditions of the world. God is present, healing us and turning us toward our neighbors and toward the beloved earth. This *ordo* does not lead individuals to techniques for getting out of here. Rather, it inserts a community into the concrete history, including the "natural history," of the earth.

16. See, for example, *Against Heresies* 4:17–18.

Liturgical Renewal, Worldview Renewal

This interest in what Crossan calls the "biographical gospels" as illuminating the classic shape of the liturgy appropriately arises in our time. The liturgical scholarship of the second half of the twentieth century showed a great interest in liturgical "shape."[17] Numerous Christian communities have used recent liturgical publications to make an ecumenically recognizable shape available as a principal local liturgical tool.[18] Then, with knowledge of this *ordo,* local communities have been able to draw from many books and many musical sources in enacting the patterned event of the liturgy. By such a conception, liturgy is not determined by the "Gutenberg galaxy." It is not a "print event," following a single book's prescriptions, marching through a set of texts, as important as these prescriptions and texts may be. Rather, the Christian liturgy is a communal participation in the meanings inherent in the juxtapositions of this received *ordo.* Furthermore, in this shape, liturgical criticism has an important tool as well. Since every kind of public meeting has its "liturgy," its public work, its ritual shape, the question for a Christian meeting is whether or not the public work of our particular meeting accords with gospel meaning. Liturgical renewal can be seen most basically as the continual renewal in the practice and meaning of the *ordo.*

But the idea of the "shape of the liturgy" is not a twentieth-century invention. In fact, it has become clear that the great preponderance of Christian liturgical history has been marked by the mutual sharing of an *ordo* for liturgy rather than the imposition of a single liturgical text. The ancient church orders, the Eastern *typica,* the Western medieval *ordines romani,* many of the Lutheran *Kirchenordungen,* the Reformed directories for worship: these all shared the idea that Christian liturgy is the order of a communal action, for which Bibles or lectionaries and then also other books of texts and of music provide variable resources. Martin Luther's two great essays on the celebration of the mass, *Formula missae et comunionis* and the

17. Most famously in Gregory Dix, *The Shape of the Liturgy* (Westminster: Dacre, 1945), and Schmemann, *Introduction.* For an end-of-century summary of this discussion, see the collections of articles in *La Maison Dieu* 204 (1995) and *Studia Liturgica* 26:1 (1996).

18. For example, the Presbyterian *Book of Common Worship,* the German *Erneuerte Agende,* the proposed new Roman Catholic sacramentary of the International Commission on English in the Liturgy, and the texts of the Renewing Worship project of the Evangelical Lutheran Church in America (www.renewingworship.org). See also the proposals for ecumenical eucharists from the Faith and Order Commission of the World Council of Churches: Thomas F. Best and Dagmar Heller, eds., *Eucharistic Worship in Ecumenical Contexts* (Geneva: World Council of Churches, 1998).

Deutsche Messe, need to be regarded in just this way. They were critical essays about how to use available materials within the received shape of the liturgy. They were not "liturgies."[19] The famous eighteenth-century American Lutheran "liturgy" of Henry Melchior Muhlenberg was much the same thing. It was an outline of the liturgical event together with an essay, written by hand and mostly circulated among pastors in manuscript form, about the use of the diverse available resources for congregations to enact the classic *ordo.*[20]

In fact, it is the idea of a single book, of the "liturgy" (conceived primarily as official text, not as communal action) being contained in one printed volume, that is the odd thing in liturgical history. The idea was especially invented in posttridentine Roman Catholicism, with the imposition of a single "Roman Missal" in 1570 on all the churches in communion with Rome, as a symbol of the increased centralism of that communion. But the idea was also promulgated somewhat earlier in Reformation England, with the imposition in 1549 of the otherwise interesting *Book of Common Prayer,* as a sign of the political intentions of the Act of Uniformity. In neither case was this central imposition very profoundly in accord with deep liturgical principles. In our present times, we will find the practice of Luther's critical but *ordo*-based approach to be the most interesting and helpful way to proceed.

Furthermore, current liturgical catechesis is frequently based on the second-century description of the Sunday eucharist given by Justin Martyr, a description which itself usefully presents the simple shape of a communal action.[21] At the end of his *First Apology* for the Christian faith, addressed to the emperor Antoninus Pius, Justin included this report of the Sunday assembly, immediately following upon his description of baptism:

> And for the rest after these things [after baptism is enacted] we continually remind each other of these things [of baptism]. Those who have the means help all those who are in want, and we continually meet together. And over all that we take to eat we bless the creator of all things through God's Son Jesus Christ and through the Holy Spirit. And on the day named after the sun all, whether they live in the city

19. English translations may be consulted in Ulrich S. Leupold, ed., *Luther's Works,* vol. 53 (Philadelphia: Fortress, 1965), 15–40, 51–90.

20. See Frank C. Senn, *Christian Liturgy: Catholic and Evangelical* (Minneapolis: Fortress, 1997), 503–4.

21. Compare *With One Voice* (Minneapolis: Augsburg Fortress, 1995), 6. See also, Lathrop, *Holy Things,* 43–53.

or the countryside, are gathered together in unity. Then the records of the apostles or the writings of the prophets are read for as long as there is time. When the reader has concluded, the presider in a discourse admonishes and invites us into the pattern of these good things. Then we all stand together and offer prayer. And, as we said before, when we have concluded the prayer, bread is set out to eat, together with wine and water. The presider likewise offers up prayer and thanksgiving, as much as he can, and the people sing out their assent saying the *amen*. There is a distribution of the things over which thanks have been said and each person participates, and these things are sent by the deacons to those who are not present. Those who are prosperous and who desire to do so, give what they wish, according to each one's choice, and the collection is deposited with the presider. He aids orphans and widows, those who are in want through disease or through another cause, those who are in prison, and foreigners who are sojourning here. In short, the presider is a guardian to all those who are in need. We hold this meeting together on the day of the sun since it is the first day, on which day God, having transformed darkness and matter, made the world. On the same day Jesus Christ our savior rose from the dead . . . he appeared to his apostles and disciples and taught them these things which we have presented to you.[22]

With Justin's report, we come again to contact with the four Gospel books. Here, too, was assembly, formed by baptism,[23] gathered around the word, celebrating the meal, and sending both the community and food "to those for whom nothing is prepared" (Neh. 8:10) and so bearing witness in the world. Justin's assembly took place within the economy and worldview of imperial Rome, and Justin himself was attentive to that context for the reorienting meaning of the Christian gathering. Indeed, the importance of Sunday, of the recurring *ordo,* of history, of the distribution of food in the world, of the presence of the triune God, of communal assembly, and of sending was shared by Justin with those very books he calls the "memoirs of the apostles," our canonical Gospels.

Is this importance shared by us? While we cannot say that all Christians everywhere have always followed this Sunday *ordo,* we can say that Justin's

22. 1 *Apology* 67. Translation in Lathrop, *Holy Things,* 45, 63–64.
23. Many presentations of Justin's eucharistic description fail to make the baptismal connection clear by beginning the quotation too far into the text. In fact, in 1 *Apology* 65–67, after a discussion of baptismal practice, Justin's report continues with an account of the Sunday meeting as the preeminent example of reminding each other of baptism and thus of helping those in need, meeting together, and giving thanks over food.

ordo accords with the four Gospels of the New Testament and that it has come to us, as our heritage, as the deep, given order of our assemblies. This *ordo* is the biblical and catholic shape of the liturgy. This *ordo* carries within itself the catholic intention of love for the conditions of the world.

But deformations are quite possible. The *ordo* of our actual Sunday assemblies can become something quite different, meaning something else. Throughout the long history of the general use of this shape by Christian gatherings, people have sometimes forgotten the world-embracing, world-saving meaning of its structure. Preaching has disappeared or the purpose of preaching has been lost, becoming any kind of exhortation, any sort of pep talk for spiritual techniques, rather than the revelation of the triune God holding the world under the hole in the heavens. The entire event has been clericalized, made essentially unavailable to the whole assembly, except as that assembly looks on at the mass turned into spiritual technique. The deep structure of the event has been overwhelmed by secondary matters, by cultural shards of "church" romantically recovered from another time, for example, or by the dominance of performers or musicians. Tragically, the prayers for all the needs of the world have sometimes disappeared. So has the sending, both as sending "portions" to the hungry or signs of justice to the poor and as sending the eschatological good news to the world. And more and more frequently since the eighteenth century, the meal itself has been lost—or so shriveled into a purely spiritual interaction that it is no longer recognizable as a meal.

These latter losses were especially fueled by the medieval misreading of Paul's exhortation to the Corinthians to examine themselves that they might eat and drink, "discerning the body" (1 Cor. 11:28-29). Contemporary exegetes largely agree that this "discernment" ought to be understood as a knowledge of the fullness and diversity of the assembly around the gift of the body and blood of Christ, as an openness to the poor and so to the whole "body of Christ" (see also 1 Cor. 12, the following section in Paul's work). But medieval practice took this warning to be an insistence upon being "shriven," upon penance and catechesis before communion. Going to confession frequently became more important than going to communion itself. The Reformation then simply continued this medieval practice. The fenced table, the ministerially issued token for admission to the table, finally the disappearing table were the result.

In America, the old sacrament meetings of the Scottish Presbyterians and the English Methodists, precisely because of this fencing, yielded to an *ordo* based on repentance before communion, but now without the table, first at Cane Ridge, Kentucky, in 1801, and then throughout the American frontier. The result was the "revival or frontier *ordo,*" systematized in the nineteenth century by Charles Grandison Finney: first, there occurs warm-up singing and, perhaps, some other drama or display; then, there follows practical and pointed preaching, based on only a few verses of Scripture; this all is intended to lead to the conversion of the individual hearer.[24] In North America—as also in places throughout the world influenced by North American evangelicalism—this *ordo* has become very widespread. Most recently, such a pattern of gathering has had its most vocal support in the so-called megachurches and their networks, although there, the third part of the pattern, "conversion," has undergone transformation to become the invitation to participation in need-based small groups and therapies.

The danger of this influential pattern should now be clear, however. Its characteristics—only a little Scripture, and that mostly verses with an accent on techniques for self-realization; the importance of the individual; preaching as concrete help; then, no prayers for the world; no meal; little sense of assembly; no sending to the poor—place this pattern far closer to the "discourse gospels," to the old sarcophobic way, than to the way of assemblies marked by the pattern of the four Gospels of the New Testament. The frontier *ordo,* in all its permutations, can easily support individualism and the gnostic tendency of American religion, doing so without reorientation or transformation.[25] This *ordo* will be of little help in inviting us again to the love of the earth and a care for its conditions.

Indeed, a liturgy so shaped may be experienced as putting divine sanction behind the absolute centrality of our own personal self-realization over all else. A newcomer or an old-timer, then, "goes to church" easily, as to a shopping mall explicitly and primarily designed to offer assistance in his or her search for "my happiness," "my fulfillment," "my family's well-being." While these are worthy goals, from a classic Christian point of view they are also always in need of challenge and enlargement. Religious language can call such self-realization by the term "salvation," the word used for the old goal of the frontier revivals but also for the old goal of world-escaping *gnosis.* Although many current American megachurches eschew the old religious word, the dynamics of their use of the frontier *ordo* nonetheless still

---

24. See further in Gordon W. Lathrop, "New Pentecost or Joseph's Britches? Reflections on the History and Meaning of the Worship Ordo in the Megachurches," *Worship* 72, no. 6 (November 1998): 521–38.

25. Compare Harold Bloom, *The American Religion* (New York: Simon & Schuster, 1992).

focus on the well-being of the individual, however that well-being may be presented. But unless either self-realization or individual salvation is subjected to the breaking and reversing work of the gospel of Jesus Christ, unless God's passion for the well-being of all the wretched and all the wounded earth is envisioned within an assembly that also cares for each person present, such talk can easily assist us to ignore or attempt to escape from the conditions of the world. Such an *ordo* does not offer us a harmless, value-free medium for the communication of the Christian idea, as is sometimes proposed. Rather, it carries within itself values that tend to be sarcophobic, values that were anciently called "gnostic." A Christianity marked only by this liturgical pattern would be rightly accused of collusion in the ecological crisis.

Instead, the serious challenge to all the churches is to recover the *ordo* of the four Gospels as the central focus and form of our Sunday meetings. This *ordo* will give us a place to stand, a place to receive and welcome the gifts of our cultures, a place from which to challenge our cultural malformations as they encounter the eschatological judgment and mercy of God, a place in communion with people beyond our cultures, a place from which to care for the earth. This *ordo* has the capability of continually reorienting our worldviews, of entering into critical dialogue with our maps of the planet. For the sake of gospel meaning and current responsibility, mutual affirmation and admonition between the churches, of whatever "denomination," should call us to the recovery of this shape of the liturgy. As a consultation sponsored by the Faith and Order Commission of the World Council of Churches put it:

> [This *ordo*] is the inheritance of all the churches, founded in the New Testament, locally practiced today, and attested to in the ancient sources of both the Christian East and the Christian West. . . . Churches may rightly ask each other about the local inculturation of this *ordo*. They may call each other toward a maturation in the use of this pattern or a renewed clarification of its central characteristics or, even, toward a conversion to its use.[26]

We need to let the *ordo* stand forth in strength, engaging participation, recovering both rich lectionary use and vigorous preaching, reclaiming

---

26. "The Ditchingham Report," 4 and 7, in Thomas F. Best and Dagmar Heller, eds., *So We Believe, So We Pray: Towards Koinonia in Worship*, Faith and Order Paper 171 (Geneva: World Council of Churches, 1995), 6–7.

attentive prayers for the needs of the world and strong communal thanksgiving at table, encouraging the full community to eat and drink, opening
the door, resisting the old penance-inspired fences around the table, recovering the sending, using this liturgy as a "manual for healing the world."[27]
We need a liturgy that has a strong center, in the central elements of the
Gospels' *ordo,* and a wide-open door toward the world.

In the renewed use of the pattern of this *ordo,* one thing next to another
always leads to a third thing. So the reading of the Scriptures—the truth-
telling of the Scriptures, the rich promises of the Scripture, the encounter
with the Risen One in the Scriptures, the gathering up of our experiences
of the world in the scriptural stories, the cosmic reversals of the Scriptures—
stands next to the preaching, the announcement that this truth-telling and
these promises have come here. If we do not cut off the implication of this
juxtaposition, then the faith that responds to such reading and preaching
must go on to sarcophilic prayer: prayer for the whole needy world; prayer
for particular needs beyond our circle; prayer for justice; prayer for the hungry, the sick, and the dying; but also prayer for endangered species and
endangered peoples; prayer for water courses and ecological networks
themselves. The juxtaposition of the sarcophilic Scriptures to present preaching must lead to prayer for others, not just for ourselves. Similarly, thanksgiving—praise to the triune God who holds all the cosmos in mercy—is
put next to the eating and drinking of the small shared meal that shows
forth Jesus' life amid our death. This juxtaposition, together with the whole
complex of the word-event next to a meal-event, leads to the final "third
thing": the faith that must share this food with the absent, send food and
assistance to the hungry, be ourselves "body of Christ" to be given away as
food in the world. Both intercessions and the sending show the assembly to
be caring again, willingly and concretely, about the interdependent networks of life in this world. Their absence makes it possible to forget the
intense sarcophilic meanings of the Gospels' *ordo.*

The son of Timaeus followed Jesus toward a reconstituted cosmology,
being immersed in the death of Jesus as if it were a baptism, then bearing
witness to the women and to us. The man born blind washed in the pool
called "Sent" (John 9:7), a sign of the Sent One and of his passion (17:3, 21),
and came seeing. The baptismal neophytes of Jerusalem, just come from the
water, were counseled by their bishop Cyril to touch their eyes with the

27. Paul Gibson, *Patterns of Celebration* (Toronto: Anglican Book Centre, 1998), 89.

wine of the Holy Communion, reorienting the senses with which they saw world.[28] For the Christian assembly, the immersion is in the juxtapositions of word and table, recalling baptism itself, cleansing the senses anew to respond to the triune God's saving embrace of the world.

What do these reflections imply for actual practice? Here are a variety of concrete suggestions. You may think of yet more. The "you" and "we" in what follows is the communal plural of the entire assembly, not just the second person singular of the leader or the presider or the first person plural of the clergy.

—Recover the full pattern of word and table as the pattern of the principal gathering of your Sunday assembly, every Sunday. If that is your pattern, ask whether its major constituent parts stand forth in clarity for your assembly, whether its actions are available as a bath to our senses, a reorientation to our cosmologies.

—Gather, remembering that you are baptized. Come past the pool; touch the water; scatter the water on each other; be forgiven again and reconciled with the locative and liberative purposes of the water in the world.

—Read the full range of the Scriptures, in as wide an ecumenical communion of such readings as is available, say in the pattern of the *Revised Common Lectionary*. Let the ministry of lectors be exercised by a diversity of trained readers and let that office be regarded as one of immense importance. Sing the psalm in response to the first reading, so that the whole assembly is actually itself in the word. Sing an alleluia or other verse to welcome the Gospel, acclaiming that text as a sign of the presence of the Risen One. Then let the preacher so preach as to make clear that the judgment and the mercy imaged in all of these texts are alive in this place now, holding the world itself into new meaning. From the parables and reversals of the Scriptures, let the preacher propose the cosmology of the holy ground, not a system of any kind but the worldview that arises when the hearers trust the only Holy One, the astonishing triune God, in faith. In the power of the Spirit, let the preacher preach the death of Christ that kills our fear and sin and death and the life of Christ that feeds us here and leads us now to live before God on the beloved earth. Let

28. See above, chapter 2.

the words of the preacher be formed by the *ordo* of the Gospels. Let them be words that go with our baptism, words that go with our gathering together, words that go with these Scriptures, words that go with this meal, words that go with our sending into the cosmos itself.

—Then sing. Let the whole assembly proclaim the word that has been celebrated here by singing it together in a great hymn. Indeed, sing your way through all of the meeting, making the whole flow of the *ordo* into a musical event, and especially drawing on a wide range of hymnody and song from throughout the world, expressing the worldwide communion of this local assembly. But attend to the words of these songs. Let them correspond to the world-affirming clarity and rich, earthly, and communal imagery of the Scriptures themselves, not to the individualism and world-escaping character of sarcophobic religion. We do not need to judge the use of such hymnody in another time, but we must not use it now. Too many of the hymns in our hymnals, still, and too many that we choose to sing, carry on as if the entire enterprise of Christianity were about "heaven" for "me." There are stunning contrary choices available.

—And pray. Especially, recover the praying. Be before the God who "knows their sufferings," on the holy ground. Find, train, and appoint leaders in the assembly who are gifted to lead us in prayer with simplicity and directness and honesty. Let each of those several leaders of prayer, taking a turn on a particular Sunday, know the great list of the intentions of the assembly and be wise to press us carefully yet further in such prayer than we may have gone before, especially bearing in mind the promises and world-containing images of the Scriptures of the day: for the poor, the hungry, the homeless, the unemployed, the war-torn, the tortured, the raped, the enslaved, the orphaned and widowed, the lonely, the sick, the alienated, the grieving, the refugees, the incurably ill, the dying, the dead; but also for our enemies, for people who see the world differently; for people filled with hate; but also for strangers and sojourners, for judges and magistrates, police and firemen, political leaders, soldiers, workers for peace; but also for threatened cultures, threatened life-ways of the various people of the earth, threatened waterways, polluted landscapes, endangered ecological systems, threatened species, whales and frogs and sea turtles, whooping cranes, and other species, perhaps also ones that are not so beautiful to us; but also for those who work with the earth and the sea, farmers, foresters, hunter-gatherers; rangers, sailors, fishers, gardeners, oil workers, explorers; but also for humankind living together, for cities and villages, families, broken families, gay and straight people seeking meaning in their sexuality, monasteries and alternative communities, babies and parents; but also for the religious communities of the world, Jews, Muslims, Hindus, Buddhists, and animists, and for their renewal in complexity and openness; but also for people who believe nothing or seek to believe and cannot; but also for the church itself, for the unity of the churches and for the clarity of the gospel, for this assembly, for its sorrows and joys, for the actual earth and actual community where this assembly gathers, and, at last, for its beloved dead; but also for much, much more. Of course, we cannot remember them all, but the possibilities are so much greater than the limits we usually place upon our prayers. Such a prayer is a concrete exercise of the sarcophilic worldview of the liturgy. Such a prayer stands in faith before the only Holy One of the Scriptures.

—Sealing the prayers with a sign of peace, turn to set the table with a loaf of beautiful and real bread and with a cup or bowl or pitcher of wine. And give thanks, all of the assembly gathering around and participating as well as it can. Give thanks for the cosmos itself, for the patterns and details of its beauty and order. Give thanks for Jesus Christ, for his life and death and the meal that is among us now as both. Give thanks for the outpoured Spirit, awakening us and all the world to hope. Then, stuttering, not quite able to pray as we ought, pray in the power of the Spirit, before the face of God, that prayer which Jesus taught us, begging for the day of justice in the earth, celebrating the presence of bread and forgiveness.

—And eat and drink, with several people helping to serve, welcoming everyone who would come, telling them clearly that it is the very body and blood of Christ, the mystery of what they now are themselves, that they receive.

—Then here—or earlier, perhaps as the table was being set for the meal—do as Justin's and Ezra's (Neh. 8) communities did. Take a collection for the hungry and the poor. Of course, you will also have to find the money for the maintenance of your building and your staff, but if that is all you do, especially if you call that by the religious term "offering," you will be undercutting the sarcophilic flow of the *ordo,* again narrowing the expansive significance of its juxtapositions. Consider finding another way to gather the money for your bills, perhaps some new version of the old "church dues," but let the Christian ritual collection exist to be entirely given away. And let yourselves be sent. See to it that the holy meal is sent to those of the assembly who cannot come today, blessing the people who will carry the bread and cup to them. See to it that the collection for the poor is given to a place or to people where it will genuinely help, especially as linked with the gifts of other assemblies. But then, follow these gifts yourselves, being staple food and festive drink for your neighbor, going to work for justice, turning again to the care for the earth.

This list will sound simply like a summary of some widespread hopes for general liturgical renewal in the churches at the beginning of the twenty-first century. How does that relate to earth-care specifically? But that is the very point. It is the Gospel-based *ordo* itself, renewed among us in strength, that can reorient our lives toward walking on the holy ground. It is the *ordo* itself, enacted every Sunday—and not for some specific earth-Sundays or earth-themes—that invites us into a reoriented, earth-loving cosmology.

Of course, the celebration of this *ordo* in different places will be richly diverse. There are, after all, *four* Gospels, not one. These four Gospels are books full of their own local speech and their own powerful images, broken to speak of Jesus Christ and his cross, broken to the eschatological purposes of God. Four different early witnesses surround the one crucified and risen Christ, using the one pattern of meeting in the triune God, just as the four beasts surround the Lamb and the One seated upon the throne in Revelation 4. Irenaeus of Lyons, again in a sarcophilic insight, saw these four books as being symbolized by those four beasts and as corresponding to the four corners and the four winds of the world, all gathered about the Crucified-Risen One.[29] The Gospel books themselves have demonstrated the importance and diversity of locality, of contextualization, from the very outset of the Christian movement. The Gospel *ordo* we have been considering is the basic tool of such localization, as the local language, the local patterns of gathering, the local music, and the local food and water come to the meeting, as if they are coming from those four corners, representing God's care for those four corners.

On the other hand, those very four Gospels—the gospels of baptism, word, meal, sending; the gospels of the historic Crucified-Risen One pro-

29. *Against Heresies,* 3:11.

146

claimed in each place; the gospels of the love for the wounded earth and of trinitarian cosmological reorientation—are the canonical foundation to authentic church. We cannot make up just any order, or center the meeting on our own brilliant ideas or techniques, without tearing the church apart. Nor ought we put the manner of music or the matter of style at the center of the meeting, as the "menu" approach to worship so easily does, making "traditional" or "contemporary" and our consumer choice between the two of far too great importance. Indeed, leaders of liturgy will do well to avoid deceiving themselves that they are celebrating the *ordo,* when the real center of the meeting has been made to be their own self-expression.

Still, this classic shape of the liturgy will be a tool for liturgy's engagement with culture, also in North America. Taught by the *ordo* itself, the strongest manner of localization, contextualization, will almost always put one thing next to another in a mutually critical pattern of meaning. Just as the shape of the liturgy puts scriptural text next to scriptural text, eating next to drinking, word next to meal, gathering next to sending—or just as classic Reformation era worship always used both chant and chorale to enact the *ordo*—so North American worship now will need to be culturally eclectic in musical style but require all the power of any music to be broken to serve the assembly, to give voice to the assembly, as it gathers around the central matters of the Gospels.[30] Such a use of the *ordo* of the Gospels can welcome many of the values of the North American cultures and yet challenge them. Here, a certain "democracy" and a critique of authority, so beloved of Americans, are mirrored in an assembly-serving leadership made up of many persons, in the midst of encouraged participation. Here, American individualism is not denied, but called, like Mary Magdalene in John 20, to come into the personal-communal assembly,[31] alive to the whole earth. Here, the interest of some Americans in finding, as the center of religion, a centralized institution or an infallible Bible or the authority of a personal vision or the charisma of a single preacher[32] will be challenged to find, rather, the strong weakness of God present in a local assembly of folks,

---

30. Paul Westermeyer, "What Music Should We Use in Worship?" in *What Is Contemporary Worship? Open Questions in Worship,* vol. 2 (Minneapolis: Augsburg Fortress, 1995), 6–14.

31. The idea that the experience of the Christian assembly ought to be a "personal-communal experience" is owed especially to Robert Hovda. See *Environment and Art in Catholic Worship* (Washington, D.C.: National Conference of Catholic Bishops, 1978), 13.

32. Peter Berger, "Protestantism and the Quest for Certainty," *The Christian Century* 115, no. 23 (August 26–September 2, 1998): 782–85, 792–96.

gathered in the *ordo* of the Gospels, sending and receiving signs of communion with other such local assemblies. Most of all, here the sometimes popular American interest in the well-being of our own environment will be challenged by God's care for the well-being of the entire blue planet and all its networks of life.

How the local is to be in communion with the universal is an old Christian and human question. It is also a question of burning importance today, for our ecological as well as our political localities. Local customs, local ethnicity, local music, local leadership, local well-being are never enough in themselves to communicate the gospel's purpose. But gathered into the assembly's purpose, made to serve its center and its open door, caused to sing not of themselves but of the experience of the Trinity embracing the world, these things are welcome, like the nations and their treasures being welcomed into the city of God.[33] For church, ἐκκλησία, assembly, is always local. Yet the *ordo* of its eucharist comes with the translocal gospel itself, a gift beyond the possibility of our locality to invent, a gift that welcomes our locality and all the world to salvation, marking the communion of our locality with the other places of the world, redirecting our attention and concern toward the earth itself.

Eucharistic Economics

The trinitarian and sarcophilic meanings of this eucharist have sometimes been made into an image. So, for example, we might think of the widely known icon of the Holy Trinity painted in the early fifteenth century by the Russian iconographer, Andrei Roublev.[34] Building on the tradition established by many other images of the visit of the three angels to Abraham and Sarah, Roublev omitted everything customary to that tradition except the angels themselves and a single cup or bowl on the table between them, presenting them together with a tree, the suggestion of a mountain and part of a tile-roofed house, showing the location of this meal. The circular composition of the angelic figures, their loving and gracious yielding to each other, represents the flowing life of the triune God. The cup in the midst of that life, containing the lamb that signifies the death of Christ and his presence and self-giving in the supper, stands in such a way that there is room at the table for the viewer also to approach the food and so be surrounded by this

33. Rev. 21:26.
34. See, for example, Victor Lasareff, ed., *Russian Icons from the Twelfth to the Fifteenth Century* (New York: UNESCO, 1962), plate 25.

flowing, communal life. And God's own communal reality embraces not only the church that participates in this cup. The circles of the icon, the circles of the divine life, also draw in the tree, the mountain, the house. Indeed, the very colors of the garments of these figures are the colors of earth and sky together, and, on the angelic figure who represents Christ, the color of blood. Such a cup, firmly on the earth, transfiguring the death we so much fear, embraced by the flowing life of the triune God, welcoming those who approach, in touch with tree and mountain and house, is the cup of the eucharist. The church that knows this cup, the house that is marked by its presence, is reorganized into the economy of the eucharist.

Of course, the eucharist itself is not a full economy. It is not the complete organization of food production and food distribution, and it is certainly not a system for the production, distribution, and consumption of yet other goods and services, or a pattern for the protection and growth of such a system. Still, the eucharist is the enacted image of a holy-ground economy, a constant economic proposal, a hole in closed and self-justifying economic systems and maps, and an invitation for all of our economic systems and maps to relate to a wider world in earth-care and in the mutual sharing of food. That cup stands amid the constantly flowing life of God, its rounded, single form inviting anyone who comes to drink. All who come, all who are thirsty, thereby drink from what seems a limited amount of food, yet, within these very limits, they are drawn into the endlessly flowing life of God, into genuine festivity. Here is the management and ordering of that house, οἰκονομία. And the house itself—the church, the assembly, the household meeting of the people of God within the household of the earth—blends in with mountain and tree, is part of the earth and not its enemy, welcomes the presence of the all-embracing Trinity.

The Benedictine tradition knows about being such an economic image. Just as the monasteries have been places where the liturgy is set out in clarity and simplicity, reminding us all of its strength at the heart of the Christian life, so also the monasteries, at their best, have been places of sustainable agriculture, local networks of food, humanized technology, and the remembrance of the poor.[35] A single monastery is not a worldwide economy. But taught by the eucharist, such a monastery is the image of an economy, an economic proposal.

---

35. H. Paul Santmire, "How Does the Liturgy Relate to the Cosmos and Care for the Earth?" in *What Are the Ethical Implications of Worship? Open Questions in Worship*, vol. 6 (Minneapolis: Augsburg Fortress, 1996), 23–24.

Or, say the matter with bread. "There is no such thing as 'my' bread. All bread is ours and given to me, to others through me, and to me through others."[36] Such are appropriate reflections by anyone who has been repeatedly fed at the eucharist as the central, world-constituting ritual of his or her life. A single loaf of bread, broken smaller and smaller to accommodate come-who-may, welcoming all the hungry, and sent away in fragments to the absent, encompasses and gives away the whole mystery of God and establishes the economic proposal of the eucharist. There is enough food in the earth to feed us all, if we use it and the earth itself with care and reverence, and if we share it equitably.

Or say the matter with the whole meal event: thanksgiving and eating and drinking, sending to the absent and collecting for the poor. All food comes from God, staple bread and festive drink, enough to live, enough to be joyful together,[37] given to us in common, fruit of the holy ground. The Holy Trinity is woven throughout all this eating: God, who is the source of food; Jesus, who makes his death into a feast of life, transfiguring our limits, welcoming the outsider; the Spirit, who hovers over all meals, creating life and connection. We eat a little limited food, finding it the holy life-giving encounter itself, practicing abundant life within limits. And what we have collected, we are learning again to send mostly away, sign of connection, sign of common life with those have too little, sign of a richer and more lively economy than we have yet learned to practice.

Of his assembly, Justin reported, "we continually remind each other" of baptism. Then, he gave that communal reminding a specific content: we "help all those who are in want"; we "continually meet together"; and "over all that we take to eat," we give thanks in the flowing life of the triune God. For Justin, the Sunday meeting of the assembly was the primary example of his assertion about mutual baptismal remembrance, that is to say, about common meeting, common thanksgiving over food, and common sharing with the hungry. In the present day, our assemblies ought to be able to do at least as well as Justin's did. Perhaps we can do more: massively significant movements toward food relief; serious organization of our common efforts toward economic justice; strong local networks for sustainable food production that care for the earth and its ecological systems; fierce resistance to the idea that more spending and more consumption of unnecessary luxuries by

36. Attributed to Meister Eckhart, quoted in Chrissy Post and Callista Brown, "A Foretaste of the Feast to Come," *Holden Village News* 41 (winter 2002): 14.

37. On the food of the eucharist as "staple food" and "festive drink," enough to live but also enough for common joy, see Lathrop, *Holy Things,* 91–93.

a few people will make those few happier and more fulfilled. Participation in the eucharist ought to be seen as fiercely questioning any easy cultural assumptions: that what we are is equal to what we own; that we may have all the energy we want, that what vehicle we drive is nobody's business but our own; that we should have a great variety of foodstuffs and clothing, building materials and consumer goods, drawn from all over the world at very low prices; that other people's salaries or poverty are not connected to our habits of consumption. Reminding each other of our common baptism will involve both the eucharist, the great feast-within-boundaries, and the continued discovery that these assumptions are lies. In any case, even to these efforts, the shared bread and cup, the body and blood of Christ poured out in this world, will always continue to propose a deeper, wider, more life-giving economics yet.

It should be clear that the economic proposal thus made by the eucharist cannot honestly be turned in such a way that justice is set in competition with ecology, care for hungry people and developing nations set against care for the earth.[38] The very biblical text at the heart of a liturgical cosmology, the text about the burning bush, shows us the God who has heard the cry of human suffering and comes to deliver. This very God declares that the ground itself is holy. When cosmology-as-ecology arises in the encounter with this God, it must never come as a cloaked form of protection for the land of the rich or for the aesthetic preferences of an elite, forgetting the hunger of the poor. Similarly, when cosmology-as-justice arises in the encounter with this God, it must never turn all land and all other species of life into "resources" over which "third world development" or "national economic growth" may always hold sway. The destroyed natural environment around the places of the life of the poor impoverishes that life yet more, threatening its very future. The actual decisions in these matters are often difficult, requiring the best of our international wisdom, the finest of our science, the most self-critical exercise of our communal honesty, the finest dialogue with other people of faith.

These questions about the care of the blue planet with its interconnected ecologies and the distribution of its food so that all people may both survive and keep festival—eat staple food and drink festive wine—do not belong only to Christians. They are the urgent questions of all humanity, of

---

38. Larry Rasmussen has been one of the wisest and most nuanced of Christian ethical thinkers in the combination of both of these themes. See his *Earth Community, Earth Ethics* (New York: Orbis, 1998).

that part of the earth that human beings are, "that part of the world through which the world as a whole can think about itself," as Roy Rappaport would say.[39] To a very large extent, people will be prepared to bring their best resources to these questions depending on their cosmologies, their understanding of the ordered world in which they live. And, to a very large extent, these cosmologies will depend upon the stories people tell each other and the rituals they mutually enact. It is now clear that the stories humankind needs include at least tales that begin at the "big bang" and continue with the development of this planet, with the surprising emergence of life and all its diversities, with the very long prehistory of the waves of humankind that emerged out of Africa to settle the earth, and with the more recent history of the human species itself threatening each other and all the rest of earth-life. The rituals that humankind needs include rituals that enact a critique of closed rituals and practice a full and hospitable life-within-limits.

But for Christians engaged with these questions and these efforts, the stories and rituals of the eucharist will continue to make their economic proposal, their house-ordering idea for household earth. The *ordo* of the eucharist will reorient us again and again to a lively love and care for the conditions of the earth. And at the shared loaf and the shared cup, we will hear both words from the burning bush: "remove the sandals from your feet, for the place on which you are standing is holy ground," and "I have come down to deliver . . . and to bring them up out of that land to a good and broad land, a land flowing with milk and honey."

39. Rappaport, *Ritual and Religion* (see above, intro. n. 3), 461.

6

Sunday, Assembly-House, Sky

L ook up. See the sky. Those birds and airplanes, those clouds and weather systems, and, most especially, beyond them, that sun, that moon, those planets, those stars and nebulae, and even, just on the edge of visibility, those galaxies—these also are a massive part of our world. Any cosmology worthy of the name must also attend to the sky. Indeed, it was promised, at the outset of this project, that this book would try to set the world-making work of the Christian liturgy in some relationship with the cosmology of current astronomy and astrophysics.

The ritual mapping that occurs in the celebration of baptism and eucharist has already been set here next to the cosmologies implied by various public symbol systems, not least when those symbol systems interact with our care for the earth. Still, while the bath, the word, and the table that are called "baptism and eucharist" make up the heart of Christian liturgy, they are not the whole of it. Christians meet and enact these things in an assembly, and that assembly often has its own space, a "house for the church," or a "church" as that space is popularly called. Furthermore, Christians mark and make use of time, praying through the day, the week, and the year. It is especially the orientations of this liturgical space and the marking of these liturgical times that may provide us with materials for a Christian communal engagement with contemporary astronomy.

Except that great pitfalls fill the path toward considering a cosmology that includes the sky, let alone considering the relationship of liturgy to such a conception of cosmic order. Three such pitfalls might be signaled here. For one thing, there really is no "sky." Or, rather, there is only the sky. Our blue planet also moves in the sky as a sky-object. We human beings live in the sky.

153

There really is no "up" or "down," except when those directions refer to the very limited point of view of one particular group of us on the surface of the earth. Such knowledge may be one of the genuine sources of postmodernism in current life: the sense that all of our points of view are constructed in relationship to our own location and that they are in need of deconstruction if they are applied too universally. Furthermore, the systems of physical existence do, indeed, include us and the rest of earth-life, but they do so only as including some rather minor parts located in one small corner of the universe. A cosmology that begins with these observations will either despair of the enterprise entirely or become primarily a reflection on the current state of astronomical knowledge, an ordered whole constructed out of the current attempts in physics toward a theory of everything. Such attempts and such knowledge struggle to imagine the place of humankind in the universe. They certainly do not leave much space for theology. Or, if "natural theology" does take up the subject of astrophysics, it often seems especially vulnerable to Occam's razor. For example, to call quantum theory "spiritual" has not really added anything to quantum theory. Such theology readily becomes an explanation that we all can do without and in which most astrophysicists have no interest. As Timothy Ferris has said: God, questioned about those matters that astrophysicists call cosmology, has responded with "customary silence."[1]

Holy silences should not be strange to Christians, if we think of liturgical practice and meaning, but we still must make the case for their cosmological importance. How do the particular silences of the liturgy relate to cosmology conceived as the whole astronomical and physical "shebang"? Does the liturgy help us peacefully to assume our real but tiny place in the universe? Moreover how does the liturgical worldview that arises underneath the trinitarian hole-in-the-heavens describe the heavens themselves?

But there is another problem as well. Most of us actually do not see much sky. We may see the birds and the clouds if we are especially attentive. Some of us may live almost entirely indoors or travel outdoors without much sky-seeing. We all probably do notice the sun, perhaps also the moon. Still, in our great, electrically lit cities and increasingly in light-polluted rural areas of the world, we see very little else of the night sky. It is quite possible for us to imagine "world" without thinking of the stars at all. The Milky Way and the great majority of the ancient constellations, the asterisms long seen by humanity and interpreted as meaningful in various cultural

---

5. Rappaport, *Ritual and Religion* (see above, intro. n. 3), 458.

ways, are increasingly unavailable to us or available only on very rare occasions. But virtually all of the ancient cosmologies oriented their conceptions of orderly world to include what could be seen in the sky. What is more, most of those cosmologies actually found their primary foundations in star patterns and in the movement of heavenly bodies. One could argue that such was the case with the perfect sphere celebrated in Plato's *Timaeus*. Such has certainly been the case with the Mayan cosmos. Among the Maya, the Milky Way was regarded as the very world-tree on which all things depended, holding up the sky itself and echoed on the earth—in stone stelae erected in ancient temples or in the use of the ceiba tree in modern shamanic rites. Those stars in the constellation Orion that our astronomers call Rigel, Alnitak, and Saiph (Beta, Gamma, and Kappa Orionis) were regarded as the three hearthstones of creation, reflected in the construction of every Mayan fireplace. The hazy patch in the midst of them, what we call the Orion Nebula, was the smoke of creation's fire.[2] Furthermore, the four points on the horizon that were marked by the rising and setting of the sun at the time of the winter and the summer solstices established the four corners of the world, the center place between them being then the place of the ceiba tree, the tree of life. Even to this day, Mayan organization of space—a house plan, an agricultural field, a regional map—makes use of this five-pointed pattern, echoing the sky.[3] Such accounts could be repeated again and again for other cultures of the world.

In contrast, most of us today do not ordinarily even see the Orion Nebula or note the rising or setting points of the sun. How, then, should our lived cosmology include the sky? Or, in the manner of our consumer culture's accent on specialization, do we abandon such vision to others, leaving such cosmology entirely to the astronomers? Will the Christian liturgy help us to see the sky?

There is yet a third pitfall awaiting us, one that can trap us in a quite opposite way. The sky, even if we do see it, especially if we regard it as establishing most of what is true about the world, can distract us from a cosmology based on the care of the earth. Ancient cosmologies were, indeed, often based on the observation of the sky. These cosmologies, therefore, invited humanity to an imitation and mirroring of the patterns that could be observed, while generally holding out little hope that human beings might significantly influence or change those patterns. Religion, of course, tried.

---

1. Ferris, *Whole Shebang* (see above, intro. n. 6), 10; compare also 303–12.
2. Friedel, Schele, and Parker, *Maya Cosmos* (see above, chap. 2 n. 6), 59–122.

But fate or the gods were seen to play such a large role, seemingly capri-
cious, just beyond human reach, that human response did not affect much,
except perhaps to stave off further evil and, sometimes, to feed the impassive
sky with words of praise and offerings of sacrifice. While some cultures
regarded the sky as the final, fateful destiny of humankind—at least of the
elite—other cultures entertained no such illusion. The Navajo, for example,
knew that earth had an argument with the sky, a struggle for equality and
solidarity, not a simple presumption of heavenly priority.[4] But sky still had the
upper hand. Although modern scientific astronomy has contributed to the
destruction of many of these archaic cosmologies, the old idea of the inability
of humankind to alter the cosmic laws has only been heightened in
astronomy and astrophysics. Roy A. Rappaport, building on the work of Stephen Toulmin, has joined others in calling for a postmodern cosmology—or
better, for him, a postmodern conception of the world-constructing logos—
that is based upon ecology rather than astronomy:

> Cosmologies based upon astronomy on the one hand and ecology on
> the other differ in fundamental respects. It may once have been plausible
> to believe that the stars' courses could affect us, but it has probably never
> been easy to believe that we could have any influence upon the stars.
> Indeed, their imperviousness to our manipulation was probably an
> important aspect of their cosmological appeal. In contrast, the reciproc-
> ity of our relations with the ecosystems in which we live is manifestly
> obvious, continuously experienced and consequently undeniable.
> Whereas the relationship of human lives to the movement of heavenly
> bodies was one of correspondences between radically separate systems,
> the relationship of humans to the plants and animals, water and soils,
> surrounding them is one of ceaseless and obvious transaction. Ever since
> plant cultivation originated, moreover, humans have become, ever more
> decisively, the most consequential actors in the systems which they not
> only seek to understand but in which they seek to live and therefore
> seek to maintain.[5]

We might, then, turn away from interest in current scientific cosmology as
a distraction from a worldview that matters for the earth. On the other
hand, we might see that the new accents in science on the effect that the
observer has on the observed and on the "anthropic principle"—the

---

3. Ibid., 123–72.
4. Zolbrod, *Navajo Creation Story* (see above, chap. 3 n. 9), 275.

observed reality that the actual universe does indeed include life and human-ity, us[6]—make it clear that astrophysical cosmology is no longer dealing with sky phenomena and human life as "radically separate systems."

Our blue planet, and our concern for its unity and its sustainability, does float among the stars. How might we acknowledge that truth and yet not, because of the vastness of the universe or the seeming intractability of phys-ical laws, abandon the quest for a conception of world that includes the quest for both justice and care for the earth? Can the Christian liturgy also join the argument of the earth with the sky, appealing for equality and soli-darity, for a new sense of sky-earth?

We look at the sky, we look at the Christian liturgy, and, if we are thinking about cosmology, these questions arise. Indeed, it used to be so that timekeep-ing and space-making in Christian liturgy were closely related to the sky. To be in the liturgical event, at the liturgical place, was in some sense to see the sky. Should that still be so for us? And, if so, are there resources in this liturgi-cal observance of time and space for a cosmology that includes the sky?

Living by the Sky, and Not

At first, the assertion that liturgical time and space are sky-connected seems simply and irredeemably archaic. Christian buildings were oriented, with the apse—or, on rare occasions, the entryway—directed toward the rising sun, sometimes with yet more movements of the sun through the year marked by the walls, windows, or floors of the building. What is more, litur-gical movement inside or outside of the building was classically supposed to be sun-wise, with circular motions around an altar, ambo, or font, or an exterior procession around the building, inscribing what we would call a clockwise pattern. "Widdershins" movement could, then, be regarded as particularly unfortunate, even as dangerously ungodly. Ceilings not uncom-monly imitated the sky, with stars painted there, for example, as if the enacted liturgy were directly under and related to the heavens. Further-more, the Christian liturgy took up and reinforced the old Babylonian planetary week. Sunday, the day named after the sun, has been the principal feast day of Christians, the day of their assembly. As well, the cardinal posi-tions of the sun have determined the Christian hours of prayer through the day. The springtime sun and the springtime full moon—"the first Sunday after the first full moon after the vernal equinox" is the old formulation—

6. Ferris, *Whole Shebang,* 290–302.

have determined the great festal cycle of Pascha or Easter, just as the winter solstice determined the Christmas cycle, Pascha in winter.

All of those arrangements may seem utterly out of touch with what is known of astronomy today, as well as irrelevant to ordinary daily life. There are more planets than are numbered in the planetary week, and the idea of relating days of the week to them, in any case, seems bizarre. Northern hemisphere equinoxes and solstices hardly work to establish festal themes ("renewal" and "light in the darkness," for example) for the whole globe. Sunrise and sunset are at very different times in far north and far south, night or day lasting even for months in places within the Arctic and Antarctic circles, places now no longer out of reach to human imagination as well as increased human settlement. Sunrise itself is a very local, very anthropocentric experience, telling us rather little about the actual planetary system in which we take part, around that local average star of ours, and deceiving us about what is actually rising. And all that concern with sun-wise movement, which is only clockwise in the northern hemisphere anyway, seems like pure superstition. How does this liturgical system give us anything to relate to contemporary astronomy or physics?

But the sky-connections of classic Christian liturgy should not be so quickly dismissed. They can give us important information about our location in the midst of things. If we grant that these old constructions do not describe an alternate, fairy-tale universe, where the sun and the stars still go around the earth and God is above the sky, then we may see their new importance, precisely as our constructions. Sun and moon, planets and stars are seen by us here. Their perceived patterns reflect our engagement, from here, with the whole massive universe. At their best, the sky-connections of the Christian liturgy are observations that make clear the actual place of our assembly and, what comes down to be the same thing since we measure time and live in it by the perceived movements of sky bodies, the experienced time in this place.

This system of sky-connections was, indeed, open to other cosmologies in other times. But it did not finally canonize those systems. Given the liturgical importance of gathering before God in the midst of the reality of the world, the liturgy of Christians can be open to the astronomy of our time as well. With only the slightest astronomical knowledge to help us, what we call the rising and setting of the sun can remind us of our turning globe and of the place on its surface where we are located. The length of the day and, thus, the season of the year in which we find ourselves are, of course, measurements at this place, not universal conditions. But they are measurements that matter to our actual symbiosis with earth and sea, sun and moon. Night and day, high tide and low, summer and winter, wet and dry, give to many of us here, wherever our "here" is, seasons of work and rest, growth and harvest—or, among hunter-gatherers, seasons of migration and then of the absence of other species, seasons of hunting and of resting or starving—and they thus give most of us real, archetypal impetus for images of death and life, loss and hope.

We probably fool ourselves to imagine that we can do without knowing where the sun and moon are in relationship to our place on the earth, as if we were absolute beings, floating outside of such connections. While we may gladly grant that electricity and central heating have freed many of us from the worst ravages of the seasons or from some of the dangers of the nightly dark, we still need the connections that are made by a knowledge of our location. We need to know how our psyche (and sometimes our biochemical makeup, as in seasonal affective disorder) responds to dark and winter, even when there is electric light. We need to know that there are poorer people for whom those daily and seasonal dangers have not been held at bay. We need to understand, in spite of what is available in our supermarkets, perhaps especially because of what is available in our supermarkets, that strawberries do not grow here year round. They grow elsewhere, our inexpensive consumption in air-conditioned rooms being dependent upon badly paid agricultural workers who are frequently nowhere near so protected from their environments, from that blazing sun and that freezing night, as are the consumers of their produce. We need to see the great sky from our location exactly as a way to relativize our frequent preoccupation with the self as the center of reality.

The orientation of the church building, the keeping of Sunday and the week, the observance of morning and evening prayer, the marking of springtime and of the winter solstice—these all enable us to know where we are in the universe. They are not pretense, make-believe. In fact, their honesty about what time it is may be more basic, more connected to the deep experience of the human psyche, than many a secular calendar with its weeks that start on Monday, workdays that never end, and holidays that keep both genuine sorrow and genuine hope at bay. The rich festival calendar that can be found in the local cultures of some temperate zone countries, interwoven as it is with the rhythms of the local earth, demonstrates the ecological uses of such archaic Christian timekeeping.[7] It may even be

---

7. See, for example, Ronald Hutton, *The Stations of the Sun: A History of the Ritual Year in Britain* (Oxford: Oxford University Press, 1996).

that sun-wise ritual movement is a good idea, if the liturgical ministers think about the value of the ritual construction involved in mirroring the perceived movement of the sun in this place and let go of ritual anxiety and superstition.

However, the sky-connections of the liturgy have been used for make-believe rather than acute observation. When Christians in the southern hemisphere import northern customs, as if these are the only proper way to keep the festivals, they are remembering a location and a time that they no longer occupy. Or when late-medieval clerics began to anticipate festivals or times of prayer, enacting them well ahead of their appointed times—the great vigil of Easter, for example, held on Holy Saturday morning, or the whole of one day's "office" recited privately the day before—perhaps out of ritual anxiety that the whole action be accomplished on time in order for the divine to be placated and time to move forward, then knowing the actual time had yielded to time-based legalism. When local folk cultures insisted on a certain way of making the midsummer fire or a particular order in hundreds of other ritual actions, then observation of actual place and time on God's good earth yielded to living by the sky, the implacable sky.

Indeed, living by the sky—in the sense of seeing the order of the sky as divine demand, seeing the dependence on the sky for sun and rain and time itself as grounds for sacrificial offering—has always been a distinct possibility and an important theme in human religion.[8] The planetary week may have originally been intended as a way of walking with the presumed power and avoiding the presumed danger of the seven visible sky-wanderers. Solstice festivity may have intended to encourage the return of the sun,[9] just as dances in Shinto shrines are understood as originating in the mythic dance that lured Amaterasu, the sun *kami,* to come back out of the cave in which she had hidden.[10] Not far away from these religious motives, there has lurked the power of the astrological observers, of the ritual specialists, or of the social elite, a power associated with the sky and reinforced by festival observance and ritual sacrifice. The political or religious hierarchy could stand for, and even become, the supposed heavenly hierarchy. Roman emperors, beginning at least in the third century, identified themselves with the sun and sometimes required its cult. Japanese emperors have been understood as

8. For North America, see Ray A. Williamson, *Living the Sky: The Cosmos of the American Indian* (Norman: University of Oklahoma Press, 1984).

9. See Lathrop, *Holy People* (see above, intro. n. 2), 216–18.

10. John K. Nelson, *A Year in the Life of a Shinto Shrine* (Seattle: University of Washington Press, 1996), 52.

descended from that very Amaterasu. Mayan kings were also identified with the sky, with the sky-tree, with figures known in myth and seen in the sky.[11] Sacrifices at Teotihuacan and then among the Aztecs fed blood to the sun.[12] Recent excavations of sites related to the Chaco Canyon civilization of the tenth to the twelfth centuries C.E. in the American Southwest suggest that this extensive archaic Pueblo culture, marked by meticulous astronomical observation and the astronomical alignment of its great buildings, came to be dominated by an elite that required not only agricultural support but also human sacrifice.[13] One ought not be romantic about religion and the sky. And all of this "living by the sky" continues among us, albeit weakly, in the daily horoscopes of our newspapers.

But the sky-connections of Christian liturgy must not be read as astrology, anxious adjustments to the sky-powers, anxious yieldings to the sky-fates. The sky-connections of the liturgy are not even beginning attempts at astronomy. They ought to be understood simply as basic, honest ways of saying what time it is and where we are as we keep assembly. In order to do this, of course, their timekeeping does need to be honest, not make-believe and not superstitious.

Powerful symbolic significances do come along with genuine time- and place-marking. Human beings live in psychic and communal symbiosis with their surroundings, finding their personal dreams and their common poetry reflecting their readings of the cosmos.[14] If we know what time it is here, then not far away may be longings for home and also for away-from-home, hope for rest and also for new beginning, the need for hard work in the daylight and the search for the communal hearth in the dusk, delight in green growth and yet the need to hide in deep darkness, the many meanings of night and day, winter and summer, and even the sense that our celebrations of these times might affect our relationship to these things. In Christian assembly, these significances should be both honestly welcomed—even treasured—and, at the same time, broken to the service of the

11. Friedel, Schele, and Parker, *Maya Cosmos,* 128, 135, and *passim.*

12. However, Inga Clendinnen thinks this action was more subtle in meaning, not intended to influence the fate of the world, but done as "a gratuitous action made by men to remind the gods of their dependence, their need and their devotion," in *Aztecs: An Interpretation* (Cambridge: Cambridge University Press, 1991), 238.

13. See Stephen H. Lekson, *The Chaco Meridian: Centers of Political Power in the Ancient Southwest* (Walnut Creek: Alta Mira, 1999), especially 140–50 and 157–61, and Christy G. Turner II and Jacqueline A. Turner, *Man Corn: Cannibalism and Violence in the Prehistoric American Southwest* (Salt Lake City: University of Utah Press, 1999), 459, 484.

14. Paul Ricoeur, *The Symbolism of Evil* (Boston: Beacon, 1967), 10–14.

gospel.[15] The triune God is our home in the midst of the earth and our connection with away-from-here. The crucified and risen Christ is our sun that does not go down, our light, our green tree. We need no emperor or king who pretends to possess the power of the Milky Way or the sun. The risen Christ holds the stars in his hand and shines beyond the sun's light. The Spirit's overshadowing wings and this present assembly in the Spirit are our dark night and our place of refuge. Yet all of these meanings can be celebrated exactly as the community is invited to know where we are and what time it is. Home and away, the green tree and the bare one, morning and evening, summer and winter are all themselves important, precious, dear. But they are not God. They are characteristics of our time and place as we are before God.

The Christian assembly's sky-connections have the capability to open its participants toward the reality that we are here at this time. We are in this place on this earth, near that moon and circling that sun, joining those planets, in one arm of our galaxy, in this universe, perhaps in this massive chaos, perhaps even in one of many universes that may be folded into the hyperdimensions of the "super-strings," according to some current theories. The Christian assembly's knowledge ought then to be quite open toward yet further research into all the astonishing and relativizing things that "here," "now," and "this universe" might mean. However, the assembly does not gather before the sun—or before the galaxy or before the universe itself, or before the ideas of time and place. The assembly does not look in any of those places for mercy or life or even order. Compassion and recognition are not to be found there; such a search misuses the universe. Rather, if the assembly gathers before God, the God known in Word and Sacrament, the God known in mercy under that hole in the perfect sphere, then it is also invited to know the God who holds all spheres and orbits and systems and even accidents and chaos itself. The liturgy, too, like the best of the astrophysicists, should keep silence before the silence of God, not being able to fill up the silence with our explanations, knowing rather only the words we are given, for example, "this is my beloved one" and "I have heard their cries" and "put off your shoes." Liturgical silence resonates with these and other words, being full of the presence and mystery of the God of these words. Christians are then invited to proclaim the faith that all things—all the grounds, everywhere, in any dimension—are held together by Christ's

---

15. On time and the Christian liturgical use of the broken symbol, see Lathrop, *Holy Things* (see above, intro. n. 2), 36–43, 68–80.

cross and embraced into mercy. Christians are invited to trust that assertion, to discover what it means continually, here and now, leaving what it means in every other place and dimension to God's great silence.

The time and the location of the Christian assembly can be seen as openings toward astronomical cosmology. So can the assembly's silence. We human beings, too, are part of what astronomers rightly study. And our liturgy has no alternative scientific explanations. Only if that astronomical cosmology leads us away from the earth itself and from responsibility for its care, then the assembly must say that we are here now. This real place, this wounded blue planet, is our connection to cosmos. We are, indeed, in the sky, part of the sky, but we see that sky from this sky-earth. Even more, if some of those cosmologists—or, more likely, a theologian or two in the guise of scientific cosmologists—present any one of the putative theories of everything as the full sphere of the truth, the total system, the new spirituality, then we will need gently to remind them that they are saying more than any of us can say, gently to invite them to that mercy that floods the cosmos through all the holes in our systems.

So the Christian assembly lives by the sky—and does not. That is, the sky-connections of Christian liturgy open toward astronomy and yet refuse the idea of the implacable sky, instead breaking both the archaic and the contemporary human sky-symbols to speak of the mercy of God in Christ. Liturgical cosmology, however, is not astronomy any more than it is astrology. Liturgical cosmology is reflection on that encounter with God in public worship in which even the galaxies, even the vibrating super-strings, are seen to be holy ground.

Sacred Time, Liturgical Time

It might seem, at first, that these sky-connections of Christian liturgy have been arranged into a celebration of sacred time. Some people have come to regard the liturgical year, for example, as a kind of comprehensive temporal metanarrative that competes with ordinary experiences of time and draws us into a salvific time-beyond-time. The seasonal round has become historicized, and the history has then transcended the natural cycle from which it was born. By this reading, the liturgical year is only incidentally associated with the flow of the seasons. The real significance is supposed to be found in our enacting of salvation history, stretched from Israel's expectation through the life of Christ, from the gift of the Spirit and the birth of the church to eschatology. In the most common popularization of this idea, the succession of feasts is supposed to take us chronologically through the events in the biography of Jesus. Such an understanding can take several forms. Call one "memory": the task of the preacher and of the worshiper alike, in this form, is to imagine what it was like in Jesus' or in Israel's day as well as in the disciples' experience, believing that such a point of view would be saving for us.[16] Call another "mystery": our celebrations insert us *in illo tempora*, in some other sacred and mythic time away from now, beyond time but saving all time.[17] Call another "fantasy": our liturgies are an elaborate imaginative game where we envision the world and the human being as other by imagining "once upon a time."

We ought not question that such reflections have provided enormous depth to some considerations of liturgical meaning. The "memory" idea seems to have found a particular home in Protestant circles. "Mystery" will be familiar to some Roman Catholic and Orthodox Christians, and "fantasy" or "play" was at home with several mid-twentieth-century reformers of all these traditions. But the ideas themselves seem to start in the wrong place, at the wrong time. Classic Christian liturgy is held here and now, inviting us to know where we are and what time it is, as we are gathered before God on the holy ground. Just so, at our best, we keep learning to pray in vernacular languages, constantly attentive to the ongoing tasks of translation, not in a fixed sacred language from another time. Such translation has, at least, been at the heart of the ongoing reform and ongoing contextualization of all of our liturgical traditions. Furthermore, the eucharist is not primarily the Jesus' Last Supper remembered and repeated, but our present communal meal, made to be the surprising presence of the Crucified-Risen One now. Baptisms are not journeys to the Jordan, but our present initiatory practices turned inside out for the sake of identification with the presence of Christ in the world today.

Certainly, memory and mystery and even fantasy have a role. But biblical/liturgical memory—$\dot{\alpha}\nu\dot{\alpha}\mu\nu\eta\sigma\iota\varsigma$—involves the proclamation of ancient presences into the present assembly, not our reaching back as if we could construct the past. Liturgical mystery involves the presence of the Mysterious One, not our transport to a place away, as if we might thereby escape the current conditions. And fantasy in Christian liturgical use ought always be

---

16. The contrast of "memory" and "metaphor" has been especially illuminated in the work of Gail Ramshaw.

17. Mircea Eliade, *The Sacred and the Profane* (New York: Harcourt Brace, 1959), 70–72.

the lifting of current false strictures,[18] not make-believe. Liturgy ought never be "as if."[19]

Of course, we do use ritual means to release our imagination and world-view from rigid present status structures. The clothing of our leaders or of the newly baptized, if it follows the practice of traditional liturgical vesture, may seem like clothes from another time. But such a practice will actually be using current but alternative clothing, albs and chasubles as current metaphors, borrowing from the tradition a radically other, more flowing and gracious, more interestingly unisex way for the human-being-in-community to be imaged and understood. Our large shared loaf or shared cup may seem like food from another time. But this is real food, eaten and drunk in an alternative way, with the idea of sharing heightened. These practices are not journeys away from here, to a sacred other-time, other-place. These are not costume dramas, with our leaders putting on Bible clothes. These ways of clothing our leaders and sharing our food are at their best when they are seen as this present place and time and our present manner of social interaction reimagined, reoriented.[20]

The most important tool for this liturgical reorientation of time and place is the way of metaphor, not the way of memory, mystery, or fantasy. When we call the assembly itself "Jerusalem" or "temple," we are intentionally calling it by the wrong name in order to say a present truth with power. If, for example, we sing "Simeon's Song" after we have received communion, taking into our own mouths those words attributed in Luke to the old man who saw the child brought into the Jerusalem Temple and took him into his own hands (Luke 2:29–32), it is not because we are acting as if we were traveling away from here and now to another time and place. Rather, the liturgy asserts that the very Light of which the song speaks fills this place, in our own hands, mouths, and lives. The very possibility of being dismissed according to the promise, of going into witnessing life or peaceful death, fills this moment. We are, to use the exact metaphor and therefore the

---

18. Robert Hovda, for example, would speak of liturgy as "kingdom play" but would mean by that expression that "liturgical celebration is . . . humanly necessary to relax the tight grip of the status quo, so that people can move and breathe and envision alternatives" (Robert W. Hovda, *Strong, Loving, and Wise: Presiding in Liturgy* [Washington, D.C.: Liturgical Conference, 1976], 20).

19. C. W. Mönnich, *Antiliturgica: Enige aantekeningen bij de viering van de kerkelijke feesten* (Amsterdam: Ten Have, 1966), 23. See further below, chapter 7.

20. On clothing for the liturgy, see also Lathrop, *Holy Things*, 96, 202. On bread, see *Holy Things*, 91–92.

wrong but revelatory name, Simeon. Such metaphors are woven throughout the liturgy. They frequently intend radically to recharacterize and so to reveal the truth about both God and the present assembly.[21] In so doing, they also give us the possibility of a newly surprising worldview, reorienting our understanding of the current time and place.[22] This hour is the time of salvation, sanctified by Christ having shared our hours. This place is the holy ground, sanctified by the story of the torn heavens.

If Christian liturgy seems to make use of the convention of sacred time—using narratives that seem like stories from a time-out-of-time, using social conventions and communal time-practices that seen archaic—then this complex of symbols will need to be one more construction that is broken to the purposes of the gospel. In fact, the narratives themselves are mostly a skein of metaphors applied to real life and death matters that have occurred on our ground. The important point about the exodus is not that it occurred historically—it very likely did not—but that images of liberation, crossing the sea, sustenance in the wilderness, being made a royal priesthood could surround and characterize a little people newly constituted by faith in the one merciful God who made heaven and earth. All of those metaphors are now made available to characterize our Sunday assembly. In exactly this way, the stories about Jesus were made by Mark's Gospel to be the means for the encounter with the Risen One in the assembly, a long resurrection-appearance story in the "wrong words."[23] Christian faith trusts that this assembly, in this time, on this ground, gathers before the same God to whom these various metaphor-laden texts bear witness. We do not travel to another time. Nor do we need to construct the stories into systematic, consequent, sacred histories in order to know that this is the place and time to put off our shoes. The presence of the triune God in the eucharist of the assembly resists any conception of sacred time as our achievement and our transportation out of here. And liturgical time at its best is our time as the time of assembly.

What might these reflections mean for actual practice? Here are a variety of suggestions about timekeeping in the Christian assembly. They focus primarily upon our reappropriating liturgical time as reoriented present time, as one important way of our seeing the sky from our own place on this beloved yet fragile sky-earth. You may think of yet more.

---

21. See Gail Ramshaw, *Reviving Sacred Speech: The Meaning of Liturgical Language* (Akron: OSL Publications, 2000), 66–81, 131–45.

22. Ibid., 82–113.

23. See above, chapter 5.

—Keep Sunday as the primary festival day of the Christian faith, the day of the resurrection and of the Trinity, the day of assembly and of weekly eucharist. Understand Sunday as the first day of our week and therefore as a day in our time. Yet teach, at the same time, that the first-day-assembly itself becomes the "eighth day," the day that our cycles of time can never deliver to us. This gift of the "Lord's Day" is not to be seen as a day out of time but the very presence of the resurrection and of grace within the limits of our time, transfiguring our time, reorienting our time.

—Treasure the week. Help the congregation to know that the week is, indeed, a human construction but that it is a construction based upon observing the sky from our place on the earth. It is not the only such construction there has ever been. But it is a currently nearly universal one, and it bears honest and historical connection to the human observation of the sky from here. So seven days correspond to the seven wanderers in the sky that can be seen with the unaided eye, even in light-polluted skies. Four sets of these seven days correspond more or less to the length of a lunar month, the period of time the moon takes to pass in our sight from new to waxing to full to waning to new again. The week, then, can really stand for our life on this earth, in relationship to that moon, those planets, that sun. Then the witness of the Sunday assembly, of the "eighth day," can be seen to be a witness like that of the burning bush. This place, this ground, this actual time is holy. Our social constructs in relationship to our environment have become a locus for the revelation of God's mercy, welcoming those constructs but freeing us from their compulsive restraints. For the whole Judeo-Christian tradition, "week" is an important and good construction if it is not made the basis for anxiety and constraint but functions rather to support a flowing rhythm in work and rest. For Christians, Sunday meeting is a magnificent, time-transfiguring gift of God.

—Encourage daily prayer. Consider restoring daily morning and evening prayer in your congregation as assembly events. Welcome whoever is able to gather, in the name of the full assembly, to mark the sunrise and the sunset each day with psalms and hymns, biblical reading and meditation, and corporate intercessions. Let these gatherings bring to expression a communal honesty about the time of day, about the primal joys and fears that do really attend these daily changes in the light. But let the gathering also mark these rhythms with reference to the gospel—using, say, the Lukan canticles to interpret the time of day[24]—and with reference to the nearest Sunday—using readings, for example, that echo the Sunday readings.[25] It may be that you will not be able to adopt this practice fully, for both morning and evening, throughout the year. But you may consider adopting it for one of these times of day in a given season. In any case, you may be able to encourage all the members of the assembly to mark sunrise and sunset with a personal use of "the office," or simply with the regular use of the old fixed Psalms—141 for the evening and 63 for the morning—or with some simple gesture of praise or prayer.[26] Knowing what time it is and where we are on this turning blue planet every day and knowing this before God—these are exercises of remembering the holy ground.

—Then, besides Sunday and the cardinal hours of each day, keep the other feasts also as feasts in our time. Let Sunday, a day of meeting, a day in our time, be the model for them all.

—Celebrate the resurrection in our time. Easter or Pascha is the occasion for the proclamation of the gospel to our springtime world. The feast has rightly been determined with reference both to the sun and to the moon. Its celebration is filled with overlaid cosmic symbolism:[27] a festival of springtime renewal of the earth and of the flocks became the occasion for the remembrance of the central "new creation" story of Israel. Then the resultant Passover Feast became the occasion for the remembrance of the central new-creation story of the church. Pascha is not a redoing of the events of our salvation, a return to another time, nor even an acting out of the story. It is meant as a Sunday to the year, an annual Sunday to our time, all the stories of

---

24. Classically, the Song of Zechariah (*Benedictus*) was sung at Lauds, at dawn the Song of Mary (*Magnificat*) was sung at vespers, at sunset and the Song of Simeon (*Nunc Dimittis*) was sung at compline, at the onset of deep night. These canticles reinterpret every day as a day for the encounter with the hope-giving, justice-making, rest-giving light of God in Christ.

25. One such lectionary is *Between Sundays: Daily Bible Readings Based on the Revised Common Lectionary* (Minneapolis: Augsburg Fortress, 1997).

26. Many fine "breviaries" exist for corporate and personal use, but one splendid resource is *Book of Common Worship: Daily Prayer* (Louisville: Westminster John Knox, 1993).

27. See Anscar J. Chupungco, *Shaping the Easter Feast* (Washington, D.C.: Pastoral Press, 1992), a revised edition of his *The Cosmic Elements of Christian Passover* (Rome: Studia Anselmiana, 1977). For one account of the history of this overlaid symbolism, see also Lathrop, *Holy Things,* 68–79.

creation and redemption giving us breath again. So Pascha rightly became a fifty-day-long feast. It rightly drew to itself the practice of Christian baptism, so that those who were coming to join the assembly of this witness to the world would be bathed in all these stories. Lent, then, is not a time to kill Jesus again but a time, now, for our baptismal preparations and remembrances, for our turning back to the font. In the southern hemisphere, this overlay continued: now, at the first Sunday after the first full moon after the autumnal equinox, the resurrection gospel offers all the biblical promise to fallow, resting earth and to the coming darkness of winter. In the southern hemisphere, the gospel will not be reinforced and illustrated by the blossoming trees (but, then, the blossoms were never themselves the gospel anyway!), but the promise must still be understood as for this earth. The time that is kept is our time, here, in this solar system. So keep Lent as baptismal time in our time. Keep the paschal vigil and the great fifty days as a Sunday to our year, proclaiming the resurrection to that year whose number is inscribed on the paschal candle.

—Celebrate the presence of God in our time. Keep Christmas as a Christian welcome and critique of human festivity at the solstice. Treasure the celebrations. But tell the truth about the inevitable sadness that comes with trying to keep the perfect light-and-fullness festival, and help people negotiate that sadness. Most important, invite the assembly to the most gracious Light, the deepest gift, present in word and sacrament. Christmas, too, is the gospel proclaimed to our time, a Sunday to the winter. The Christmas feast, together with its twelve days and its echoing Epiphany feast, is a way of preaching the gospel of Jesus Christ in the midst of the winter solstice of the northern hemisphere. It is not the time that Jesus was born, constantly revisited as if we could thereby encounter an eternal, unearthly, mythic birth. The infancy narratives are told because the feast celebrates the presence of God among us in the very barren and needy time of northern hemisphere winter. The feast celebrates the incarnation, finding its central text in the hymn of John 1. The infancy texts may also be told simply because ancient Christians were part of societies that began their year at the winter solstice, and with the new year may have come the Christian custom of starting once again to read one of the Gospel books from its beginning.[28]

28. Thomas J. Talley, *The Origins of the Liturgical Year* (New York: Pueblo, 1986), 129–34.

—Keep Advent, uncompromised. Advent may have been yet another ancient Christian reaction to general human solstice festivity, a reaction in abstention, fasting, waiting, prayer, all as honest ways to express the need of the world and to resist the compulsion and anxiety of religious practice meant to force the sun to return. In any case, the modern Advent/Christmas cycle is a remarkable blending of the fierce honesty of abstention with the graciousness of transformed winter festivity. But Advent, too, is our time. It is not a time to pretend as if we are Israel waiting or as if Jesus were not yet born. Rather, the Christian assembly tells the truth about a world still full of waiting and want. Yet the assembly also tells about Christ who already now identifies with the hidden and waiting ones. Each Advent Sunday, after all, is also still a Sunday.

—But, then, precisely in order to underscore what time it is and where your assembly gathers, resist the ways in which this timekeeping can be malformed. Let Sunday be the primary feast, and resist the theme Sundays, special-group Sundays, sales-based Sundays. If you pray the office communally or personally, do not anticipate the hours just to get them done. Pray at morning and evening—perhaps at noon and night—and if you cannot, do not fear some retribution from the unsatisfied sky or a discontented god. The community prays for you. The hours come anyway, by God's gift. Keep Lent for baptismal preparation and remembrance and Easter for all the stories of deliverance, centered in the resurrection and proclaimed to our time, to our year. Resist the ways in which various commentaries or liturgical resources want to urge you to make the feast into either "memory" or "mystery," away from here. As you tell parts of the story, tell them as facets that always introduce the assembly to the whole gospel, as on Sunday. On Palm Sunday, tell of the passion as well as the victorious, resurrection-anticipating entry. On Good Friday, tell of the all-embracing resurrection as well as the death; tell the Johannine passion with its paradoxes: the one called "I am" is arrested; the very source of the Spirit is killed. And know all the time, all through Lent and Holy Week, that Jesus is already risen now. Keep a real Advent, all the way to Christmas, as a way of telling the truth about the world's need. Be gracious to the frenzied quest to find a perfect gift, but resist the use of the church assembly as another place to support or lengthen the shopping season and avoid the truth-telling rhythm of genuine festivity. And keep the Christmas feast for twelve full days. Consider holding Christmas concerts and Christmas programs then.

—If you fail in any of these things, be at peace. These feasts are there, not as constraints, not as offerings to the implacable sky, but as gifts to reconfigure our experience of time now.

—Furthermore, if your assembly meets in the southern hemisphere, in the tropics, or within either the Arctic or the Antarctic circle, consider how the trajectory of this proclamation of the gospel to our time and place may need to continue. If Christmas is kept in the southern hemisphere with an explicit intention to relate it to the experience of the summer solstice, remarkable gifts in poetry, liturgy, and proclamation may be given to us all. But if Christmas is kept only in nostalgia for the north, its connection to honest time and place will be lost. It may well be even more important that other real-time festivals—sun-return and sun-loss in the Arctic; the coming of the rains in the tropics; the winter solstice itself in the southern hemisphere; and yet other locally observed changes—become themselves the occasion of new liturgical creativity: the insertion of place-specific, time-specific assembly eucharists within the general Christian calendar.

As with the earlier suggestions regarding baptismal and eucharistic renewal, this list will at first appear to be simply a wish list of one approach to contemporary liturgical renewal. But then, the cosmological significance of such renewal may become clear. If we can recover the practice of timekeeping as knowing what time it is here, we may find ourselves invited to see the sky from our place on the earth. Then, if the celebration itself accords with the ecumenical liturgical renewal, it will juxtapose the grace of the triune God, known in word and sacrament, to our place and time on the earth. As a result, the assembly will simply and faithfully be proclaiming that God holds our sky-earth, that we are gathered here on holy ground, and that fidelity to this God includes care for this planet.

Holy Place, Open Place

Should we also reclaim the practice of orienting our church buildings toward the east? That is, if Sunday, daily prayer, and the principal feasts help us to see the sky from our place on the earth, should the arrangement of the assembly-house also help us to know where we are?

This eastward orientation is not a bad idea if it is practicable. It is an old arrangement, rich with global resonances, utilizing an old cosmology that came to be connected to ancient Christian eschatology: the daily rising sun recalls for us both the resurrection and the promise of Christ's final coming with open justice and mercy. Yet orientation can also coincide with current astronomy. It can help us to see a wider location for our assembly than we usually remember and begin to train us to see the connection lines that run out from this house. But it should not be compelled. Even if it is used, it is certainly liable to misunderstanding. Christ will no sooner come from the rising sun than he has gone up. These are linguistic constructions, arising from our place on the surface of the earth. To be useful now, their symbolic force needs to be tempered with a simple knowledge of astronomy. The way our house is ordered toward the dawn must be seen as primarily celebrating that this liturgy takes place here, on this planet, at this latitude, circling this sun, held in God's mercy. Even more, the emotional force of sunrise must be reinterpreted of the triune God's presence among us: the Light rises now, mercy and justice are openly known now, in this word, this bath, this meal.

For our time, however, there are probably more urgent orientations. We have argued that the Christian liturgy does, indeed, situate its participants in a reoriented map in which the cardinal directions are toward God, toward the assembly, toward the poor, and toward the earth itself.[29] Here we may call that fourth direction an orientation toward "sky-earth," toward our place in the observed universe. We have also argued that this assembly needs to be marked by a public symbolization that always balances "here" with "away from here."[30] The assembly-house we use could best be marked by these orientations, its lines and structures coordinated with and reinforcing the map proposed by the *ordo*.

The ways that the house of the church can be so oriented are diverse. But the principles for such orientation can be simply delineated. Let the house be a gracious space for an assembly, accessible to all people, open and human-sized, hospitable but serious, an "agora" or a pavement on which "to transact the public business of death and life."[31] Let it have strong and weighty centers in the place of the word, the place of the table, and, if the baptistry is not a separate building, the place of the bath. Let the places of presiding and of music, the presence of visual arts, the use of other symbols and lighting all support the community in doing the events that flow in and

29. See above, chapter 2.
30. See above, chapter 4.
31. Aidan Kavanagh, *Elements of Rite: A Handbook of Liturgical Style* (New York: Pueblo, 1982), 21.

out of the primary centers for word, bath, and table. Let the house have wide and accessible doors for coming in and for going out, for easily welcoming the poor and for easily going out to serve them. And let the connections to the earth and the sky be an important consideration—demonstrated by honesty in the use of local materials, by the utilization of arts that recall the lines of connection that run out from this assembly, perhaps by clear windows that allow the earth-location of the assembly to be seen from within the building.

The principles may be clear, but enacting them may not be so easy. In fact, the history of the house of the church demonstrates a frequent loss of balance between matters that function best when they are kept in vigorous, balanced tension. The ancient house-for-the-church needed to be made larger, remodeled for more than a small group in a dining room. Then the ancient basilica needed to be tempered, focusing on an assembly around word and table and not just on an imperial representative.[32] Our times will not be different. Balancing a strong center with an open door, a weighted center with open access, holiness with hospitality, public event with personal attention, center with the eccentric, here with connections to not-here will take creative skill. So will the careful creation of a space that can work as an assembly hall for all three of the major functions of this assembly: a place for a word service, a room for a large communal meal, and a communal bathing place.

But the most useful space for the Christian assembly will be marked by just these tensions. After all, the juxtaposition of one thing to another can be taken as the classic way that meaning occurs in Christian liturgy. Word next to table next to bath—and strong center next to open door—may help us continually to remember the location of this liturgy under the torn sphere, on the holy ground.

Then, in Christian liturgical use, sacred time best yields to liturgical time, understood as the present moment reconfigured as the time of assembly. And, just so, sacred place best is understood as this local place, now organized for an open assembly, around these central things. Such a conception of the timekeeping and place-marking practices of Christian liturgy can help us to see the sky while standing together gladly on this ground.

Paul's sermon at the Areopagus may provide us with a wise summary of such liturgical place and time. God has provided all the nations of the whole earth with "the times of their existence and the boundaries of the places

---

32. See Lathrop, *Holy Things,* 222–23, and Lathrop, *Holy People,* 41, 129.

where they would live" (Acts 17:26). Liturgy, first of all, acknowledges our times and places, both of which have to do with our location on the earth, under the sky. That is not the end of the matter, however. These boundaries and times remain permeable, open toward God, first "so that they would search for God and perhaps grope for and find God." But, then, the times and places become the location of the celebration of the gospel itself, for "indeed God is not far from each one of us" (17:27).

Christian liturgy is not astronomy. Neither, as we have seen, is it ecological studies or economics or politics or the only system of public symbols by which we live. But the practices of the Christian assembly can make modest though critically important proposals about economy and politics, can reorient us in the use of public symbols, and can show us the godly hole in our spheres and systems. In regard to astronomy, similar proposals may be made. An assembly around Word and Sacrament, held in our time, can be seen to say this: Our place in the universe now is this sky-earth, this blue planet. It is a good place. From this place, we rightly observe what we can and consider what our observations might mean for theories about how all things are connected—or not. We also rightly resist any theory if it is taken to undermine our increased common care for both social justice and the well-being of the planet's many systems of life. And while we have no easy explanations, we meet before the mercy of that triune God who holds all those systems, on this planet and far beyond, into healing and hope.

In Advent, as the Christian assembly begins to count the last week of days before its own celebration of God's presence and mercy at the time of the winter solstice, several antiphons have been used to surround the singing of Mary's song at evening. These are timekeeping texts. They bring to expression the need of the world and the confident, waiting hope of the church. They give ancient, metaphoric names to the incarnate One, whose presence among us is the grounds of our hope and the deepest reason for our festival. The first of these antiphons, appointed to be sung on the evening of December 17, is called O *Sapientia:*

O Wisdom, coming forth from the mouth of the Most High, reaching from end to end, strongly and delightfully ordering all things, come and teach us the way of good sense.[33]

---

33. The classic Latin text was as follows: O *Sapientia, quae ex ore Altissimi prodiisti, attingens a fine usque ad finem, fortiter suaviterique disponens omnia: veni ad docendum nos viam prudentiae.* These antiphons are perhaps most widely known now in the form of the Advent carol, "Oh, Come, Oh, Come, Emmanuel."

Even and especially in these postmodern times, the faith of the church can be refreshed that, as it gathers in clarity and simplicity around word, bath, and table, the assembly does, indeed, gather around this holy, world-ordering Wisdom. We cannot recite all the traits of this strong and delightful world order ourselves. We cannot always even see it, in the midst of the death and loss and injustice around and in us. But we can trust in faith that the lines that run "from end to end" run through here. We can trust that in following those lines as we shape our ethics, we will be following something like the way of good sense. We can see that the reoriented map of the world that begins to be set out in the liturgy corresponds to those lines. It is a map of the holy ground.

PART THREE

One Is Holy
Liturgical Poetics

IN SACRED MANNER MAY WE WALK
UPON THE FAIR AND LOVING EARTH,
IN BEAUTY MOVE, IN BEAUTY LOVE
THE LIVING ROUND THAT BROUGHT US BIRTH.
WE STAND ON HOLY GROUND.

—*Susan Palo Cherwien*

7

Antiliturgica:
On the Ritual Making of False Worlds

D oes the Christian liturgy really do all this? Does Christian assembly in Word and Sacrament gather its participants into a worldview marked by reorientation and the hole in the heavens? Does liturgical life enable an open but critical dialogue with the other cosmologies by which we live? Does it propose a set of radically reoriented maps for our ethics?

No, not necessarily. It must even be said that in some Christian experience, the rituals that the community celebrates do something quite different. This book has already said as much in the cautionary catalogue carried in the margins of its reflections. Christian liturgy can be organized to serve and reinforce an ideology in which humanity is the crown of creation and sacramental grace can be seen as always involving a restoration of that preeminence without regard to anything else. Or Christian liturgical poetry can utilize, unbroken, a language filled with ideas of an earth-centered universe or of the immortality of the soul or of going away to somewhere else called "paradise." Christian celebration can be construed as deeply sarcophobic. Or it can be exclusively locative, supporting the status quo, or exclusively liberative, in one way or the other inviting us out of here. Or a Christian meeting can be focused upon the hopes and dreams of individual participants and their self-realization. Going to church can be going to a celebration of our own unchallenged identities and worldviews. It can be attending a romantic pageant that recreates imaginary times and places, or joining a consumer gathering in which consumer values are themselves never challenged and the world is seen as a great shopping mall, or participating in a sacred drama in which a closed, sacred ideology is celebrated. Christian liturgy does not automatically have something interesting to say in critical dialogue with cosmologies. The hole in the heavens—or the burning bush or the foliage of the tree of life—does not automatically appear in our assemblies because of our own excellent efforts. In fact, our liturgies can be quite destructive, quite actively unhelpful, in the midst of the current cosmological need. So, no, Christian liturgy as it is actually practiced does not necessarily make all of the cosmological proposals we have discussed. We ought to hold ourselves in this negation for a while.

In 1966, C. W. Mönnich, a Lutheran professor of the history of dogma at the University of Amsterdam, published an elegant and yet caustic little book entitled *Antiliturgica: Several Notes on the Celebration of Churchly Feasts*.[1] His goal was paradoxical. He intended to write against the liturgy or, at least, against liturgical pretensions. At the same time, he intended to propose that his beloved Christian liturgy should be seen as something like Ionesco's *antithéâtre*, an event that admits no spectators but rather engages all those present in the work that is being done in the room. Some of Mönnich's comments are dated. But many of his conclusions are still worth attention, if only for their marvelous ability to goad toward thought by holding us in a significant *no*.

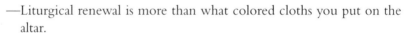

—Liturgical renewal is more than what colored cloths you put on the altar.

—The assembly, the "guests of the Lord's hospitality," make up no elite, but are a ragtag, unrighteous lot. Only the presence of the Messiah makes them into God's people.

—Nothing is "consecrated" by us in the liturgy, including bread and wine, but the Lord does really give himself away there.

—Supposed "purity of liturgical style" is probably mostly made up of the style mistakes of an earlier time. "A foolish mistake in A.D. 600 is still no holy law in A.D. 1966."[2]

—The creed does not belong in the usual Sunday liturgy, where it too easily becomes "a sort of shibboleth of a stagnant orthodoxy";[3] it belongs in the celebration of baptism where it genuinely functions.

—Liturgy ought never be acting "as if." The event is real, here, now.

1. C. W. Mönnich, *Antiliturgica* (see above, chap. 6 n. 19). The book has never been translated into English.
2. Ibid., 19.
3. Ibid., 51.

movement?   *Sitting &*
Standing

Choir
reading
Communion

ANTILITURGICA

Singing

—"Liturgy is no esoteric matter of the initiated who can follow the secret language of signs. It is no theosophy."[4]

—Liturgy is always a movement, from the gathering around the word to the table of the Messiah, and probably ought to involve a communal movement in space between differently arranged rooms or spaces. Most of our usual spaces deceive us about the nature of the event, creating a passive audience.

—Pastors do not interpret the Scripture because they are pastors. They are pastors because they interpret the Scripture.

—And this:

Christ is no mathematical point, but God's action itself, from the foundation of the world to its completion. Everything that the church, the body of the Messiah, does in his name and authority is sacrament, is the service, the liturgy itself, is movement, action, blessing, help. Whoever prays for another enacts a sacramental action, because it is done in Christ's name. Precisely the same is true for a sermon, a conversation, the laying on of hands, economic or social or medical or administrative help.[5]

—And finally, this:

Whoever regards the preceding comments as barbarism and as a misunderstanding of the heritage of the fathers and of the higher symbols does not know what liturgy is. Respect for the heritage of the Lutheran fathers? Those fathers also had an unwavering faith in the importance of the persecution of witches. Still further back in the rich past of the church and we bump up against the murder of heretics, the worldview of Ptolemy (the earth in the center and the sun going around it), sacrosanct government, inviolable churchly authorities, divinely willed social classes and yet more things that presumably the most fervent restorationist and most enthusiastic lover of the tradition will reverently, but determinedly let go. Regarding the liturgy: it is time to be done with worship in which bourgeois solemnity, venerable conservatism, gerontocracy, the ethics of the china cupboard, taste for higher symbolism, and restoration fanaticism have set a conspiracy afoot wherein the communication of the Messiah with those who have not been initiated into these holy mysteries is practically impossible. . . . I am, however, genuinely not pleading for a complete destruction of our liturgical heritage. For one thing:

4. Ibid., 23.
5. Ibid., 70–71.

181

hands off the structure of the liturgy! Not because it is ages old, but because it is so freshly alive: everything a celebrative movement toward the messianic meal.[6]

But the most useful thing from Mönnich's book is the paradoxical idea itself: *antiliturgica,* writing against the liturgy that is also an encouragement toward participation in the liturgy. That is a paradox that may well accord with the breaking of symbols and the reorientation of cardinal directions. Might we engage in the same undertaking, now for liturgical cosmological purpose? Can a liturgist write against the liturgy precisely in order to encourage full participation in the liturgy?

Of course, a great deal might be said about the dangers and distortions of human ritual in general. But that is not the point here. Rather, here we need to ask in what ways Christians may build their own false or closed or self-serving estimations of the cosmos, using the liturgy to sacralize the result. Here we need to reflect on the Christian ritual construction of worlds that are not marked by the biblical reversals or reorientations we have earlier explored. One way we can do so is by focusing on two common liturgical distortions. Then we might, nonetheless, let ourselves be invited to liturgy as antiliturgical event.

The Hierarchical Distortion

"The liturgy is hierarchically structured," Aidan Kavanagh asserts flatly.[7] In a book like Mönnich's devoted to the brilliant skewering of liturgical pretension, but also, unlike Mönnich's, engaged in articulating extensive practical liturgical wisdom, Kavanagh nonetheless makes this assertion one of his ten central affirmations. For all that Kavanagh adroitly turns this hierarchy continually toward service of the assembly, the constitutive structure of those who are "higher" and those who are "lower," those who rule amid the sacred things and those who are ruled, remains.

Such an assertion should be widely recognized among those who practice traditional Catholic liturgy. The idea of the "hierarchical nature of the liturgy" recurs in no less a source than that basic document of the twentieth-century liturgical movement, the *Constitution on the Sacred Liturgy,*[8] perhaps

6. Ibid., 25–28.

7. Kavanagh, *Elements of Rite* (see above, chap. 6 n. 31), 10.

8. For example, "liturgical services pertain to the whole body of the Church; they manifest it and have effects upon it; but they concern the individual members of the Church

as part of the Second Vatican Council's famous ambiguity, mixing old ideas with new, a mixture undiscussed and unresolved in the documents themselves.[9] Hierarchy in liturgy is also popular with those liturgists who have found help in the anthropological work of Victor Turner and his assertion that the inevitably absolute authorities of cultic practice ought to be understood as reversed images of the status structures operative in ordinary life.[10]

But hierarchy is best known simply in practice. You know the list: The presider's chair looks like a throne, the entrance procession like the arrival of a monarch. The servers hold books for that presider and pour water for the washing of his hands. The pulpit rises several feet—yards?—above contradiction. Indeed, the central matters of the liturgy all take place at higher elevations, at places generally accessible only to clergy. The Holy Communion may be put into the mouth of the communicant, the higher order thus feeding the lower. The preacher-presider is the most powerful person in the room, taking that power as appropriate, natural, correct. Sometimes while the presider stands at the holy table, everybody else kneels. Sometimes, the presider's voice simply gets to be the loudest, the presider's style the most intense among all the participants. The bishop wears a phallic hat that makes the episcopal stature look even taller, even higher than it is. The "sacred order of priests" all are wearing stoles, even though they may be doing nothing in this large-group liturgy. Everyone hushes in order to listen to the choir sing or the organ play. More, all the orders and ranks of participants stay in their appropriate place. And even in a small church, the pastor tells the liturgy committee or the parish council or any number of detractors a thing that is manifestly true: "liturgy is not democracy." One impious definition seems near at hand: "liturgy comes down to this—clergy marching around, telling other people what to do."

These practices, even though they may be traditionally or anthropologically defended, reflect a distortion of the Christian conception of "church."[11] Even more, for our purposes here, they manifest and reinforce a

in different ways, according to their differing rank, office, and actual participation." *Constitution on the Sacred Liturgy,* vol. 26 (Collegeville, Minn.: Liturgical Press, 1963), 19.

9. See Michael J. Tkasik, *Compromising the Eucharist: The Parallel and Parting Theologies of the Second Vatican Council* (Ph.D. diss., McAnulty College and Graduate School, Duquesne University, 1996), 126–34.

10. Victor Turner, *The Ritual Process: Structure and Anti-Structure* (Chicago: Aldine, 1969), 166–203.

11. For one articulation of that conception and for alternative views on liturgical leadership, see Lathrop, *Holy People* (see above, intro. n. 2), 73–98.

problematic cosmology. The "throne" reflects the conception of a single center to the universe, away from here but represented here, with God as a lone monarch, not as a triune perichoretic dance. The elevation of the sacred things, while it may serve the practical purpose of communal vision and thus participation, inevitably suggests that old "up" as the most sacred direction away from here, toward the truth and the light. The very organization of the body into ranks and orders and offices, ritually arranged and enacted as a pyramid of knowledge and power—archbishops or patriarchs or cardinals above bishops above priests above deacons above cantors above lectors above doorkeepers or ushers above widows or other dominant women above the people above the outsiders—suggests those orbits within orbits within the great sphere of the *Timaeus*. Indeed, "hierarchy" itself carries along the Platonic idea of the emanation of being, knowledge, and light flowing from the single, ideational, divine center until, working their way down through the great chain of heavenly hierarchy and subservience, these come to be thinly manifested in the merely and grossly physical world. Hierarchy is, at its root, a cosmology.

And it is false, wrong. Not only does this conception of the cosmic order not at all accord with current astronomy. It also does not have much room for the balanced dialectic between here and away from here, between the locative and the liberative. It gives no support to considering our earth, our actual location in the merely physical, as holy ground. And it does not seem to have heard of Mark's rending of the Timaean sphere or of Jesus' inveighing, just before the healing of the blind son of Timaeus, against the hierarchies of the Gentiles: "it is not so among you; but whoever wishes to become great among you must be your servant" (Mark 10:43).

Hierarchy does indeed seem to be the stuff of "going to church." For many people, elevated ideas, elevated actions, and elevated music, clerical authority and gestures toward that "up" are all they know of church, the very symbols that make the event to be church. For others, only fragments of the hierarchical world remain. But these fragments are real enough: those clergy, for example, marching around and telling others what to do. It is not only the churches that call their clergy a "hierarchy" that maintain hierarchical liturgical practices, even if only in fragments. Wherever they occur, these fragments do propose a world. From a cosmological point of view, hierarchy, in any form, always seems to carry along Platonism and that Timaean sphere.

But the "hierarchical nature of the liturgy" is an old mistake, and "a foolish mistake in A.D. 600 is still no holy law" in the present time. Or, at

identification with powerful

least, it ought not be. Perhaps hierarchy does inevitably occur whenever an event becomes ritually intense and serious as cult. Perhaps Victor Turner was right. Or, perhaps, in Christian circles, hierarchy attended all sorts of other second- and third-century cultic borrowings from the mystery religions. In the history of Christian liturgy, however, some of the practices that came to be called "hierarchical" seem to have especially accompanied the important fourth- and fifth-century achievement of imperial status on the part of bishops. Perhaps the story could be told in this way: When that status was achieved, after centuries of official persecution, the sad and usual thing occurred. The persecuted began to mirror something of the characteristics of the old persecutors. Bishops began to behave with imperial insignia, and attendants, imperial ceremony and buildings, even imperial religious authority as *pontifices*.[12] At the outset, the domestic actions that still claimed the heart of the liturgy to which these imperial personages arrived—the simple serving of food to the people, set out in the center of the imperial building and remarkably reorienting that building's purpose—had the effect of juxtaposing another conception of leadership to this hierarchical one, potentially breaking its symbolic power. But as the old imperial purpose of the building reasserted itself, as that table was withdrawn and hidden, as the food was minimized, as the thanksgiving prayer began to sound like an imperial petition to a yet higher Authority, as the leadership of the bishop became crucial in the absence or failure of other civic leaders, and as Christianity gave its weight to the widespread, mostly unrealized patriarchal longing for a king, the imperial and ruling character of the ecclesiastical hierarchy came to be occupied unambiguously, without critique, unbroken by the gospel word, unchallenged by actual liturgical practice.

In any case, the massive Neoplatonic rationalization of the idea of hierarchy was articulated in the fifth or sixth century by Pseudo-Dionysius. His writings, which ultimately came to be very important for the Western church as well as for the Eastern churches and which were universally regarded to be the first-century works of a companion of Paul the apostle, included both extensive cosmological speculation and an important liturgical commentary.[13] The idea of "hierarchy" wove the cosmology and the

12. See Anscar J. Chupungco, "Eucharist in the Early Church and its Cultural Settings," in S. Anita Stauffer, ed., *Worship and Culture in Dialogue* (Geneva: Lutheran World Federation, 1994), 93–97.

13. For translations of "The Celestial Hierarchy" and "The Ecclesiastical Hierarchy," see Colm Luibheid, Paul Rorem, et al., eds., *Pseudo-Dionysius: The Complete Works* (New York: Paulist, 1987), 143–259.

liturgical commentary together. Indeed, Dionysius may well have invented the word "hierarchy,"[14] using it to discuss the descending cosmic orders of angels but also the threefold orders of sacraments (baptism, eucharist, and chrism), of ministers (bishops—who were regarded as hierarchs per se—followed by priests and deacons), and of the whole sacramental economy (sacraments, initiators, and initiated).[15] In all of this, there was an above and a below, that which is below not being able to exist without mediation from and participation in that which is above. In the liturgy, by this conception, everyone was to participate "according to their order," the hierarchs, for example, perpetually deigning to initiate the people.

The whole conception is simply wrong. Dionysius is not a first-century apostolic voice, as he was for so long uncritically regarded. That idea, still hovering behind church documents that discuss "hierarchy" as if it were ancient, holy tradition, is bogus. If the liturgical assembly has anything to do with the Jesus of the Gospels, then above and below must be radically reconceived. While leadership, even powerful and solemn leadership, is certainly needed in liturgical events, that leadership must always be subject to the breaking of symbols. Liturgical leadership must not become the focus of an ideology that weaves its assumed power into the essence of the church, let alone into the very structure of the universe. Every one of us—bishop and priest included—do not first of all participate in the liturgy "according

14. Ibid., 1. Compare ibid., 197 n. 11. See Dionysius's own definition ("Celestial Hierarchy" 164d–165a, ibid., 153–54): "In my opinion a hierarchy is a sacred order, a state of understanding and an activity approximating as closely as possible to the divine. And it is uplifted to the imitation of God in proportion to the enlightenment divinely given to it. The beauty of God . . . reaches out to grant every being, according to merit, a share of light and then through a divine sacrament, in harmony and peace, it bestows on each of those being perfected its own form. The goal of a hierarchy, then, is to enable beings to be as like as possible to God and to be at one with him. . . . Hierarchy causes its members to be images of God in all respects, to be clear and spotless mirrors reflecting the glow of primordial light and indeed of God himself. It ensures that when its members have received this full and divine splendor they can then pass on this light generously and in accordance with God's will to beings further down the scale."

15. On this last triad, see "The Ecclesiastical Hierarchy" 501a–b, ibid., 233–34: "In our sacred tradition every hierarchy is divided in three. There are the most reverend sacraments. There are those, inspired by God, who understand and purvey them. And there are those who are sacredly initiated by these. . . . These first beings around God lead others and with their light guide them toward this sacred perfection. To the sacred orders farther down the scale they generously bestow, in proportion to their capacity, the knowledge of the workings of God. . . . The ranks coming in succession to these premier beings are sacredly lifted up by their mediation to enlightenment in the sacred workings of the divinity. They form the orders of initiates and they are named as such."

to our order." We first of all participate, hands out as beggars with all beggars, for the sake of once again encountering mercy, once again coming to faith. Bishops should not be kings. Martin Luther, who in the early controversies of the Reformation found Dionysius being used by Eck and Emser to support everything from papal primacy to seven sacraments to clerical prerogatives, was right: Dionysius "is downright dangerous, for he Platonizes more than he Christianizes. So if I had my way, no believer would give the least attention to these books. So far, indeed, from learning Christ in them, you will lose even what you already know."[16] We should heed that judgment, also in our liturgical work.

The resistance to hierarchy has been one of the major unifying themes of late-modern feminism.[17] This theme itself may have come to feminism from similar themes in Christian liberation theology. In any case, throughout the twentieth century, many of the concerns of feminism have become widespread concerns of renewal movements generally. For that reason, it may, in fact, be true that the liturgical movement itself—at least in its quests for shared leadership, for dispersed centers of authority, for a circle of participation, as well as for accessible and metaphoric symbols—might be regarded as one of the fruits of a Christian feminism.[18] But whether that is true or not, those who care about authentic liturgy in dialogue with a cosmology that matters ought to join hands with feminists in the resistance to hierarchy.

If we meet "hierarchy" when we go to church—and many of us do—we thus meet an old mistake. If we persist in uncritically continuing the idea and the symbolic expressions of hierarchy, however, we will not only be distorting the identity of the church. We will also be helping to make that church a cosmological anachronism. This will not be a salutary anachronism in the sense that the archaic is sometimes most profoundly relevant, in the sense that the archaic can help us to imagine healthy alternative ways to

16. *De captivitate babylonica ecclesiae praeludium, WA* 6:562 (see above, chap. 3 n. 17): "etiam pernitiosissimus est, plus platonisans quam Christianisans, ita ut nollem, fidelem animum his libris operam dare vel minimam." Christus ibi adeo non disces, ut, si etiam scias, amittas. Translation altered from Abdel Ross Wentz, ed., *Luther's Works,* vol. 36: *Word and Sacrament II* (Philadelphia: Muhlenberg, 1959), 109. See also Karlfried Froelich, "Pseudo-Dionysius and the Reformation of the Sixteenth Century," in Luibheid, Rorem, et al., *Pseudo-Dionysius.,* 41–44.

17. See, as a leading example, Rosemary Radford Reuther, "Sexism and God-Language," in Judith Plaskow and Carol P. Christ, eds., *Weaving the Visions: New Patterns in Feminist Spirituality* (San Francisco: Harper, 1989), 151–52.

18. See, for example, Gail Ramshaw, *Under the Tree of Life: The Religion of a Feminist Christian* (New York: Continuum, 1998), 93.

conceive the world. The alternative imagined in hierarchical liturgical practice will generally be an alternative that devalues the actual conditions of the earth and invites us to get out of here, at least in our spiritual life, under the tutelage and initiatory powers of those "above us." If we continue uncritically with hierarchy, we will be building up a fortress against current astrophysics, against helpful critical dialogue with a variety of active public symbolisms, against seriousness about the care for the earth. Most important, by the constant reference up and away, we may even be found to be resisting God's holy ground. In any case, we will be refusing to give ecclesial service, refusing to give even a cup of cold water, to the world-making requirements of the present needy and fascinating time. We will be engaged in a cosmological distortion, proposed and reinforced by our liturgical practice.

In the seventeenth century, in Denmark, the absolute Danish monarch lived in a world that did not require of him any encounter with contradiction to his authority. Still today, at Rosenborg Slot, the tourist can see one version of the dwelling place of this monarch, every corner of the rooms filled with pictures of kings that hung around that of the king at the time. Even the royal nightclothes are preserved, replete with the lace crown the monarch could wear to bed. Nothing, night or day, needed to gainsay the world-construction of kingship. If we maintain hierarchical liturgical practice, it may well be as if we are trying to live in such a castle, putting such a pathetic nightcap upon our clergy. But we will hardly be seeing the whole contradictory world.

The Closed-Circle Distortion

The hierarchical distortion is not the only liturgical cosmological distortion available to us. There is also the matter of the closed circle. If hierarchy tempts the Catholic tradition, is most obviously known in the Catholic tradition, the closed circle bedevils the Protestants.

Not that the closed circle is unique among Protestant Christians. The strong communal identity that may arise in whatever shared ritual can lead any group of us humans to the Dover Beach syndrome: "Ah, love, let us be true to one another!" against all the ignorant others.[19] Intense ritual involvement and shared ritual knowledge can easily draw a line around our group, even when we do not want such a line. Simply to have a formal dinner together is to include some—the invited guests—and exclude others—ev-

19. See above, intro.

erybody else—even if we treasure the virtues of openness and hospitality. And just as Protestant communities have powerful fragments of hierarchical liturgy in their practice, Catholic Christians, for all of their longing to avoid the sect type of religious social structure, can also shelter together against the world, against the others, especially in some forms of the ethnic catholicisms and some forms of monasticism and the religious institutes. Thus, massive distortions are found where a fierce devotion to the hierarchical has been combined with the embattled sect mentality, as in the various societies for the Latin liturgy among the Roman Catholics. This same poisonous combination of both distortions can also be found outside of Roman Catholicism: in various high church groups among the mainstream Protestants, for example, or various sect-like Protestant groups that also have a strong commitment to the absolute authority of their "shepherds."

Still, even apart from these comments on the sect type among Christians and on the generally exclusive character of ritual, Protestants have a tendency to the closed circle. Classic Reformation concerns have included such salutary things as widespread education of the laity, the "priesthood of all believers," and a sense of the local communal responsibility for what occurs in the room. The Puritan version of Calvinist Protestantism in North America has added the accent on the covenant into which the believers enter. It is no wonder, then, that a classic Protestant call for parish renewal may well include one or the other call for greater communal discipline, dreaming of the knowledgeable and committed congregation. You may recognize some of the formulations: "Purge the membership list of inactives. We want no deadwood here." Or, "the church is the company of the committed. There is a cost to discipleship." Or, "everybody in this parish must sign a covenant and renew this covenant yearly."[20]

But how are these practices liturgical practices? And what are the implications of such practices for cosmology?

For proponents of such parish renewal, liturgy may form one leading indicator that the longed-for discipline has been taken seriously. Baptism is not to be practiced indiscriminately, they may assert. Leadership in the assembly should fall to those who are involved in the initiatory practices of the church, those who teach and those who have been taught. The liturgy ought to have a continuing didactic character. Perhaps, as in one widely known and very Protestant experiment, the real members of the church

---

20. For a further evaluation of the ecclesiological practice of the closed circle, see Lathrop, *Holy People,* 92–93.

meet on Wednesday nights, for gatherings of the committed, so that Sundays may be freed for seeker services, attracting the as-yet uncommitted. Perhaps, then, the Lord's Supper is celebrated primarily with this committed group, as if to maintain the old "close communion," or as if to perpetuate the old "communion tokens" that admitted the examined and catechized to the disciplined meeting house in the midst of the much more populous and tumultuous frontier revival.[21] Or, perhaps, as among most Protestants, the liturgy of Holy Communion is still observed on Sunday. But the advocates of discipline may wish that this liturgy might especially celebrate the covenant of the committed, say with the strict maintenance of close communion, or the periodic observation of a covenant renewal ceremony, or the regular invitation for the assembly to recite the local disciplinary covenant as if it were the creed of the church, or the understanding of the recitation of an historic creed as that covenant, or the teaching that the meal itself is primarily a demonstration of our commitment. In any case, liturgy can be seen to involve the gathering of the committed into an identified circle and then the dispersal of that circle in mission. In regard to this conception and practice of liturgy, in spite of other differences, the megachurch movement, conservative Protestant practitioners of close communion, and the proponents of covenanted congregations of "resident aliens" all share a similar, profoundly related view.

Of course, in order for us to celebrate a communal liturgy at all, there must be widespread and continued education and a level of widespread commitment. Of course, for us to do together the rituals that make up Christian liturgy, we will inevitably have something of a closed ritual circle about us. Of course, there must be education, especially for the leaders of the assembly, together with the dream of deepening the knowledge and ownership of the communal rituals by all of their participants. But this ritual competency, this membership, this insiderhood, must also be open to the breaking of symbols. If we make our own commitment to one of the central symbols we gather around, without further critique, we will have paid little attention to the Gospel stories of Jesus eating with the traitors, the compromised, the unclean, and the sinners. The closed circle is also an old mistake.

---

21. For further discussion of the history of Holy Communion amid the revivals of the "second great awakening" and the implications of this history for the liturgy of the current "megachurches," see Gordon W. Lathrop, "New Pentecost or Joseph's Britches: Reflections on the History and Meaning of the Worship *ordo* in the Megachurches," *Worship* 72, no. 6 (November 1998): 521–38.

To quote Mönnich again, "Liturgy is no esoteric matter of the initiated who can follow the secret language of signs. It is no theosophy." So, for example, Paul fiercely urged the Corinthians to discern the body of Christ, that is, to open the circle of the eucharist more widely than any ancient triclinium, any ancient dining room of the wealthy, could possibly admit (1 Cor. 11:17-34). And the same Paul urged the same church to evaluate the apparently beloved and central assembly practice of ecstatic speech on the basis of its accessibility to the outsider (1 Cor. 14:16). Similarly, Jesus in the Gospels turns toward the excluded women, thus reconfiguring the way in which ritual space is seen (Luke 7:44), and welcomes those who tear a hole in the roof of the inaccessible house (Mark 2:4-5). These Synoptic stories, probably told originally with the house of the church in mind, must all be juxtaposed to our membership practices, our ritual circles, our inaccessible houses.

For those practices and circles also imply a cosmology. The world built by the closed-circle distortion will not be quite as obvious and systematic as the Platonic structure proposed by hierarchy. But it will be there. For one thing, closed-circle ritual is never far away from reducing liturgy to ceremony.[22] It is easier, if our commitment is one of the most central matters, to be clear about the things to which we are committed. So advocates of discipline may seek to let the ritual become an unambiguous expression of a univocal idea, without reference to contradictions in actual experience. Just so, an academic commencement ceremony celebrates academic achievement, only very seldom welcoming any criticism of our learning or any reflection on the relationship of that learning to wealth and class. Just so, the ceremony of a military parade celebrates our national preparedness, without reference to the death and destruction these weapons may work, perhaps justly, perhaps not. In both cases, these ceremonies propose unbroken worldviews. In the same way, although Christian liturgical tradition has resources to refer outside of our circle and to call our very ritual seriousness into question, we may think that, in our committed circle, it will be easier to embrace ceremony. For example, we may let one biblical text be used, with a single practical and didactic message, without the confusions and tensions of other texts. Or we may let thanksgiving predominate without the sour note of beseeching and lament. We may let commitment be praised and the virtuous be unambiguously indicated, with no mention of the danger of self-righteousness. The

22. For the distinction, see Ronald Grimes, *Beginnings in Ritual Studies* (Washington, D.C.: University Press of America, 1982), 41–45.

world so proposed will be a world of our own closed projection, with no room for the hole in its consequent system, the hole in the heavens above God's holy ground.

Then, for another thing, if our commitment is the central matter, the world so proposed finds its center in us. Or, said more subtly, that world will be conceived as a duality: inside, here, and outside, there. God will be identified with here, and the missional task will be to take God over to there, to bridge the gap between the dualities.[23] Worse, that task may be conceived simply as resistance at all costs to the strange world-ordering patterns of the strangers over there. Christian ritual and Christian rhetoric, when they are shaped by the closed-circle distortion, can play an important role in helping to make local cultural phenomena brittle, resistant even to needed change. Thus, the Greenlandic Christian Norse of the late Middle Ages seem to have become extremely conservative of their Nordic life and of their hard-won Christian ceremonies and Christian worldview. They were resistant to the needed skills of the "skraelings," the Inuit people around them, and this resistance should probably be regarded as the cause of their finally complete demise.[24] So also, the nineteenth-century, cross-Australia explorers Bourke and Wills were famously resistant to the assistance of Australian Aboriginal people, to their own hurt. Worse yet, the task may be conceived as imposing the values and language, the world-ordering methods of here on the outsiders over there, even at the cost of their lives, as the Puritan New Englanders did on the representatives of the feared wilderness, the Algonquian peoples who surrounded them. Ritual, including Christian ritual, can play an important role in the world-destroying, world-making tasks of war.[25] The closed-circle distortion is an old, tragic, sometimes violent liturgical cosmological mistake.

Liturgy as Antiliturgy

There are still other distortions. We could explore yet further, for example, the consumerist distortion and the Romantic or make-believe distortion, though these have figured prominently in the cautionary catalogue already

---

23. John F. Hoffmeyer, "The Missional Trinity," *dialog* 40, no. 2 (summer 2001): 108–11.

24. Thomas H. McGovern, "The Demise of Norse Greenland," in William Fitzhugh and Elizabeth Ward, *Vikings: The North Atlantic Saga* (Washington, D.C.: Smithsonian Institution, 2000), 327–39.

25. Jill Lepore, *The Name of War: King Philip's War and the Origins of American Identity* (New York: Knopf, 1998), x, 91–121; and Elaine Scarry, *The Body in Pain: The Making and Unmaking of the World* (New York: Oxford University Press, 1985), 60–96.

present on the edges of the foregoing chapters. Then, there is the sacrificial distortion. Some Christians, too, like other religionists, seem to be able to believe that the world is at least partly constructed or maintained by their sacrificial gestures toward the divine, their participation in the ancient tit for tat of religion. Some of these sacrificial gestures are ritual gestures. Although the classic Christian liturgy is made up of texts and songs, preaching, a bath and a meal, a collection for mission and for the poor—nothing that could reasonably be called "sacrifice"—that word has been applied metaphorically to the actions of the liturgy, and some liturgical theologies have made it a central concept, though they have not often pursued its world-making implications.[26] But for now, for a consideration of malformations in liturgical cosmology, let these reflections on hierarchy and the closed circle be enough.

These reflections could evoke a response. "We have no powerful leaders in our liturgy," we might say. "God is our leader, and we only do what God commands." Or, "Our celebrations are quite open." The problem is that, for all of their good intentions, such responses might be among the greatest distortions of all, evidencing our abilities at self-deception and self-righteousness.

Say it again: If we have a focused, important meeting, we will have powerful leadership. To act as if there is no leadership, as if God is our group leader, will only disguise and hide what should be the manifest actions and clear responsibilities of those who plan and decide and focus the group attention in the meeting. In a deep sense, liturgy is not a democracy. Though Christian liturgy seeks to engage a whole people, there are given centers for that engagement and appointed custodians of those centers. Those given centers—"Word and Sacrament," we call them—ought not be up for a vote, and the authority of those custodians should be clear, though not misused or used for other ends. Furthermore, if we have a focused meeting, we will have ritual boundaries and degrees of ritual competence, and we ought to have a liturgical educational program. We will have something of a circle about us, even if we wish we did not, even in the most open gathering. We will do better to be honest about that circle. Whatever else it is, the Christian liturgy is a human ritual, and it will have the characteristics of a human ritual. Just by being a ritual, this liturgy will be marked by the

---

26. For a critical discussion of sacrifice and offering in Christian liturgical practice, see Lathrop, *Holy Things* (see above, intro. n. 2), 139–58; and Lathrop, "The Bodies on Nevado Ampato: A Further Note on Offering and Offertory," *Worship* 71, no. 6 (November 1997): 546–54.

profound dangers of strong leadership and ritual competency. We could say more: if we keep this ritual in the present Western or Westernized world, then the meeting itself will be on the market. It will inevitably be present amid all the other competing consumer claims. That is where we live. Moreover, if the meeting matters to us, then of course we will use its material to dream alternatives. And we may indicate our seriousness about the interchanges in the ritual by calling them, in some sense, "sacrifice."

But every one of these assertions needs to be held in tension. And the concrete symbolic expressions toward which they point need to be repeatedly juxtaposed, in the ritual itself, to their contraries. This sacrifice is like no other sacrifice. This dreaming of alternatives is open-eyed about here and now. This consumer good is being given away.

Indeed, the poetic tradition of Christian liturgy—the way liturgical celebration makes meaning, its poetics—constantly employs juxtaposition, "one part against another across a silence."[27] We have argued that this juxtaposition makes up the most important way that Christian worship signifies something. Strong leadership and widespread ritual competence will mean something interesting for the dialogue with cosmologies, will not get lost in the cosmological distortions of hierarchy and the closed circle, will turn toward the service of the gospel of Jesus Christ, precisely as they are unfolded in the manner of this poetics.

So, in Christian liturgy, leaders are invited to serve. This assertion may imply many things in concrete practice, in the concrete and local poetry of the liturgy. Here are some possibilities. The presider will honor and work to enable the assembly, preside "not over the assembly but within it," be "the speaker of its house of worship,"[28] attend to the stranger and to the margins of the meeting, and yield to other leaders. Indeed, yielding to others will be one of the principal tools of leadership. All the leaders will resist the current tendency to lead by being charismatic, bright, like a celebrity, interesting. "The minister at the liturgy, like a Zen master, should be as 'uninteresting' as a glass of cold, clear, nourishing water."[29] The minister will be one of many ministers, organized horizontally in mutual honor and respect, in mutual service, according to the needs of the rite. One of those ministries will be the service of presiding. Another will be the ministry of the cantor whose primary responsibility will be to enable the voice of the assembly,

27. See above, chapter 5, note 2.
28. Kavanagh, *Elements of Rite,* 13.
29. Ibid., 53.

also welcoming the least singer. If one minister is served, that minister should also be seen to serve, each holding the book for the other, for example. Each of the ministers of communion will come to communion, perhaps last, after the rest of the assembly, in a sign that befits current understandings of the hospitable gesture. And congregations newly building might think about making the central places in the room lower rather than higher, banking the room to enable vision and celebrating how grace roots into our land.

So, in Christian liturgy, the insiders, the ritually competent, are invited to understand themselves as needy beggars with the rest of humanity. "The truth is, we are beggars," wrote Martin Luther on the scrap of paper found by his deathbed.[30] This summary statement ought to matter for liturgy influenced by the Reformation, and this assertion as well may imply many things in the actual local liturgical poetry. Here are possibilities. Those engaged in teaching the faith will also be learners, listening to the newest ones who come. The entire assembly will always be asking to be taught how to pray again, for example, adding the old beginner's prayer, the Lord's Prayer, to even its best efforts. Sermons, themselves ritual speech, will regularly criticize ritual practice and ritual exclusion. Prayers will add beseeching to thanksgiving. Intercessions will pray humbly for as many needs and people beyond our circle as we can think of. The holy bath and the holy table will be regarded as centered, powerful gifts, full of the presence of the triune God, leading us deeper and deeper into the mystery of grace, needing our best formation practices, and yet they will be unprotected, unfenced, given away to all who come.

Such is one account of liturgical poetics. Were the liturgy to be practiced in something like this way, it would be an antiliturgy in both possible senses. That is, it would contain within itself a critique of at least some of those inevitable concomitants of serious ritual, while maintaining serious ritual. And it would be like Ionesco's *antithéâtre,* an appeal for all comers to join in the action and resist becoming an audience.

The liturgical poetics of this antiliturgy, like Mark's Gospel, may evoke various cosmologies, but it will canonize none. Ritual itself may entail holy leadership, but Christian liturgical poetics will resist the hierarchical cosmological implications. The triune God comes through that torn sphere, onto this holy ground, among us in concrete signs, identifying most profoundly

---

30. Peter Manns, *Martin Luther* (New York: Crossroad, 1982), 217.

with the least and the neediest. God does not come slowly down that ladder of the rulers and the ruled. Ritual itself may imply a cosmic inside and out, a dually constructed universe that we are supposedly bridging. But Christian liturgical poetics will gather us to the one who is always outside, Jesus Christ, and will send us to be part of the Spirit's great continued ingathering of all the world to God's promised table. "We enact that sending precisely as we go from our worship gatherings to share communion with the sick, to invite others to the next celebration of the eucharist, to fill grocery bags in food pantries, to advocate for legislation that will reduce the number of hungry people, to refuse to cross picket lines where workers are striking to be able to feed their families, etc."[31] Liturgical poetics turns things inside out:[32] gathering is sending and sending is gathering. The cosmology of this poetics is not a consequent ideology, not a coherent system, but the experience of standing surrounded by the grace of the Holy Trinity and hearing, "Remove the sandals from your feet."

This poetics should be familiar from the entire structure of the Christian liturgical *ordo,* not just from what is done with leadership and the ritual circle. In that *ordo,* silence is set next to speech, concrete symbol juxtaposed to lengthy discourse as if we always needed both, never just one or the other, in order to speak the truth about God. Collections of food and money are called "offerings to God" and yet are given to the hungry. The assembly is called to "lift up your hearts," and in the very next movement hears about God among us, sharing our need and our death, sending out the Spirit to renew all the earth. That "up" seems to be rather more like "down"—or like the "up" of the Fourth Gospel, presenting the cross in response to the search of the Greeks to see: "And I, when I am lifted up from the earth, will draw all things to myself" (John 12:32). By means of such contained contradictions, the tradition of worship can be taken to stand in continuity with the tensions contained in the Bible itself. The Bible speaks about God—as it has ever since the writings were gathered into a single codex—with both Leviticus and Amos, both Deuteronomy and Job, both Paul and James held explosively between one set of book covers. In the same way, the poetics of the liturgy does not so much first of all orient its participants in the world as disorient them in relationship to the usual cosmological readings,[33]

31. Hoffmeyer, "The Missional Trinity," 110.
32. See further, Thomas H. Schattauer, "Liturgical Assembly as Locus of Mission," in *Inside Out: Worship in an Age of Mission* (Minneapolis: Fortress, 1999), 1–21.

including the readings that seem to flow from holy leadership and ritual exclusion.

In fact, our hierarchies and closed circles are never pure. We cannot seem to bring off putting that Rosenborg nightcap on our clergy anymore, in any lasting and convincing way. It seems too silly, not to say too dangerous. Further, even the most severe of our disciplinary undertakings always seems to have its exceptions. And most important for the undercutting of our false cosmologies, God is faithful. That is, in the midst of our hierarchical parades, if the Bible is still read, we will hear, "I am among you as one who serves." In our very closed circles, we will still hear, "Come to me, all who labor and are heavy laden." It is true that the hole in the heavens or the foliage of the tree of life or the burning bush itself does not show up in our meeting because of our own excellent efforts. But the Christian faith maintains that they do show up. If even fragments of the Word and Sacraments of God's gift are alive in our meetings, those very fragments will finally undermine and reverse all ritual meanings, break open our ceremonies, engage us in the poetics of the liturgy, and immerse us in the cosmology of the holy ground.

Only one is holy. So the liturgy may freely let in what does not fit. The triune God, not our cosmology, is what is holy, whole, holding all into mercy.

But there is much more to cosmological implications of the poetics of liturgy than can be expressed in this negative exercise. In the final chapters of this book, we will explore this poetics further, considering again how liturgical juxtapositions may become liturgical cosmology and how that cosmology, for Christians, is finally theology itself.

33. I owe this insight to my colleague, Dirk G. Lange.

8

The Unmapped:
Three Homilies in the Wilderness

Here is a test for the cosmology implied by any liturgical poetics:
put the liturgy in the wilderness.
At first glance, liturgy and wilderness do not seem to go together.
Liturgy is an ordered, patterned event, seeming to propose an ordered world.
Liturgy implies cosmos, sets out maps, indicates centers and paths. Wilderness, on the other hand, epitomizes the end of all of our patterns, the limits to our ordered world.

Wilderness: the human dwelling places thin and then disappear; the streets and the street lamps run out; the signs by the wayside cease; or, in another kind of venture into wilderness, the coastline recedes. The walker or the rower comes into a place in which the usual systems by which we hold our worlds together seem no longer to pertain. The very observant, perhaps the scientifically schooled, may observe other kinds of systems: the local ecology, for example, including the local water systems and the local patterns of eating and being eaten; the current weather system; the long-lasting rock patterns of the shifting earth or the tides or great sea currents. In true wilderness, however, even these systems seem to be at least partially our own fragile, temporary constructs, always on the edge of disruption. Earthquakes are not yet predictable and never controllable. The wind and temperature, too, change beyond our constraint, frustrate our predictions. Moreover, the flyway for bird migration that runs through this wetland today may not run through here next year. The fish may spawn somewhere else—or not at all. Sometimes, in the forest or at sea, we may be the ones who are eaten. In any case, our words, our songs, our meanings, our very survival do not matter to the animals, fish, rocks, streams, currents, mountains, and trees. The wilderness has frequently been made a screen for the projection of a society's hopes and fears. The chaotic sea means death, and the dark forest brims with evil, some cultures have said. Or wild places are all that remain of purity uncontaminated by human touch, others have asserted. But the wilderness itself remains unconcerned with such projections. Liturgy and wilderness, celebration of meaning and refusal of meaning, seem to be an odd juxtaposition.

Some people visit wild places precisely in order to experience a suspension in our world-patterns. The experience of wilderness enables one to consider the basic necessities for human life—food, water, companionship, rest, adequate clothing and shelter, and meanings that are basic enough to survive contact with the beautiful but uncaring wild—and then to use that reconsideration as a basis for rethinking the value and meaning of the more complex systems and maps by which we live. In a wilderness journey, those ordinary networks of connection are temporarily set aside, perhaps so that they will not be absolutized, perhaps so that they may remain malleable to needed change. It would be no surprise, then, if liturgy—especially hierarchical or closed-circle liturgy—were one of the systems left behind. Wilderness and churchgoing do not seem to go together.

Of course, the whole exercise of the wilderness trek, important as it is to some of us, is more than a little artificial. The food in the backpack may be freeze-dried, the well designed tent fabulously expensive. The time of the journey may be a carefully regulated vacation or a socially condoned period of youthful wandering. The water filter or the iodine tablet reduces the danger of too direct a contact with such wildness as is present in the *Giardia* bacteria that may inhabit the beautiful stream. The manufacturing and marketing systems of contemporary life—not to mention the network of friends who lend you equipment—are never far away. Just so, Henry David Thoreau had his quintessential Walden Pond experience supported by the relatively unacknowledged gifts of food and tools from the Alcotts and from Ralph Waldo Emerson. Ah, solitude! One might better ask for honesty. Furthermore, the wilderness trek belongs especially to the world's rich, to those with the leisure and resources to walk into the wild with something else in mind than that most widespread and persistent of human preoccupations: the responsibility of finding the next day's food for one's family and oneself.

Still, everybody, rich and poor, may go for a walk. Or they may find some way to consider that many of the things they see—that flight of birds, that windstorm, those streaking meteors—lie outside of the immensely important systems by which they themselves live. Sometimes, cultural systems have actually included moments for such relativizing vision within the ritual structure of the culture itself. One thinks of the walkabout of some Aboriginal Australians or the vision quest, the *hanblecheyapi,* of the Oglala Sioux of North America, both of which wilderness journeys are moments of defining ritual significance for their cultures. In the latter example, a Lakota youth, surrounded by the prayers, instruction, and support of the community, goes alone into the wild, seeking from the Great Mystery, from *Wakan Tanka,* a personal way toward harmonious life together with kin and cosmos, with "all my relatives," *mitak' oyas'in,* in earth and sky. The vision achieved, the person who went on the quest then returns to the community to discuss with holy persons or elders the meaning of that vision for the community, for the course of its life, as well as for the individual who had the vision.

The current North American walk into the wilderness may play, for some people of the dominant culture, something of the role of the walkabout or of that Plains Indian "crying for a vision." While many backpackers may think that they are leaving ritual and liturgy behind, the communal ritual character of their trek might at least be suggested by their widespread acceptance of the phenomena of wilderness ethics: "walking softly," "leaving no trace," minimum impact camping, protection of lakes and streams, catch-and-release fishing, as well as the expected exchange of information and needed support in the encounter of different parties on a trail. That ritual character may also be present in the things some backpackers have to say when they return, speeches about what they have seen and about implications for personal and communal ethics. In any case, the growing North American passion for the preservation of wilderness areas should probably be understood as a socially needed call for areas where the usual world-patterns are at least partially suspended, where a hole is created in the consumer system, and room is left for the consideration of another way to understand the world, another cosmology than that drawn by global marketing. In such an arrangement, ordinary patterns of commerce and life would need to remain malleable to this other way. The saying that summarizes this possibility for an alternative cosmology is usually attributed to Henry David Thoreau: "In wildness is the preservation of the world."

Only, one may ask, is there any true wildness left? Virtually all the land-masses of the earth have been mapped. Even more, satellites assure the working of hand-held Global Positioning System monitors, as an electronic grid is drawn over all the planet. Roadless areas are disappearing. Backpack-ers walk with cell phones, even satellite dishes in their packs. Discarded cola cans may be found in the deepest recesses of, say, the Gobi Desert or Kam-chatka. And intrepid adventurers carry all the systems and values of the consumer society into the wilderness: competition in expensive gear or competition in bagging mountain peaks are both widespread. What too many trekkers find in the wilderness may only be a further image of them-selves: themselves as strong; themselves as winning. So much for wilderness ethics. So much for a hole in the ordinary structure of the world. Honesty, please. Is "wilderness" then only a preserved space set aside for the privi-leged to prove themselves to themselves?

These questions and these phenomena, however, ought not fool us into thinking that there is no wildness left. Our most detailed maps and our sat-ellite grids do not include all that is there. The parkway along the busy highway, the ledge of an office building, our backyards themselves may shel-ter a red-tailed hawk's nest, an extensive colony of beetles, a coyote's den, a resting place for birds on a thousand-mile migration, a whole world not usually considered part of the system of the city. We ought, indeed, to pre-serve areas as wildernesses, precisely for the sake of cosmological refresh-ment as well as for the support of species-diversity in the earth, but that preservation ought not lead us into a cosmic dichotomy, dividing the land in two, with protected land minimized and with all of the unprotected space regarded as ripe for consumer development. Wildness is everywhere. It includes us. It needs to be seen, protected even, most certainly respected, everywhere. It even needs to be included, if only as a hole, in our concep-tions of the systems of the city and the neighborhood.

Such an assertion of the nearness of wilderness becomes especially clear when the force of a storm or the quaking of the earth overwhelms all of our systems of meaning, all of our vaunted control, also and especially in settled areas on earth. Our words, our meanings, our songs, our survival do not matter to the hurricane or the blizzard. We are never really that far from the unmapped chaos of the sea in a storm, a chaos not all that different from that of the surface of Mars or of outer space. Our constructed order, our cosmos, is fragile.

That fragility is sometimes known most acutely in personal agony. Remember *Beowulf*'s old man who had watched his own son being killed:

Alone with his longing, he lies down on his bed
and sings a lament; everything seems too large,
the steadings and the fields.[1]

"The steadings and the fields," the very places of ordered civilization, not just the untamed woods or the wild sea, were too large, exceeding any meaningful order. When such personal agony is multiplied—as in war, for example—the inability of any ordered values, including especially the order and the values for which the war is being fought, to contain the largeness of disorder becomes acute.

The real question for us is not whether backpackers will take the liturgy with them when they go into the wilderness, realizing and enacting the ritual nature of their quest. It is rather whether we have any liturgy at all to celebrate honestly in the face of that "too large." More, the question we must consider is whether any liturgy can carry cosmological significance while it is still quite aware of the fragility of all of our systems, the great unmapped wildness all around us, including us. The whole argument of this book has been that liturgy that proceeds from the burning bush, from the hole in the heavens, from the holy ground—the liturgy of the strong center and the open door, of strong leadership broken to service, of ritual adepts who come as beggars—can indeed respond with respect and meaning, both to the wildness around us and to the lamenting cry of disorder, doing so without imposing a false order. Not just any liturgy, not just any beautiful poetics, but liturgy around the triune God, full of the gifts of that God of the torn heavens, full of the paradoxes that can only point to that God as their resolution—such a liturgical poetics can indeed respond to those holes in our cosmic order represented by wildness.

If the backpackers take along what they need for church, that might be a good test case.[2] It will be hard—though not impossible—to keep up hierarchical and closed-circle forms of liturgy when surrounded tangibly, visibly, by "all of our relatives" in earth and sky and by their terrible beauty. If those backpackers are honest about their continuing though bracketed connections to the structures of their world, if they are drawn to the exercise of wilderness ethics, if they pay attention as they walk, if they report back—in some form—what they have seen that matters for our common life, then

1. Seamus Heaney, trans., *Beowulf* (New York: Farrar, Straus & Giroux, 2000), 167, lines 2460–62. See above, introduction.
2. On backpacking as a test case for church, see further in Lathrop, *Holy Things* (see above, intro. n. 2), 88–118.

their journey may indeed be a cosmological adventure, a temporary experiment in an alternate way of constructing world. And their common prayers—even their gathering as church—may bring that adventure to expression before God, on God's holy ground.

But the deepest cosmological adventure will simply be holding an ordinary assembly of Christians, in an ordinary place, aware of suffering, aware of wildness beyond our control, critical of false order.

We cannot hold such an assembly or do its liturgy together in a book. This book can only be an appeal for you to go into your own assembly, attend to its cosmological meanings, work on its continual reform, refresh its poetics. But might we take that part of the liturgy that ought to bring the whole event to verbal expression—the sermon—and consider how that sermon does cosmology within the wildness of the world? Might we explore the meanings of liturgical cosmology further by considering written examples of preaching? Could a homily be one form of primary liturgical theology that we can consider in a book?

What follows are three homilies or sermons—I make no distinction—that might be given at Christian assemblies. The sermons imagine a eucharist as their context. The liturgies envisioned are neither special Earth Day observances nor camp liturgies. Rather, every Sunday or festival offers the opportunity to propose the relationship between liturgy and the unmapped, between liturgy and all the senses of cosmology. So these are simply Sunday or festival homilies. In these sermons, each of the three senses of cosmology we have considered provides, in turn, at least part of the question addressed—shared worldview in the first, ecological concern in the second, location in the universe in the third. Yet, in all three, some attempt has been made to be aware of our postmodern hesitancies at any universal systems and to be aware of the aching truth of the "too large," the wildness that calls all of our cosmologies into question. You might imagine the preaching that should occur in this context and from these texts quite differently. The point here is not to propose these sermons as models but to engage quite concretely in the poetics of liturgical cosmology.

Of course, written sermons are not preaching itself. Preaching takes place in living communities, in actual assemblies, addressed to real and present needs, articulating the present good news. Preaching occurs between people, words in the air, images and ideas in the hearts, the preacher knowing the participation and support of the assembly. Therefore, written sermons cannot be primary liturgical theology, after all. Indeed, sermons ought not, in the first place, be thought of as written, individual affairs, available for personal reading. Nonetheless, there is a long tradition of written sermons. In Lutheran homes in past centuries, the "postil," the collection of Sunday sermons by Luther or by another, more local preacher—Bishop Jon Vidalin in Iceland, for example[3]—often was the next most important book, after the Bible and the hymnal, and was intended to foster further reflection on Sunday meaning, to extend the Sunday poetics also into the home. So here follows a tiny, abbreviated postil with cosmological themes in mind. Here follows an extension of liturgical poetics. The texts for these sermons are drawn from the Revised Common Lectionary and the Roman Catholic Lectionary, the most widely read lectionaries in the ecumenical world, out of the deep conviction that we should always attend to the lectionary in preaching and that, in the mutual giving and receiving of gifts, each other's lectionary also always is our own.

While such written sermons are not liturgical preaching itself, they may represent something of the biblical word that enables a liturgy to be both strong and open, theocentric and broken, ordered yet in touch with wildness. After all, the poetics of the liturgy that ought to come to expression plainly in preaching will leave its mark also in a written sermon.

What is such poetics that comes to expression in preaching? Preaching is a set of words set next to the central bath and table of the assembly, a single voice set next to and supported by all the voices in the room, and those very juxtapositions occur as sources of meaning. Moreover, in preaching the preacher should be able to articulate something of what is happening when biblical text is set next to biblical text next to biblical text, when prayers are set next to concrete signs, law set next to gospel, honest speech about our deathly need set next to honest speech about God's life-giving mercy, the word about the death of Christ set next to the word full of the resurrection and full of a vigorous trinitarian faith. Preaching should be words for our common baptism, words for our assembly, words for the reading of these texts here, words for the eucharist, and words for our sending into God's beloved world. Precisely in all of these things, and not alongside them, a homily may also then have something helpful to say about cosmos.

And what is the purpose of this poetics of liturgy come to expression in preaching? Preaching means to bring us again to faith and so gift us again with the reoriented view of the world that belongs to the whole liturgy.

---

3. Michael Fell, trans. and ed., *Whom Wind and Waves Obey: Selected Sermons of Bishop Jon Vidalin* (New York: Peter Lang, 1998).

Imagine that we are celebrating the eucharist in the wilderness, in a place where our mapping knowledge is thin or nonexistent. That is always where we celebrate, everywhere. How are we to find bread in this wilderness? How might we articulate worldview in this wilderness? Here follows a little postil, a homiletical attempt at liturgical cosmology.

Bread in the Wilderness

A sermon at eucharist, celebrated using the Revised Common Lectionary texts for Proper 12 B, the Sunday between July 24 and 30, in the second year of the three-year cycle:

2 KINGS 4:42-44
PSALM 145:10-18; ANTIPHON: "You open your hand, satisfying the desire of every living thing."
EPHESIANS 3:14-21
VERSE: "Alleluia. Lord to whom shall we go? You have the words of eternal life."
JOHN 6:1-21

Bread and wilderness do not go together. Bread is the result of a long development in human culture, one of the earliest products of agriculturally settled humankind but possible only as grain and cultivation, tools for grinding, and fire for baking came to be discovered. "Wilderness" is usually a word used for the absence of such culture and development, a place where the ordered fields and the ordered patterns for the distribution of the products of the field cannot reach.

Assembly and wilderness do not ordinarily go together, either. Wilderness is no place for a crowd of people or for a meeting. They could die there. So when a crowd nonetheless gathers in the wilderness, far away from farms and shops, Jesus rightly asks, "Where are we to find bread for these people to eat?"

In the narrative tradition behind this text, other figures have asked this same question.

In Mark, it is the disciples: "How can one feed these people with bread here in the desert?" (Mark 8:4). In the story of the exodus, it is the people themselves, complaining: "If only we had died by the hand of the LORD in the land of Egypt, when we sat by the fleshpots and ate our fill of bread; for you have brought us out into this wilderness to kill this whole assembly with hunger" (Exod. 16:3). In the story from the Elisha cycle, the first reading for today, a story not of bread in the desert but bread in the wild-making circumstances of a famine, it is Elisha's servant who asks of the twenty barley loaves: "How can I set this before a hundred people?" (2 Kings 4:43). But here, in John, it is Jesus himself. The Johannine Jesus sums up the questions of the Israelites, of Elisha's servant, of the disciples.

We ask those questions as well. Not that we are necessarily wandering in the wilderness or enduring a famine. But the deep human question—indeed, the deep and usually inarticulate animal question generally—is always a question after food. Most people who ever lived had these questions: How shall I find food for myself? How shall I provide food for those for whom I bear responsibility? Can I organize the world so that we get bread? Shall we die without it? What else can we eat?

Of course, these questions are very largely cloaked in a consumer society of plentiful and diverse food. But they remain alive for us nonetheless, perhaps unacknowledged, perhaps only trembling in the back of our minds, perhaps only in the oddly reversed form: Am I eating too much food? What is the right food? Or, perhaps as the underlying questions: When and how shall I die? What is it for me truly to live? How shall I help those I love to live? In the context of that anxiety, every place I may come is a wilderness, essentially unconcerned with my survival, threatening, not organized to help me. Food that tames that anxiety, truly gives life in the face of death, responds to our deepest hungers, seems not to be available.

The questions are more basic, more acute; yet in spite of the rich availability of food in some parts of the world, bread and other staples are not at all so richly available elsewhere. There really are, at this very time, famines, parched earth, bloated bellies, dying children, people stupefied by their malnourishment, and this in spite of the adequacy of food supplies in the world. There really are, now, people whose very suffering makes every place seem a hostile wilderness. There also really are, at this very time, dying species, starving fish, famished birds, hunger-crazed mammals. If we have any imagination or any ability at compassion, these situations become our own, forming themselves as burning issues in our own minds, connecting our own needs to the wider need, provoking us to be questioners. Such a picture makes the gracious, faithful assertion of the psalm we have sung difficult to believe: "The eyes of all look to you, and you give them their food in due season. You open your hand, satisfying the desire of every living thing." Is this true?

Jesus articulates that question, inhabits that question, becomes that question with the hungry and with us. The Johannine Jesus is both the great truth-teller and the great questioner. Indeed, throughout the Fourth Gospel, Jesus becomes the question itself, from "Do you believe because I told you that I saw you under the fig tree?" (1:50) to "Woman, why are you weeping?" (20:15) and "Have you believed because you have seen me?" (20:29). So here, Jesus is the one who asks the great question, "Where are we to find bread?"

That question about bread is also a question about faith. In the Israelite narrative, "wilderness" functions precisely as a place of testing. Will the people trust God as the life-giver? Or will they make a god to their own order or turn back to the gods and the conditions of Egypt, either shaping their own worldview or submitting to the Egyptian one? According to John, Jesus forms and inhabits exactly that testing question. Hidden in his "where?" is a reference to God as bread-giver, God as known in the stories of the exodus and of Elisha, God as praised in Psalm 145. Shall God be trusted for bread? Can we live in the world, with each other, with that trust? After all, according to the Psalms, the true God does not eat the animals nor the produce of the earth but does, indeed, know of the hungers and needs with which the earth is filled (Ps 50:9-15). Can God-as-lifegiver and wilderness-as-bread-absence go together? Can the juxtaposition of these two form the foundation of our worldview?

According to this story in the Gospel (John 6:1-21), what follows is bread in the wilderness. From the five barley loaves and two fish there flows a great feast, with basketfuls left over. The crowd itself becomes an ordered meeting, a paradigm for assembly, with a strong center in Jesus and in the food, but without walls, welcoming all, in the midst of a wilderness now seen to be a friendly place, green and blossoming. Those basketfuls of further bread seem to be intended, one for each of the twelve disciples, to be distributed in yet other assemblies, extending the rich feast of this gathering yet further into the wild, needy, and hungry world.

This story is told, however, not in order for you to imagine that if you had ever seen such a miracle, you, too, might become a believer. The story is told, not to make you wish that you had been there at some supposed past event. The story is told for this meeting on this Sunday. "Glory to you, O Lord! Praise to you, O Christ!" we sing around this text as it is read here. Those acclamations invite us to see that the bread-giver has come here. If we join the world in the question after bread, then where else can we go?

More: if Jesus articulates and inhabits the question about bread and about faith in God as bread-giver, he most deeply does so in his death. In the event of the cross, Jesus shares with all of us the agonizing question: Is the praise of the psalm true? Does the hand of God open to feed everything with life? According to John, Jesus' refusal to become king makes a little down payment on his cross-death, a little sign that he is not the permanent system-chief organizing the hungry world into one closed ideological answer. Rather, he still remains the question. That Crucified One has come here, sharing the hunger of the poor, sharing your hunger, sharing the question of the wild, wounded, and hungry world.

But in the resurrection, Jesus Christ has also become the living bread himself, given away to all who will come to him. The bread-question and the bread-gift foreshadow the death and resurrection of Jesus and proclaim them both here. Here, in the eucharist, bread is shared with as many as will come. We, too, will send some of the food—or money to buy food—to the absent and the hungry, making our own links to other assemblies in the wilderness. At our best, by the gift of the triune God, we, too, will be an assembly with a strong center and a very porous circumference. At our best, we want the house of our meeting, if we have one, to be a house in the wilderness, not the fortress of a closed worldview. The Spirit of God, poured out from the death and resurrection of Christ is forming us together into trusting the God of the open hands, is bringing us to faith, is gathering us into the life of the Holy Trinity. In that faith, we may begin to see that whatever wilderness we are in also has its green grass, also lies around us as holy ground. Whatever the sea storms, the Crucified-Risen One is the presence of God's own "I AM."

There are still famines, dying species, personal agonies and hungers, food-destroying storms, devastating wars. The wilderness that is unconcerned with our own life-survival still surrounds us. But this little assembly, gathered by the Spirit into the living Bread and before the Bread-giver, forms us to live in this world in faith, rooted and grounded in Christ's own love. We—the postmodern folk who make up this assembly—are invited by the very bread we have together in our hands, by the stories we tell of it, and by the view of the world that both bread and stories propose to be committed to this faith. We do not need to make the fear of death or our own lonely quest for bread for ourselves or for our own kind into the central ordering principles of our lives. We also do not need to think that we can blot widespread need out of our imagination, forbid wilderness, or establish the bounds of our own organizing canons, our own kind of kingship, our own fortress world.

A healthy Christian cosmology in the past has sometimes suggested that stewardship of the earth, that is to say, the action of careful farmers to whom the whole had been entrusted as to stewards, was a wise way for believers to proceed. Such an assertion is partly true, but it acts a little too much like all the world is a farm for our use. We could say that faith in the God who gives bread in the wilderness proposes that respect for the earth and all its wildness, letting it be, acknowledging its mystery and otherness, respecting and praying for the other species, seeking to understand sympathetically every form of the question after bread, meanwhile laboring for better networks of food distribution, also belong to such a cosmology. Faith that God gives bread in the wilderness—and what is the same thing, faith that God makes an assembly in the wilderness—enables us to stand beside the hungry, sharing what we have, allowing the wild that is beyond our organizing ability, and nonetheless, in that faith, somehow comprehending "the breadth and length and height and depth" of all things as all are held in God's love.

How do we receive such faith? Here is a beginning: put out your hands for this bread, together with all the others, and eat. Then share bread with—be bread for—your neighbor in this wild world.

Do Not Hurt the Trees

A sermon at eucharist, celebrated using the Roman Catholic Lectionary texts for the Feast of All Saints, November 1, every year:

Do not damage the earth or the sea or the trees

REVELATION 7:2-4, 9-14
PSALM 24:1-6; ANTIPHON: "This is the company that seeks your face, O Lord."
1 JOHN 3:1-3
VERSE: "Alleluia. 'Come to me, all you that are weary and are carrying heavy burdens, and I will give you rest,' says the Lord."
MATTHEW 5:1-12a

An old biblical tradition holds that a city may be spared destruction if it contains just a few righteous persons. The story goes that Abraham argued with God—bargained with God—over the fate of Sodom, daring to steadily reduce the number of the righteous for the sake of whom the city would be spared, until just ten were deemed enough (Gen. 18:16-33). Perhaps the Christian community was called "salt of the earth" with exactly the preservative character of salt and therefore this same idea in mind: "you are the ones through whom the earth is being preserved." In any case, Christian tradition regarded that Jerusalem itself was spared as long as James the Just still lived. And some Jewish interpretations of the *minyan* needed to hold synagogue prayers propose that these ten righteous persons are functioning like Abraham's ten: their prayers are holding the fabric of their cities in existence, against the real threat of divine wrath.

Such an understanding lies behind this festival's first reading. Only now, it is all the earth that is being preserved. "Do not damage the earth or the sea or the trees," calls out the angel who is coming from the sunrise to mark all the servants of God throughout the world. Thus the wind-angels, powers who have been given God's own authority and strength to harm, are restrained for the sake of that sealing. Here, however, it is not so much that the righteousness of all the saints preserves the earth, sea, and trees. Rather, God's own powerful intention to claim and mark that great multitude from every tribe and people and language—an intention embodied in the rising angel and in the seal in the angel's hand—itself puts off the threatened destruction. The winds are held back, at least until the full number have been sealed, and that full number "no one could count." This assertion is rather like another later assertion of the Revelation about the city of God: "Its gates will never be shut by day—and there will be no night there" (21:25). So here: the earth and the sea and the trees will not be harmed until all the saints are sealed. And their number is countless.

Only the earth and the sea and the trees are being harmed. According to the Christian faith, this sealing with the seal of the living God still proceeds now. Nonetheless, winds—both real and metaphoric—do their destructive work. Forests fall to wind storms and firestorms—and to clear-cutting, to the timber requirements of the massive building and packaging needs of a global economy, to swarms of loggers working to enrich a few global companies, to swarms of beetles out of balance because of global warming. Seas are roiled in hurricanes—and in overfishing, in silting from the erosion of clear-cut forests, in industrial runoff and widespread garbage dumping, in algae blooms encouraged by global warming. The earth itself is hurt by tornados—and by soil erosion, by overplanting, by industrial and nuclear waste, by drought that accompanies global warming. Where is the promise? The earth and the sea and the trees are being harmed.

This day's feast celebrates the many little and nameless ones throughout the world and through history—the poor, merciful, peacemaking, persecuted ones, many of whose stories have been forgotten—who have been so sealed as God's own. But the stories of their being claimed by God have not stopped the parallel stories of their suffering and of the earth itself being hurt. We ourselves may long to be in their number, to be among all the saints. But the story of our washing whatever unclean garments we have, making them white paradoxically in the blood of the Lamb, does not stop the ongoing damage to earth and sea and trees.

"In the blood of the Lamb," the text says. There is the key. The Christian faith trusts that God has joined us amid the damage. The center of the cosmos, by the biblical account, is not just the "throne." It is also the wounded Lamb. In the cross-death, Jesus shares the lot of the little, powerless, and persecuted ones. But he also comes among trees torn down to become execution posts, seas overfished by starving people, and the earth desperately farmed for the sake of absentee landlords and unjust taxes. Those realities fill the stories of the Gospels. Jesus comes among our history of social and ecological sin. He does not stop it. Rather, he is killed by it. But in the resurrection, he does become another, foundational word, a word that describes the meaning and God-intended fate of the world. He becomes bread shared on the holy ground, the healing sabbath that is rest from the hurting of the earth, the tree of life itself, the sea of peace, the down payment on the earth restored. Furthermore, the Risen One invites us to forgiveness for our own participation in world-hurting sin and to the faith that God's intention with the world is this: "Do not hurt the trees!" Such faith trusts that the earth is the Lord's, in spite of all appearances.

If you wish to be part of the company that the Spirit of God gathers around this Jesus, the assembly—the countless number—is still open. Everyone is welcome. Joining that number, you will indeed be sealed. But the seal of the living God marked upon your forehead will be the mark of the wounded tree. Baptism is that great washing whereby we all join this company, this gathering of all the saints. That washing immerses us in the death of Christ in order to raise us together with Christ. The signing with oil is the sealing on the forehead with which new Christians are still marked, the seal that old Christians still remember. But that seal upon our foreheads is the sign of the death of Christ, in order that we might be raised with Christ. Gathered by the Spirit of the Risen One before the throne and the Lamb, raised together with Christ, every Sunday this assembly is together made a living word of God to the world: do not harm the earth or the sea or the trees; the earth belongs to God; do not hurt it. Indeed, every Sunday the word read and sung in the assembly, in one way or another, says this same thing about God's intention for the beloved earth, the holy ground. And every Sunday, we are invited to live the course of our lives in accordance with the word that we have been made, to come away from destructive ways and be healed from that overuse that proceeds as if we owned earth and sea and trees.

God knows that the Christian churches have often not understood this gift and task. We have acted as if our vocation were away from here. We have even sometimes said, to others as well as to ourselves, "Go ahead with the harming. It does not really matter." We have not heard—certainly not been—the word about God's intention for the undamaged earth.

We do not yet see such an undamaged earth, such restrained powers of destruction. It takes an act of faith to trust that this word really resounds through the cosmos—that there is a God and the Spirit of God and the resurrection and the promised restraint of the winds. But the death and resurrection of Jesus Christ, washed over us, proclaimed here, given to us to eat and drink, marked on our foreheads, pull us again and again out of unfaith to faith. That pulling is the purpose of this meeting.

In Sadao Watanabe's modern print of the scene of this Revelation text, "The Angel Ascends from the Rising of the Sun" (1967),[4] we see the great diversity of the servants of God throughout the world, gathered in several different open assemblies. We see the curve of the earth itself and its rich flowering. We see the sea and its wealth of life. One tree—the tree of life? the unburned bush?—stands for all the others, extending the shade of its branches over the gathered peoples. The angels hold back the damaging winds and the sealing angel arises with the very sun. The print is a picture of God's intention with the earth, of God's word, of the word that the risen Christ is, of the word into which the Spirit is forming this assembly.

We do see this print, but we do not see such things actually in the world, where earth and sea and trees are hurt and where we are participants in the hurting. Or we do not quite see such things. We do see a diverse assembly, an assembly that longs to see God and God's enacted intention for the earth. We are in it now. We do see the promising freshness that still lives in earth and sea and trees, a freshness beyond our control. We do see the rising sun. And in baptism and its remembrance, we do see the seal.

Dear sister or brother, will you help keep our assembly open for yet others to join us in a resistance to the inevitability of sin and damage as the lot of the earth, open for yet others who long to see God working in the life

---

4. This print is reproduced on the cover of this book. It is also found in Sadao Watanabe and Masao Takenaka, *Biblical Prints by Sadao Watanabe* (Tokyo: Shinkyo Shuppansha, 1986), no. 18. Watanabe was the distinguished Japanese artist who took the great print tradition of his country and turned it to the expression of biblical and Christian themes.

of the world? And will you trust that seal on your forehead? It is not make-believe, not a Pollyanna wish for happy times. It is the seal of the wounded tree, of God come among our wounded cosmos. But it is also the sign of the resurrection, a constant invitation for you yourself, with all the saints, to be this word in the world: "Do not hurt the trees."

Where Christ Is

A sermon at eucharist, celebrated using the Revised Common Lectionary texts for Proper 13 C, the Sunday between July 31 and August 6, in the third year of the three-year cycle:

ECCLESIASTES 1:2, 12-14; 2:18-23

PSALM 49:1-12; ANTIPHON: "No ransom avails for one's life; there is no price one can give to God for it."

COLOSSIANS 3:1-11

VERSE: "Alleluia. Jesus says, 'Those who love me will keep my word, and my Father will love them, and we will come to them and make our home with them.'"

LUKE 12:13-21

With the texts of this Sunday, we are invited into wisdom. The preacher or assembly-crier of Ecclesiastes uses wisdom to search out for us "what is done under heaven," that is, the conditions of our life on earth. The psalmist sings with us, "My mouth shall speak wisdom." The Pauline letter invites us to think and conduct ourselves in a certain way, to "set your minds," one way to describe wisdom. And the parable of Jesus in Luke's Gospel describes a fool, always a contrary image intended instead to urge wisdom's way.

The concern of all this wisdom centers on death. According to these texts, the wise person knows that she or he will die. Ecclesiastes says it most baldly: all of our frantic activity qualifies only as "chasing after wind," since we die. Nothing we do will avert this end. All our toil, even if this has been toil with "wisdom and knowledge and skill," will yield only an inheritance for others—sometimes for quite foolish others, who have done no toil—not an escape for ourselves. For Ecclesiastes, as for much of the biblical wisdom tradition, the great characteristic of wisdom consists in the assent to human limits, the peaceful ordering of life to the sure reality of death.

Then the psalm reinforces the same word: Riches will not ransom you out of death. Human pomp cannot last forever or put off the grave. We all are also among the animals that perish. And the Gospel parable seems to continue the sense of both the psalm and the preacher of Ecclesiastes: Only a fool thinks that all that labor for a larger barn full of goods means many years of being merry. Death and someone else's inheritance are always lurking. Indeed, in the parable, this death is God's inevitable judgment.

According to Christian faith, these judgments, these wise sayings, these truths about limits are the word of God. On this Sunday—on any Sunday—we gather around the proclamation of this word: We die. Our lives occur within limits. Pay attention to the limits. All talk about unlimited human life and the endless possibilities that any one of us may grab for the self are lies. "Do not lie to one another," says the second reading. There is, indeed, endlessness around us, but it is not ours. We are among the animals that die. We are earth, and to earth we shall return.

But have not we Christians now come beyond this word? Is not Ecclesiastes behind us, part of the old, transcended covenant? Does what we do with the earth, on the earth, really matter so much if we are going to get out of here? If we die, do we not go to heaven, beyond all limits?

Not in these texts. The Gospel here sounds just like Ecclesiastes. Of course, the deep trust of Christian faith is that God "gives life to the dead and calls into existence the things that do not exist" (Rom. 4:17). God does that, not some invincible life or soul that is within us. But what does this assertion mean? That it means "going to heaven" and getting out of here once and for all can be found in the Bible very, very much less than is popularly thought. And it is not found at all in these texts.

What about heaven, then? Is there one? What about life after death? I do not know. Neither does most of the Bible. Here is a better answer: Trust God. Die into God. In your death, let your life—and the life of your beloved ones—be hidden where it has always been hidden since your baptism: in Christ, appearing where Christ appears. But, in any case, do not use some idea of "going to heaven" to justify the misuse of the world.

Here we come to see that there are a lot of fools in the world—ourselves included—who try to live as if there were no limits, consuming and consuming, goods and food, things from the earth, things that might rightly be shared with other limited creatures as well, all of this consumption and hoarding supposedly for the well-being of the self, while that self is not at all rich toward God. Rich toward God? What is that? Treasure in heaven? Put there, perhaps, by a little almsgiving on the side, while we keep most of the stuff for ourselves?

There is one who is rich toward God. Look there. He comes among our hoarding ways, refuses to be an arbiter of wealth and inheritance, takes on the lot of the poor, is at last robbed of his dignity, of his garment, and then, too soon, of his life. But in that poverty, he gives and gives and so has more to give: witness to the truth, forgiveness, mercy, bread, himself. And raised up by God and standing among us, he becomes the very source of the riches of God poured out forever here, transfiguring our limits: witness to the truth, forgiveness, bread, life.

Ah, Christ is raised! Does that not mean raised beyond our limits? Perhaps here is the chink in the wall of Ecclesiastes, and we will get out at last. Does Colossians not say that we are to "seek the things that are above, where Christ is, seated at the right hand of God"?

Be careful with that "above." It is, of course, a word drawn from an old cosmology, where heaven and God were up, beyond the sphere of the sky, and earth was down. That cosmology will not work anymore. The sky is down as well as up. There is no "sphere of the sky." Our planet also swings through the sky. The limits of life and death would be known even more fiercely by us were we able to go up in any direction, away from this watery home, or down, into its crushing depth. And, in any case, what the Pauline writer means by "above" and "on earth" quickly becomes apparent. The directional, cosmological words are being used metaphorically for what belongs to God and what belongs to sin and death. If we take this metaphor literally, as too many recent generations of Christians have, we will be newly foolish, using an old cosmology to justify a bad lifestyle and missing the deep point of the passage. As the passage proceeds, the metaphor changes to one of clothing: in baptism, the old has been stripped off and the new has been put on. Christ has been put on.

But then, where is Christ? What does the resurrection of Christ mean? Where are those "things that are above," to use the metaphor? At the right hand of God. And where is that?

Christian faith trusts that this "hand"—another metaphor, this time for the power of God and the ability of God to act—is everywhere in the real world. Is here. Within our limits. Jesus Christ, the eternal riches of God, has been raised to be giving away those riches within this world, everywhere, especially among the poor, especially among those whose condition of life is nothing but crushing limit.

But if you wish to see that presence—so usually hidden, hidden as God is hidden, hidden as the true fullness of our own life is hidden—then look here, at this little gathering. Here the Scripture is read and sung and preached. According to the promise, where that word is present, there is the very home of the triune God. Here the bath that puts us to death with Christ is remembered and celebrated. According to the promise, where that water is, there, now, is real life, beyond the fear of death. Here the meal of Christ is kept. According to the promise, in that meal, the Spirit draws us into the very body of Christ present and so before the face of God. In that meal, we are surrounded by the presence of the Holy Trinity and by all those little ones, poor ones, dead ones, limited ones, who are hidden in the Trinity.

If you wish to know wisdom, come to that meal. If you want to "seek the things that are above, where Christ is," come to that meal. Here is wisdom, tasted and seen at this very meal: Look. You are not alone. You are with many others. You are welcome to eat and drink but only to your own needs, sharing the food with others, within limits. You are loved, honored even. You are given Christ and the mystery of yourself, together with the others—a new us. Christ appears. Your life appears. Although this is limited food, here and now, it is a feast, thick with the richness of God, intense, alive. And nothing is hoarded. What we have is used or sent to the absent or the hungry. This meal of wisdom, of life transfigured within limits, is then an icon of all real life. Eating and drinking, beholding the others eat and drink, we may say to ourselves, "Soul, be like that." Be part of the world, gladly, acknowledging your limits, living on the surface of this planet within this solar system within this galaxy, taking what you need with thanksgiving and sharing with the others, not fooling yourself that more stuff will get you beyond death, finding life in the mercy of God for you and the sharing of that mercy with others.

Where is Christ? Still sharing the lot of the poor. Still witnessing to the truth. Still transfiguring our limits. And he is here, in this community of the Spirit, here on this ground holy to God, and he is making you alive, now, here.

9

One Is Holy:
Liturgical Theology, Liturgical Cosmology

In the mercy of God, Word and Sacrament, enacted in assembly, do hold us on the holy ground, before the Holy One. Celebrated faithfully, they do cast a new light on the world, suggest cosmic meanings, relativize structures that misconstrue and misuse the world, propose paths for us to walk, reorient us in the material and social realities of our context. Such has been the argument of this book. Word and Sacrament do not give us a full cosmology, finally revealed in detail. They do not give sanction to one or the other cosmic ideology, one or the other all-embracing metanarrative, one or the other all-organizing closed structure. Rather, they set their proposals, their cosmological sketches, in critically helpful dialogue with the many cosmologies by which we live. They do so simply by doing what they most basically do: hold us before God and bring us to faith in God.

Liturgical poetics thus undertakes a modest but essential task. If we attend to what occurs when Scripture is set next to bath and table, amid all the other meaning-making juxtapositions of the liturgy, then what we will see—hear, learn, be gathered into—will only be a little thing. It will be "knowing something a little," to use one phrase that has summarized the self-critical, limited but absolutely essential cosmological knowledge and orientations that mark many of the ancient peoples of the land around the

---

1. For a reflection on borrowing this phrase to serve as a summary for what Christians may know together, see Lathrop, *Holy People* (see above, intro. n. 2), 101. Careful yet critical attention to the wisdom of the ancient peoples of the land—American Indians and Inuit, the Aboriginal peoples of Australia, the Sami of northern Scandinavia, the Ainu of Japan, Mary Douglas's "positional cultures"—can provide one important source for relativizing dominant

world.[1] But the "little" of the Christian liturgy will be enough for us to walk in faith and love upon the holy ground, enough continually to reorient our basic views of the world, while we freely admit that we do not know everything of the mysteries and powers that surround us.

The "little" of the Christian liturgy will be that unburned burning bush. After all, the point of all the juxtapositions, reversals, and paradoxes of Christian liturgy, many of which we have explored here as liturgical poetics, is to draw us before the living God. The liturgy is not God. Our gestures toward God, our metaphors for God are not God. Rather, let them be thought of as our removing the sandals from our feet. Only one is holy. Still, the mercy of that Holy One also entails the holiness of the ground. Indeed, such is the meaning of "holiness" here: God is holy as the one who in mercy and love intends the wholeness of all things, the one who gives holiness away.

Our gestures toward God are on the ground beloved of God and are, amazingly, inhabited by this same God. The Holy Spirit of God is poured out in the assembly to make the holy things and this odd, holy people to be full of God, and yet, at the same time, to make them an openness to God. Henceforth, to be in an openness toward God is to be in God. Christian faith says that this very same Spirit is renewing the face of the earth, making it an openness to God. Further, by the word and promise of Jesus Christ, the holy things here are full of Christ's presence as he makes an unholy, needy people to be God's people. Henceforth, to be in such need and such forgiveness is to be in God.[2] Christian faith says that this same Crucified and Risen One remains identified with all the broken ones of our wounded world, holding all things—even the stars—in his hands. For an assembly to be in the central matters of Christian liturgy is for that assembly to be before the God—indeed, to be surrounded by the God—who holds all things into mercy and wholeness. We call this assertion of faith "the doctrine of the Trinity." Trinitarian faith is the soul of Christian liturgy, the heart of

worldviews, a relativizing that we have argued is sometimes analogous to the work of liturgical poetics. For one example of that relativization—in the quest to protect the Arctic National Wildlife Refuge—see Anthony Lathrop, "People of the Caribou in the Land of the Oil," *Wisconsin Environmental Law Journal,* spring 2002 (8:2), 169–96.

2. This sentence and the earlier sentence about the Spirit, also beginning with "henceforth," both build upon the "henceforth" in the remarkable trinitarian meditation of Hans Urs von Balthazar, *Heart of the World* (San Francisco: Ignatius, 1979), 37–57. So, of Jesus Christ: "He alone would henceforth be the measure and thus also the meaning of all impotence. He wanted to sink so low that in the future all falling would be a falling into him, and every streamlet of bitterness and despair would henceforth run down into his lowermost abyss." (43); and of the Holy Spirit: "Distance and proximity coincide" (55).

liturgical theology. Such a theology necessarily entails a cosmology. To find words appropriate for God, as that triune God is encountered in the liturgy, is inevitably to find words appropriate for the world. Liturgical cosmology, at its root, is an exercise in liturgical theology.

Still, be careful. These assertions begin to sound awfully grand. Our liturgy is not God. Only one is holy. What we have before us, at best, is the bush. And we think we hear a voice telling us that the ground is holy. That same voice speaks of the deliverance of the poor and of the resurrection. "I have heard their cry" (Exod. 3:7). And "Have you not read in the book of Moses, in the story about the bush, how God . . . is God not of the dead but of the living?" (Mark 12:26-27).

Liturgy is a little thing, some words, some water, a meal, a gesture, all as those very words from the bush, all as a sketch of the world. Think again of "knowing something a little."

An analogy might be found in the classic Sami drum. While reconstructions of the religion of this ancient people of northern Scandinavia should be entered upon with care, it does seem that this religion was shamanic, and that the Sami shaman, the *noaidi,* like the shamans of many other boreal peoples, used a drum in achieving ecstasy and in seeing visions for the sake of the people. But among the Sami, unlike many other peoples, the drumhead itself came to be dealt with as a cosmic map.[3] It was marked with numerous figures and symbols—people, animals, birds, fish, gods, trees, dwelling places, boats, sun, moon, stars, all drawn very much like the prehistoric rock carvings found in much of the same geography. This map was later used for divination, as a marker moved between these graphic symbols during the beating of the drum, but it was probably originally intended to assist the shaman's orientation to the surrounding world and to the world of the gods and of the dead while on the ecstatic journey. Of course, the collection of symbols on the drumhead could not include everything. The drumhead itself was only a cosmic sketch. While divisions in the drawing, sometimes represented by lines dividing the space into two, three, or six areas, may have indicated different parts of the world or worlds, and while the edge of the drumhead may have corresponded to the horizon, the sense of this map seems to comport with life as it was lived in the great open

---

3. Rolf Kjellström and Håkan Rydving, *Den samiska trumman* (Stockholm: Nordiska Museet, 1988, 1993), 6. See also the classic work, Ernst Manker, *Die lappische Zaubertrommel* 1 and 2, Acta Lapponica 1 and 6 (Stockholm: 1938, 1950), and the study of religious change among the Sami, Håkan Rydving, *The End of Drum-Time* (Uppsala: 1995).

spaces of the north. A few known centers are established. The known world coheres in these centers. Surrounding these centers there is mystery, unknown distance, the wilderness. Using these centers—"knowing something a little" and following the counsel of the shaman interpreting what is known—there is life.[4]

The Christian liturgy is like that drumhead. A few known centers are marked, and thereby a partial cosmic map is set out. Cardinal directions are established. Christians are invited to live within the surrounding wilderness from these centers that they know together. But unlike shamanic religion, among Christians this cosmological knowledge is not achieved by ecstasy, nor is it given to and through religious experts, technicians of the sacred. It belongs rather to the whole assembly together—women and men, adults and children, insiders and outsiders—and is given in the concrete experience of word and sacrament set side by side. In fact, it is not really "knowledge" but faith in the triune God. And it is given by grace.

The Christian liturgy is a little thing. Yet it is full of God's grace, enabling faith, entailing the holy ground. Both.

For the Healing of the Nations

One of the graphic symbols of the Sami drum bears further attention. In the center of the drumhead of the great majority of the more or less seventy drums that have survived from the practice of this old religion, there is a figure probably representing the sun.[5] This figure, found especially as the identifying characteristic of south-Sami drums, takes the form of a diamond-like central figure, with four long rays reaching out toward the directions, organizing the whole of the rest of the map. But one of these rays—the bottom ray, as understood from the orientations of the other figures—frequently ends in what looks like roots. And one or more of the other rays not infrequently ends in leaves or branches. This sun, this organizing center of the Sami cosmos, can be perceived as a great tree, under which the animals and people and gods and corners of the earth all shelter. The shaman could find a way only working with this cosmic principle, metaphorically climbing this tree.

Other cultures beside that of the Sami have embraced the image of the tree of life as a major, world-organizing symbol. A good deal can be told

4. A fictional representation of the way in which a Sami community might follow such counsel and find a way toward survival is presented in the Norwegian-Sami film *Pathfinder* (*Ofelas*), written and directed by Nils Gaup.
5. Kjellström and Rydving, *Den samiska trumman*, 8–9.

about the cosmology of those cultures by considering the ways in which this symbol functions, sometimes in ritual, often in mythology, sometimes in both. Thus, in that ancient Near Eastern world reflected in much of the Old Testament, the king was the great tree of life and urban kingship the great organizing principle of meaning and world structure. All the birds of the air—all the people of the city and all the foreigners as well—should find order and refuge in him.[6] No wonder kingship meets us in so many of the cosmological psalms.[7] Or, in Norse mythology, all things, all locations, all gods had their place in the structure of the great, world-embracing ash tree, Yggdrasil. But the dragon or serpent, Nidhogg, was gnawing away at its root.[8] Underneath all things, fate and doom were the surest principles. Or, among the Gbaya of the western African savannah, the little *soré* tree ritually held all things together, its leaves being used in virtually every important initiation, reconciliation, purification, or blessing.[9] The "coolness" or slip-periness that characterizes this malleable and humble tree calmed hurt and danger and held the social world intact.

One could go on. In Japanese Shinto, the *kami* descend the sacred *sakaki* tree to establish a ritual center, and the local world is held in existence and under blessing by ritual contact with the gods who are then enshrined at that center, the devotees and priests bearing *sakaki* leaves in hand as they pray to those gods.[10] In Plains Indian life, the sun dance pole is both the world tree and the sun itself, recalling the south-Sami drumhead, and the sacrifice of the dancers holds the community into an orientation to the order and blessing established by the sun.[11] And more: there are also the maypole, the summer solstice pole, the *bodhi* tree, the pagoda, perhaps even the menorah.[12] These symbols are not all the same. But they do all evidence interest in a communal sense of cosmos, a shared sense of world order, using

6. See Daniel 4 and Ezekiel 17 and 31. For an older history of religions study of this image, see E. O. James, *The Tree of Life* (Leiden: Brill, 1966).

7. For example, the urban king in Pss. 18, 72, and 89, and God as king in Pss. 24, 29, and 74.

8. Snorri Sturluson, *Edda*, "Gylfaginning," 15-16, Anthony Faulkes, trans., (London: Dent, 1987), 17-19.

9. Thomas G. Christensen, *An African Tree of Life* (New York: Orbis, 1990), see especially 137–39.

10. John K. Nelson, *A Year in the Life of a Shinto Shrine* (Seattle: University of Washington Press, 1996).

11. William K. Powers, *Oglala Religion* (Lincoln: University of Nebraska Press, 1982), 95–100.

12. See further in Roger Cook, *The Tree of Life: Image for the Cosmos* (New York: Thames & Hudson, 1988).

221

the figure of a tree to image that order, and finding ways in which a community can live in accordance with the cosmic order by living in accordance with that tree.

Does Christianity also make use of a tree of life to express its cosmological themes? Does a cosmic tree also stand at the center of the drumhead that is Christian liturgy? Yes. The cosmological chapters that frame the Bible—Genesis 1–3 and Revelation 21–22—hold exactly such a tree, at the center of the original garden, in the second creation story (Gen. 2:9; 3:24), and in the heart of city in the heart of the new heaven and new earth in the final vision (Rev. 22:2, 14). "The leaves of the tree are for the healing of the nations" (Rev. 22:2). These very chapters play an important role in the lectionary—in Lent, at the Easter Vigil, and in the Sundays of Easter. Furthermore, the image recurs in liturgical iconography, in liturgical texts, in contemporary eucharistic prayers, and in ancient and modern hymnody. "O tree of beauty, tree most fair" many Christians sing on Passion Sunday.[13] And for centuries, the Christian community at the Church of San Clemente in Rome has gathered before an apse mosaic of the Crucified One shining forth as brilliant vine-tree, swirling branches reaching out toward the assembly. It is as if this very image, in Christian liturgical use, willingly and sympathetically gathers up all the human hopes for order and survival—for cosmology as a shared and workable worldview, describing a life-giving place for our community in the universe—all the hopes that the Sami drum-tree and all the other mythic and ritual images evoke.

Only in Christianity, as so often with other images, the references of the myth are turned upside down, reversed, broken. For Christians, the world-holding tree is no king, but a servant, a crucified man. This tree, making room for all things to nest, is not the sun or any other magnificent object. If anything, it is an annual bush (Mark 4:30-32 and parallels); that is, it is the cross on which Jesus Christ was killed, understood as giving refuge and life to everyone, everything. For the Christian assembly, the water flowing from under this tree, the leaves and the fruit from its branches are not just mythic hopes, achieved perhaps by our sacrifice. They are available now, given away here, in these words, this bath, this meal. In these things, in the heart of Christian liturgy, the death of Jesus is met as the resurrection and the gift of the Spirit. Water, healing, food flow where we thought they could not. As used in Christian ritual, the tree of life always stands for grace, for God's

---

13. In the translation of the classic hymn "Vexilla Regis" by Venantius Fortunatus, published in *Lutheran Book of Worship* (Minneapolis: Augsburg, 1978) as hymns 124 and 125.

mercy that receives our hopes for life and fulfills them unexpectedly, beyond our dreams, in spite of our religion, forgiving our sacred techniques and failed rites, undercutting our sacrifices and our kingships, against our sense of fate and doom and luck. If we let the tree symbol function as cosmology for us, we will find our worldview radically reoriented. There will still be such a great life-giving tree, but in a way and at a place we had not expected. A hole forms now in the sphere of the tree of life myth, and through that hole streams the healing of the nations, beginning with a healing of our cosmologies.

For Christians, the tree of life image points to the only Holy One. The tree of life myth itself is not holy. It can inspire anxiety, oppression, hierarchical order, violence, a sense of fate. All human hopes, all human cosmologies—and the actions they inspire—are not innocent. Finally, the myth can only express our hopes and our failures. If forced to hold the world in order, it will do so only as false order, disorder. But, in the mercy of God, that very myth, with its extensive human history of cosmological hope, can be healed and turned to speak of God come among us, making our places of death and loss and sin and otherness and wilderness—the very places usually ignored or excluded in our patterns of order—into the place of life.

Let the tree of life image stand for all cosmologies. The reorientation that happens with this image, as it is used to express world coherence, can happen also with other cosmologies. Be careful in saying this. What Christians have in their liturgical practice is not a massive and assured polemic against all other cosmologies. All these other cosmologies are part of the cultural treasure of the nations, due a sympathetic hearing from us. All these other cosmologies also belong to us, also parallel our own worldviews: Christians should freely say, "Everything that is human is of us." What is more, Christians are as likely as others—sometimes more likely, as we have explored—to absolutize and misuse their own worldviews. But what Christians should have in their liturgical practice is this: they gather around a few central things, a hole in any sphere, a mustard-bush tree, knowing something a little. That is, they gather around the mercy of the triune God. Under that mercy, as we have seen, the leaves of the tree of life are applied to the cosmological treasures of the nations, including whatever is the cosmological treasure of our nation. Cosmology as shared worldview is invited to continued revaluation, seeking to include the excluded others; cosmology as astrophysics is gladly accepted yet fiercely relativized; cosmology as ecology is strongly encouraged and yet paired with cosmology as justice; postmodern cosmological hesitancy is affirmed yet called to commitment;

and those mourners for whom everything is "too large" are simply held. The arms of God's mercy are world enough. For the business of the liturgy is not consequent cosmology but the burning Mercy. As we stand before that Mercy, surrounded by that Mercy, we stand on holy ground.

Bath, Table, Prayer, Word

But what liturgy, what communally enacted symbols, may hold us before this Mercy?

This book has been a further reflection on the meaning of a few such symbols, proposed as central to biblical promise, central to Christian tradition, and central to current Christian practice. The inscription on a church bell that used to hang in northern Wisconsin says it all:

> To the bath and the table,
> To the prayer and the word,
> I call every seeking soul.[14]

These few things—when they are enacted communally, when they are communally sung, just as the bell sings, and when they are set out openly, inviting all—make up the primary matters of Christian worship. These few things may be seen as rooting us in the Scripture and in the life of Jesus. They are accessible in many cultures. They are generally, even universally recognizable gifts, yet they are always preeminently local. They are the stuff of participation, of gracious hospitality and welcome to the stranger, to all of us as strangers: "I call every seeking soul." They can form a strong center around which open doors, a permeable boundary, may be rightly constructed. They can make up the matter for mutual affirmation and admonition between the churches as we call each other to faithfulness in their use. They can be enacted with greater clarity, with "the fullness and integrity of the sign," as Martin Luther said,[15] being continually refreshed in the actual practice of bath, word, prayer, and table. They may be received by local communities as gifts.

---

14. For the bell at Luck, Wisconsin, and for reflection on the meaning of its inscription, see Lathrop, *Holy Things,* 89–91; and Gordon Lathrop, "The Bath and the Table, the Prayer and the Word," *Grundtvig Studier* 51 (2000), 104–7; revised as "Strong Center, Open Door: A Vision of Continuing Liturgical Renewal," *Worship* 75, no. 1 (January 2001): 35–45.

15. Or, "a true and complete sign," "The Holy and Blessed Sacrament of Baptism," 1, translation in E. Theodore Bachman, *Luther's Works,* vol. 35 (Philadelphia: Muhlenberg, 1960), 29: in the original German, "ein rechts volkommens zeychen geben" (*WA* 2:727; see above, chap. 3 n. 17).

And these few things have cosmological significance. We have set the bath next to politics, the word and the table next to economics, and prayers through time next to astrophysics. But we might have done it otherwise. The multivalence of the washing that forms the community, for example, so exuberantly celebrated in the readings of the Easter Vigil, holds forth a multiplicity of images for the world: the world after the flood, the world resisting tyrants, the world learning to share food freely, and, most especially, the world itself pulled up to life by the body of the Risen One. The point remains: these communal enactments are capable of holding a community under the hole in the heavens, on the holy ground, in dialogue with all of our theoretical and practical cosmologies.

Say it this way: Christian worship is primarily word and sign on Sunday and festival, in assembly, following an ancient shape musically, openly, with focus and flow, to speak the Holy Trinity, for the life and meaning of the world.

Chapters in this book have called for the renewed centrality of these things in detail: for word and table as the clear shape of the Sunday meeting; for baptism as a communal process, continually remembered; for festivals as marking our actual times and avoiding make-believe; for preaching that articulates the full meaning of the meeting. The agenda for reform given here echoes ideas for renewal that have been widely discussed in many Christian circles, Protestant and Roman Catholic, Western and Eastern. There is nothing particularly new here, even though in this book these agendas are, indeed, articulated in the diction and from the viewpoint of this one commentator, this one participant in the meeting. But say it again, as others have said: these reforms are needed, at least partly, so that the Christian liturgy may make its critical contribution to our operative conceptions of the world. These communal interactions are "the public business of death and life."[16] Bath and table, prayer and word, continually and openly set out, are "for the life of the world."[17] Such a liturgy is about this world, now, before God.

There are indeed "catholic exceptions" to the central practice of these primary things.[18]

Quakers and Salvationists do not keep bath or table. Baptists and Mennonites welcome only the confessing, adult members of the assembly to the

---

16. Kavanagh, *Elements of Rite* (see above, chap. 6 n. 31), 21.
17. Schmemann, *Life of the World* (see above, intro. n. 28).
18. For "catholic exceptions," see Lathrop, *Holy Things,* 157–58.

bath. Feminists must sometimes lock the door when the liturgy hopes safely to welcome abused women to a celebration of honesty and healing.[19] But even these exceptions, when held in critical dialogue with the wider liturgical practice of the churches, can be seen as intending the renewal of the primary things for the sake of the life of the world. Those Quakers who are Christian can find every meal to be the Lord's Supper. The Salvation Army hopes that the giving away of help to the wretched in the world is the giving away of the body of Christ. Anabaptists call all the churches to baptismal responsibility. The feminist liturgy can be seen as the hope for an open door in a safe world. Left to themselves, allowed to harden into institutions, each of these exceptions runs the significant danger of the closed-circle distortion. But when the Salvation Army captain who labors in the poorest section of the city also goes to communion, sometimes at a Lutheran or Episcopal church, when the preacher at the feminist eucharist both supports and criticizes the closed door, when the Baptist congregation welcomes one baptized as a child as a full member while still maintaining the usual adult-baptizing practice, then the protests can be seen as arising out of the deep trust that these central things are, indeed, meant for the life of the world, not just as markers of our circle against the world.

Tree of Life, Burning Bush

Two hymns available to the current English-language repertoire of many churches, may together give a final word. They each may stand for the whole assembly, gathered in its liturgy, doing its poetics, before God, but they do so best together. Together they sing out a worldview. The cosmology thus poetically proposed is not complete, but its exercise nonetheless engages us in a critical, transformative dialogue with all the ways in which we see the world.

The hymn "There in God's Garden," written by the seventeenth-century Hungarian pastor Király Imre von Pécselyi, was translated in 1973 by Eric Routley.[20] The hymn makes use of that ancient Christian tree-image—found in the traditions of Fortunatus and of San Clemente—that we have explored as receiving and transposing a widespread human cosmological symbol. Now, in the personal-communal assembly, the individual

---

19. I thank my colleague Ninna Edgardh Beckman for this insight. See her *Feminism och liturgi—en ecklesiologisk studie* (Stockholm: Verbum, 2001).

20. The hymn is found in *With One Voice* (Minneapolis: Augsburg Fortress, 1995) as hymn 668. ©1976 by Hinshaw Music Inc., Chapel Hill, N.C. Text used with permission.

Christian may be gathered with all the others into mercy and hope, into resurrection itself, now, and so into a new sense of the world. The tree of the cross, encountered in word and sacrament, is the burning bush that entails the holy ground. After singing of Jesus as the tree of life, the source of the leaves for the healing of the nations, two of the final stanzas of the hymn sing this of that tree:

> See how its branches reach to us in welcome;
> hear what the voice says, "Come to me, ye weary!
> Give me your sickness, give me all your sorrow,
> I will give blessing."
>
> This is my ending, this my resurrection;
> into your hands, Lord, I commit my spirit.
> This have I searched for; now I can possess it,
> This ground is holy.

The hymn "In Sacred Manner" was written in the late twentieth century by Lutheran poet Susan Palo Cherwien.[21] It makes use of American Indian prayer—familiar, for example, in the Navajo songs we have explored—set next to biblical imagery. Now, in the communal-personal assembly, the whole body of us together is beckoned to learn to walk on the earth, in our location in the universe. After inviting us to attend to earth, stars, trees, sea, fire, and wind, the two final stanzas of the hymn sing:

> In sacred manner may we live
> Among the wise and loving ones,
> Sit humbly, as at sages' feet,
> By four-legged, finned, and feathered one,
> The animals will teach.
> The animals will teach.
> In sacred manner may we walk
> Upon the fair and loving earth,
> In beauty move, in beauty love
> The living round that brought us birth.
> We stand on holy ground.
> We stand on holy ground.

21. The hymn is found in Susan Palo Cherwien, *O Blessed Spring* (Minneapolis: Augsburg Fortress, 1997), 26–27, 64–65, 102.

What will the animals teach us? Job says, "Ask the animals, and they will teach you; the birds of the air, and they will tell you . . . that in the hand of the LORD is every living thing" (Job 12:7-10). Woven in with all the Scriptures, the voice of Job should also be heard in the assembly, surprising us, inviting us to see the world differently, to keep a wider company than we had thought. And where might we find that blessed exchange where we may give our sorrow in exchange for blessing, learning to turn to do the same with our neighbors? In word and table, in the prayers that surround them, in the bath that introduces us to them, we encounter the outreaching arms of that tree, utterly reconfiguring all the exchanges of our world. The presence of the triune God in the assembly, the very presence of that tree, burns in these few central things as the burning bush.

We stand on holy ground.

Indexes

Biblical Texts

Classical Texts and Sources

Modern Authors

Subjects